I0117327

EARLY MEDIA EFFECTS THEORY & THE SUGGESTION DOCTRINE

EARLY MEDIA EFFECTS THEORY & THE SUGGESTION DOCTRINE

Selected Readings, 1885–1935

edited by

Patrick Parsons

media
studies.
press

Early Media Effects Theory & the Suggestion Doctrine

edited by Patrick Parsons

© 2024 Patrick Parsons (new materials)

Works not in the public domain are licensed under a Creative Commons Attribution-NonCommercial 4.0 International (CC BY-NC 4.0). This license allows you to share, copy, distribute and transmit the text; to adapt the text for non-commercial purposes of the text providing attribution is made to the authors (but not in any way that suggests that they endorse you or your use of the work).

Published by:
mediastudies.press
414 W. Broad St.
Bethlehem, PA 18018, USA

Copy-editing: Emily Alexander

Cover design: Mark McGillivray

Landing page: mediastudies.press/early-media-effects-theory-the-suggestion-doctrine

Public Domain series - issn (*online*) 2770-2480 | issn (*print*) 2770-2472

isbn 978-1-951399-28-3 (*print*) | isbn 978-1-951399-26-9 (*pdf*)

isbn 978-1-951399-29-0 (*epub*) | isbn978-1-951399-27-6 (*html*)

doi 10.32376/3f8575cb.f1e0489e | lccn 2024931261

Edition 1 published in December 2024

Contents

An Overview of the Origins and Evolution of Suggestion Theory

Patrick Parsons

While much has been written on the history of media effects research in the United States, a casual review of the literature could reasonably lead one to believe that little if any such work was conducted until the 1940s. Most textbooks place the start of investigation during and just after World War II, with the work of Carl Hovland and colleagues at Yale University and Paul Lazarsfeld at Columbia University. Wilbur Schramm (1963), who did as much as anyone to set the historic timeline, declared that the beginning of serious work on media influence began with four scholars: Hovland, Lazarsfeld, Harold Lasswell, and Kurt Lewin. Steve Chaffee and John Hochheimer (1985) similarly observed that nothing that could be considered systematic scientific research on media effects began much before the late 1930s.

According to some versions of the origin story, to the extent that the public, policy makers, and even academics posited ideas about the power of media before the war, they were cast in the form of a "hypodermic effect" (Klapper, 1960) or "magic bullet" model of influence. Quoting Schramm, "Communication was seen as a magic bullet that transferred ideas or feelings or knowledge or motivation almost automatically from one mind to another" (1971, 8–9). Not everyone has accepted the magic bullet tale, arguing that such a model never, in historical fact, existed (see Lubken 2008; Wartella and Reeves 1985). And indeed, Schramm concocted the term, in application to media effects, if not the concept. Overall, the exploration of effects research before World War II has been somewhat contentious and has left a cloudy picture.

In 2021, this author entered the conversation with a new view of that history (Parsons 2021). The anthology presented here is an extension of that work. It is centered on the concept of "suggestion," which was a specific and clearly articulated psychological process of attitude formation and change that dominated social science from roughly the late 1800s until World War II. What media scholars know today as "persuasion," social psychologists of the early 1900s would have understood as the process of suggestion. Suggestion, as defined by one leading theorist of the period, was *"the process of communication resulting in the acceptance with conviction of the communicated proposition in the absence of logically adequate grounds for its acceptance"* (McDougall 1909, 97; italics in the original). At first glance, the description appears to emulate the primary characteristics of the magic bullet model in the nature of its direct effects assumptions, and in fact suggestion does share, to some degree, that attribute. But where the magic bullet was said to exact uniform effects across all consumers of a message, suggestion theory was held to vary widely in its effects across individuals and circumstances. As will be seen, the contingent character of suggestion drove much of the research in the early 1900s. One of the consequences was the discovery of psychological processes that anticipated research on cognitive selectivity and cognitive dissonance conducted many decades later. The eventual decline of suggestion theory and its erasure from the memory of the field are discussed in detail in the prior work (Parsons 2021) and this process is briefly sketched at the end of this introduction.

This anthology, then, seeks to provide contemporaneous substance and context in a review of the history of the suggestion doctrine. By one count, there were more than 230 studies published on suggestion theory by 1939. While a mere thirty-one are presented here, they include the original statements on the subject from many of the leading social theorists of the age, including figures such as Gabriel Tarde and Gustave Le Bon in France and James Baldwin, Edward Ross, and Floyd Allport in the United States. The anthology also draws on the extensive record of experimentation published in the early 1900s on the topic of attitude formation and modification and the role of media in the process.

The collection is divided into three sections: "Foundations," "Evolution and Variation," and "Applications." The first section presents the founding statements in suggestion theory. Suggestion was the child of French crowd theory and arose primarily from the work of Tarde and Le Bon just before the turn of the century. It was mated at the time with the theory of imitation, and the two in combination were employed in the analysis of crowd behavior, with special attention to "the mob." The core idea was that individuals in a crowd were prone to shed their rationality, joining in an automaton-like "crowd mind" and becoming susceptible to powerful charismatic speakers. In such a state, declared Le Bon, "all feelings and thoughts are bent in the direction determined by the hypnotizer . . . Under the influence of a suggestion, [the individual] will undertake the accomplishment of certain acts with irresistible impetuosity" (1903, 35).

The suggestion-imitation doctrine of attitudinal and behavioral control emigrated to the United States around the turn of the century, and it quickly found a home in the embryonic field of social psychology. In his history of social psychology, Gordon Allport (1968) declared that this doctrine came to dominate the field by the 1930s. As late as 1948, Solomon Asch, a Gestalt critic of suggestion, complained that the doctrine had become *the* theory "of the formation and change of opinions and attitudes. In consequence the psychology of attitudes is well-nigh universally (both in social psychology and in the social sciences generally) treated as at bottom an affair of suggestion and bias. This approach has penetrated nearly all regions of social psychology" (251). In short, social psychological analyses of opinion formation and change, across interpersonal and mediated communication, were dominated in these early decades by the doctrine of suggestion.

Theorizing and exposition from the early social scientists, therefore, constitutes the start of this anthology, where the emphasis is on definitions, categorization, and qualifications. Typical in these passages are efforts to identify various types of suggestion, stipulate conditions of suggestibility, and speculate about the impact of "social suggestion." The statements are broadly theoretical but with frequent allusion to potential real-world implications for both individuals and the general public.

The "Evolution and Variation" section first considers work done by social scientists to integrate suggestion into then-emerging models in social psychology, specifically instinct theory and behaviorism, as US researchers abandoned French crowd theory and advanced new models of collective behavior. Passages from William MacDougall and Wilfred Trotter on instinct theory and from Edward Thorndike and Floyd Allport on early behaviorism are featured here. One continuity of particular relevance is the manner in which suggestion is transported into their models without losing its essential nature as non-rational and automatic cognitive response to suggestions. Describing a stimulus-response process, Allport, for example, explains suggestion as a situation in which "[the individual] who gives the stimulus controls the behavior and the consciousness of the recipient in an immediate manner, relatively uninfluenced by thought."

The selections on variation deal with the early recognition that the suggestion process, although psychologically non-rational and automatic, was nonetheless contingent in practice. The term "suggestibility" was adopted to illuminate the differences in the susceptibility of individuals to suggestions. Typically, and early on, psychologists identified age, ethnicity, and gender as variables in the process. The analyses, moreover, were usually racist and sexist (sometimes outrageously so), with some exceptions. As experimentation on the factors that affected suggestibility expanded, more and more variables, some having to do with situational context and some with the internal nature of the message itself, were identified as influential in the efficacy of the attitudinal impact. In many of the early experiments, the researchers produced findings and developed explanations for attitude change that predated by decades similar work conducted after World War II. By way of example, Carl Hovland and his colleagues (see, for example, Hovland and Weiss 1951–52), working in the 1950s, famously offered findings on "source credibility" as a significant variable in the process of persuasion, but the perceived authority of the source was heavily studied many years prior to that under its original label, "prestige suggestion."

This section also draws from some of the principal textbooks in social psychology to illustrate the taken-for-granted ubiquity of the doctrine at the time. The list of early researchers involved in this work, and presented here, includes names largely forgotten today, such as Robert Gault, Henry Moore, Frederick Lund, and Luther Bernard.

The final section, "Applications," reviews studies that used suggestion theory to explain and analyze propaganda, advertising, and, in one case, newspaper-incited crime and antisocial behavior. While the first two sections present work that often used real-world messaging to illustrate a theory or the implications of laboratory findings, this section considers writing that starts with problems in practice to show how social scientists of the period engaged suggestion theory to either explore troubling social issues, especially political propaganda, or advance guidance and advice to professional communities on how to better sway consumers.

The section begins with a 1910–11 double article from the *American Journal of Sociology* that was one of the first rigorous empirical studies of the effects of newspaper reading and, moreover, was authored by one of the few women scholars in the field. The subsequent excerpts, on propaganda, include a journal article by Harold Lasswell that adds some illuminating detail to his more famous 1927 book on the topic, *Propaganda Technique in the World War*. Suggestion theory, which Lasswell referenced in both the article and his book, was a natural fit for the analysis of propaganda, given its assumptions about the inherent malleability of social consciousness.

As concern about and research on propaganda accelerated in the interwar years, the suggestion doctrine came to dominate public and scholarly understanding of the phenomenon. Leonard Doob's (1935) *Propaganda: Its Psychology and Technique* offered one of the best examples. While not included in this anthology due to copyright restrictions, it was a leading work on the subject from one of the field's preeminent social psychologists. In it, Doob crafted a version of suggestion theory alloyed with behaviorism and elements of Gestalt theory, ultimately describing suggestion as "the psychological process which causes men and women to change and to be changed" (1935, 405–6). He considered in detail the use of suggestion in propaganda across all forms of media, from newspapers, to radio, to cinema, qualifying the analysis with all the by then well-established conditions and contingencies of the process.

Another historically important text, published the same year, was Hadley Cantril and Gordon Allport's *The Psychology of Radio*. Again, copyright issues precluded its inclusion here, but it was the most thorough and comprehensive study of radio to date and focused special attention on its implications for social life. "Radio," declared the authors, "is an altogether novel medium of communication, preeminent as a means of social control and epochal in its influence upon the mental horizons of man" (1935, vii). And they left no doubt as to the psychological process by which influence was exercised: "The mental mechanism upon which the propagandist relies is not reason but *suggestion*, which brings about the acceptance of a proposition for belief or action without the normal intervention of critical judgment" (62; italics in the original).

Suggestion remained at the heart of Cantril's theory of influence even in his more famous *Invasion from Mars* study five years later (Cantril, Allport, and Herzog 1966). There, he and his colleagues looked at the so-called public panic caused by Orson Welles's 1938 CBS radio production of H.G. Wells's *War of the Worlds*. In assessing why some, but not all, listeners mistook the radio play's depiction of a Martian invasion for a genuine news broadcast, the authors explained: "Those persons who were frightened by the broadcast were, for this occasion at least, highly suggestible. Those who were not frightened and those who believed the broadcast for only a short time were not suggestible" (190). From Le Bon to Cantril, then, the social scientists of the early twentieth century called on suggestion theory to unwind and explain the effect of communicative influence in the context of advertising, political propaganda, and antisocial behavior, in dyads, groups, and disaggregated masses. It was the dominant paradigm of the age.

By 1940, however, suggestion theory was losing its intellectual luster. An underlying assumption of the rising spirit of Progressivism was human rationality. Through the 1930s, scholarly optimism about our potential for reasoned judgment grew, with implications in social psychology and sociology for suggestion's inherently irrational character. Christian Borch suggested it even had an ideological dimension, stating that "[suggestion] was hard to digest for liberal sociologists who launched a vendetta against the concept, eventually rendering it sociologically inappropriate" (2012, 17). At the same time, suggestion came under direct attack from an emerging Gestalt theory whose proponents privileged an explanation for attitude change based on thoughtful human evaluation. By the start of World War II, suggestion was largely out of fashion.

The convergence of these theoretical and even philosophical changes helps explain why suggestion theory faded from social science but does less to explain why the memory of its dominance disappeared as well. And in fact, this is only true in media studies. Any standard text on the history of social psychology—from Le Bon to Doob—will include a recitation of the role played by suggestion. It's reasonable to ask, then, what happened in the study of media? Briefly stated, the research conducted by Hovland's team at Yale after the war, and heralded as the start of media studies by subsequent scholars, eschewed the term suggestion. It was replaced by a new label: "persuasion." And even though the new nomenclature implied psychological process grounded in rationalism, much of Hovland's research still found irrational processes at work. In such cases, Hovland applied the label "gullibility." So even though many of Hovland's findings echoed research conducted decades before, his linguistic pivot from suggestion to persuasion had the effect of cleaving suggestion theory from the historical record (Parsons 2021).

Subsequent histories only served to further seal off that past. Through the 1960s, as noted above, a number of influential books were published that in one way or another designated the work of Hovland and Lazarsfeld as the starting point for serious research on mass media effects. These included Joseph Klapper's (1960) summary of media effects research, Melvin De Fleur's (1966, 1981) textbooks on media theory, and, of course, Schramm's pronouncement on the founding fathers. In none of those works, nor in the many textbooks written by others in the field, did the history or even the existence of suggestion theory receive mention.

The problem was exacerbated with the post–World War II growth of academic schools and departments in media and communication, which frequently arose out of existing professional programs in journalism rather than in the social sciences. This evolution entailed the creation of graduate programs as the newly emerging field of communications or media studies began training its own PhDs. To the extent that these young scholars received any introduction at all to the intellectual history of the field, it was that crafted by Schramm and De Fleur. At the same time, sociology and social psychology were largely abandoning the subject area and moving on to other topics, a movement memorialized by Bernard Berelson's (1959) famous obituary to the field.

So the fields diverged, with the well-known intellectual insularity of the disciplines growing only more pronounced with increasing sub-division and specialization. For media effects scholars, suggestion, grounded in early twentieth-century social psychology, became a lost doctrine.

The following selections, then, are offered in hopes of repairing the historical record and providing greater insight into the extensive work on attitude formation and alteration conducted by psychologists, social psychologists, and sociologists in the first decades of the twentieth century.

Refereneces

Allport, Gordon. 1968. "The Historical Background of Modern Social Psychology." In *The Handbook of Social Psychology*, Vol. 1, edited by Gardner Lindzey and Elliot Aronson, 1–80. 2nd ed. Reading, MA: Addison-Wesley.

Asch, Solomon. 1948. "The Doctrine of Suggestion, Prestige and Imitation in Social Psychology." *Psychological Review* 55, no. 5: 250–77.

Berelson, Bernard. 1959. "The State of Communication Research." *Public Opinion Quarterly* 23, no. 1: 1-6.

Borch, Christian. 2012. *The Politics of Crowds*. New York: Cambridge University Press.

Cantril, Hadley, and Gordon Allport. 1935. *The Psychology of Radio*. New York: Harper.

Cantril, Hadley, Hazel Gaudet, and Herta Herzog. 1966. *The Invasion from Mars: A Study in the Psychology of Panic*. New York: Harper Torchbooks.

Chaffee, Steven, and John Hochheimer. 1985. "The Beginnings of Political Communication Research in the United States: Origins of the 'Limited Effects' Model. In *The Media Revolution in America and in Western Europe*, edited by Everett Rogers and Francis Balle, 267–96. Norwood, NJ: Ablex.

De Fleur, Melvin, and Everett Dennis. 1981. *Understanding Mass Communication*. Boston: Houghton Mifflin.

De Fleur, Melvin. 1966. *Theories of Mass Communication*. New York: David McKay.

Doob, Leonard. 1935. *Propaganda: Its Psychology and Technique*. New York: Henry Holt.

Hovland, Carl, and Walter Weiss. 1951–52. "The Influence of Source Credibility on Communication Effectiveness." *Public Opinion Quarterly* 15, no. 4: 635–50.

Klapper, Joseph. 1960. *The Effects of Mass Communication*. New York: The Free Press.

Lasswell, Harold. 1927. *Propaganda Technique in the World War*. New York: Alfred A. Knopf.

Le Bon, Gustave. 1903. *The Crowd: A Study of the Popular Mind*. London: T. Fisher Unwin.

Lubken, Deborah. 2008. "Remembering the Straw Man: The Travels and Adventures of Hypodermic." In *The History of Media and Communication Research*, edited by Jeff Pooley and David Park, 19–42. New York: Peter Lang.

McDougall, Wiliam. 1909. *An Introduction to Social Psychology*. 2nd ed. London: Methuen.

Parsons, Patrick. 2021. "The Lost Doctrine: Suggestion Theory in Early Media Effects Research." *Journalism & Communication Monographs* 23, no. 2.

Schramm, Wilbur, and Donald Roberts. 1971. *The Process and Effects of Mass Communication*. Rev. ed. Urbana: University of Illinois Press.

Schramm, Wilbur, ed. 1963. *The Science of Human Communication*. New York: Basic Books.

Wartella, Ellen, and Byron Reeves. 1985. "Historical Trends in Research on Children and the Media, 1900–1960." *Journal of Communication* 35, no. 2: 118–33.

PART ONE

Foundations

CHAPTER ONE

The Crowd: A Study of the Popular Mind (1896)

Gustav Le Bon

New York: MacMillan, pp. 1–14, 125–44 [with elisions]. Originally published in French in 1895.

EDITOR'S INTRODUCTION

Gustave Le Bon (1841–1931) was, along with Gabriel Tarde, one of the leading French social theorists of the late nineteenth and early twentieth centuries. With a doctorate in medicine from the University of Paris (1866), his interests and publications spanned psychology, sociology, medicine, and archeology. His research on crowd psychology was motivated in part by his witnessing of the mob destruction wrought by the Paris Commune of 1871, and in 1895 he published his seminal work, *The Crowd: A Study of the Popular Mind*. There he developed and applied his theories of suggestion and imitation, making them central in the understanding of collective behavior.

Neither suggestion theory nor crowd psychology were strictly original with Le Bon. Tarde and the Italian criminologist Scipio Sighele had pioneered work on the latter, especially as it related to criminal behavior. And research on hypnotic suggestion as a therapy had been ongoing through the mid-1800s by both Auguste Liebeault at the influential Nancy School of Psychology and Jean-Martin Charcot at the Salpêtrière Clinic in Paris.

Le Bon's approach to collective behavior, including the behavior of crowds and especially mobs, sought to synthesize and extend Tarde, Charcot, and even Emile Durkheim with an emphasis on the influence of the collective over the individual. According to Le Bon, the psychology of crowds was such that individuals brought together in large assemblies, under certain conditions, could lose their capacity for rational thought and mentally conjoin in a "crowd mind" or "crowd spirit" which would rapidly diffuse through the group by "suggestion or contagion." With the individual's rationality and sense of self lost or displaced, the crowd became susceptible to the influence of a powerful, charismatic speaker, who could manipulate, through a force much like hypnotic suggestion, the assembly's will and action. As Le Bon famously stated, "all feelings and thoughts are bent in the direction determined by the hypnotizer . . . Under the influence of a suggestion, he will undertake the accomplishment of certain acts with irresistible impetuosity."

The following passage, taken from *The Crowd,* highlights Le Bon's major themes, including the definitions and nature of crowds and the collective mind, along with crowd-based suggestibility and the processes of psychological contagion. Le Bon also speaks to specific techniques of influence, such as affirmation and repetition, invoked not just by the street orator but, presaging volumes of later social science, advertising. "When we have read a hundred, a thousand, times that X's chocolate is the best, we imagine we have heard it said in many quarters, and we end by acquiring the certitude that such is the fact."

A full section is also devoted to the power of speaker "prestige," which would become an important and heavily studied characteristic of information sources through the early 1900s, and morph, unattributed, in 1950s communications research into "source credibility."

Through this work, Le Bon became a prime mover in applying suggestion, or imitation-suggestion, to mob behavior, and, with Tarde, helped shape early US social psychology. —*P.P.*

The Crowd: A Study of the Popular Mind (1896)

In its ordinary sense the word "crowd" means a gathering of individuals of whatever nationality, profession, or sex, and whatever be the chances that have brought them together. From the psychological point of view the expression "crowd" assumes quite a different signification. Under certain given circumstances, and only under those circumstances, an agglomeration of men presents new characteristics very different from those of the individuals composing it. The sentiments and ideas of all the persons in the gathering take one and the same direction, and their conscious personality vanishes. A collective mind is formed, doubtless transitory, but presenting very clearly defined characteristics. The gathering has thus become what, in the absence of a better expression, I will call an organised crowd, or, if the term is considered preferable, a psychological crowd. It forms a single being, and is subjected to the LAW OF THE MENTAL UNITY OF CROWDS.

It is evident that it is not by the mere fact of a number of individuals finding themselves accidentally side by side that they acquire the character of an organised crowd. A thousand individuals accidentally gathered in a public place without any determined object in no way constitute a crowd from the psychological point of view. To acquire the special characteristics of such a crowd, the influence is necessary of certain predisposing causes of which we shall have to determine the nature.

The disappearance of conscious personality and the turning of feelings and thoughts in a definite direction, which are the primary characteristics of a crowd about to become organised, do not always involve the simultaneous presence of a number of individuals on one spot. Thousands of isolated individuals may acquire at certain moments, and under the influence of certain violent emotions—such, for example, as a great national event—the characteristics of a psychological crowd. It will be sufficient in that case that a mere chance should bring them together for their acts to at once assume the characteristics peculiar to the acts of a crowd. At certain moments half a dozen men might constitute a psychological crowd, which may not happen in the case of hundreds of men gathered together by accident. On the other hand, an entire nation, though there may be no visible agglomeration, may become a crowd under the action of certain influences.

A psychological crowd once constituted, it acquires certain provisional but determinable general characteristics. To these general characteristics there are adjoined particular characteristics which vary according to the elements of which the crowd is composed, and may modify its mental constitution. Psychological crowds, then, are susceptible of classification; and when we come to occupy ourselves with this matter, we shall see that a heterogeneous crowd—that is, a crowd composed of dissimilar elements—presents certain characteristics in common with homogeneous crowds—that is, with crowds composed of elements more or less akin (sects, castes, and classes)—and side by side with these common characteristics particularities which permit of the two kinds of crowds being differentiated. [...]

It is precisely these general qualities of character, governed by forces of which we are unconscious, and possessed by the majority of the normal individuals of a race in much the same degree—it is precisely these qualities, I say, that in crowds become common property. In the collective mind the intellectual aptitudes of the individuals, and in consequence their individuality, are weakened. The heterogeneous is swamped by the homogeneous, and the unconscious qualities obtain the upper hand.

This very fact that crowds possess in common ordinary qualities explains why they can never accomplish acts demanding a high degree of intelligence. The decisions affecting matters of general interest come to by an assembly of men of distinction, but specialists in different walks of life, are not sensibly superior to the decisions that would be adopted by a gathering of imbeciles. The truth is, they can only bring to bear in common on the work in hand those mediocre qualities which are the birthright of every average individual. In crowds it is stupidity and not mother-wit that is accumulated. It is not all the world, as is so often repeated, that has more wit than Voltaire, but assuredly Voltaire that has more wit than all the world, if by "all the world" crowds are to be understood.

If the individuals of a crowd confined themselves to putting in common the ordinary qualities of which each of them has his share, there would merely result the striking of an average, and not, as we have said is actually the case, the creation of new characteristics. How is it that these new characteristics are created? This is what we are now to investigate.

Different causes determine the appearance of these characteristics peculiar to crowds, and not possessed by isolated individuals. The first is that the individual forming part of a crowd acquires, solely from numerical considerations, a sentiment of invincible power which allows him to yield to instincts which, had he been alone, he would perforce have kept under restraint. He will be the less disposed to check himself from the consideration that, a crowd being anonymous, and in consequence irresponsible, the sentiment of responsibility which always controls individuals disappears entirely.

The second cause, which is contagion, also intervenes to determine the manifestation in crowds of their special characteristics, and at the same time the trend they are to take. Contagion is a phenomenon of which it is easy to establish the presence, but that it is not easy to explain. It must be classed among those phenomena of a hypnotic order, which we shall shortly study. In a crowd every sentiment and act is contagious, and contagious to such a degree that an individual readily sacrifices his personal interest to the collective interest. This is an aptitude very contrary to his nature, and of which a man is scarcely capable, except when he makes part of a crowd.

A third cause, and by far the most important, determines in the individuals of a crowd special characteristics which are quite contrary at times to those presented by the isolated individual. I allude to that suggestibility of which, moreover, the contagion mentioned above is neither more nor less than an effect.

To understand this phenomenon it is necessary to bear in mind certain recent physiological discoveries. We know to-day that by various processes an individual may be brought into such a condition that, having entirely lost his conscious personality, he obeys all the suggestions of the operator who has deprived him of it, and commits acts in utter contradiction with his character and habits. The most careful observations seem to prove that an individual immerged for some length of time in a crowd in action soon finds himself—either in consequence of the magnetic influence given out by the crowd, or from some other cause of which we are ignorant—in a special state, which much resembles the state of fascination in which the hypnotised individual finds himself in the hands of the hypnotiser. The activity of the brain being paralysed in the case of the hypnotised subject, the latter becomes the slave of all the unconscious activities of his spinal cord, which the hypnotiser directs at will. The conscious personality has entirely vanished; will and discernment are lost. All feelings and thoughts are bent in the direction determined by the hypnotiser.

Such also is approximately the state of the individual forming part of a psychological crowd. He is no longer conscious of his acts. In his case, as in the case of the hypnotised subject, at the same time that certain faculties are destroyed, others may be brought to a high degree of exaltation. Under the influence of a suggestion, he will undertake the accomplishment of certain acts with irresistible impetuosity. This impetuosity is the more irresistible in the case of crowds than in that of the hypnotised subject, from the fact that, the suggestion being the same for all the individuals of the crowd, it gains in strength by reciprocity. The individualities in the crowd who might possess a personality sufficiently strong to resist the suggestion are too few in number to struggle against the current. At the utmost, they may be able to attempt a diversion by means of different suggestions. It is in this way, for instance, that a happy expression, an image opportunely evoked, have occasionally deterred crowds from the most bloodthirsty acts.

We see, then, that the disappearance of the conscious personality, the predominance of the unconscious personality, the turning by means of suggestion and contagion of feelings and ideas in an identical direction, the tendency to immediately transform the suggested ideas into acts; these, we see, are the principal characteristics of the individual forming part of a crowd. He is no longer himself, but has become an automaton who has ceased to be guided by his will.

Moreover, by the mere fact that he forms part of an organised crowd, a man descends several rungs in the ladder of civilisation. Isolated, he may be a cultivated individual; in a crowd, he is a barbarian—that is, a creature acting by instinct. He possesses the spontaneity, the violence, the ferocity, and also the enthusiasm and heroism of primitive beings, whom he further tends to resemble by the facility with which he allows himself to be impressed by words and images—which would be entirely without action on each of the isolated individuals composing the crowd—and to be induced to commit acts contrary to his most obvious interests and his best-known habits. An individual in a crowd is a grain of sand amid other grains of sand, which the wind stirs up at will. [...]

The Means of Action of the Leaders: Affirmation, Repetition, Contagion

When it is wanted to stir up a crowd for a short space of time, to induce it to commit an act of any nature—to pillage a palace, or to die in defence of a stronghold or a barricade, for instance—the crowd must be acted upon by rapid suggestion, among which example is the most powerful in its effect. To attain this end, however, it is necessary that the crowd should have been previously prepared by certain circumstances, and, above all, that he who wishes to work upon it should possess the quality to be studied farther on, to which I give the name of prestige.

When, however, it is proposed to imbue the mind of a crowd with ideas and beliefs—with modern social theories, for instance—the leaders have recourse to different expedients. The principal of them are three in number and clearly defined—affirmation, repetition, and contagion. Their action is somewhat slow, but its effects, once produced, are very lasting.

Affirmation pure and simple, kept free of all reasoning and all proof, is one of the surest means of making an idea enter the mind of crowds. The conciser an affirmation is, the more destitute of every appearance of proof and demonstration, the more weight it carries. The religious books and the legal codes of all ages have always resorted to simple affirmation. Statesmen called upon to defend a political cause, and commercial men pushing the sale of their products by means of advertising are acquainted with the value of affirmation.

Affirmation, however, has no real influence unless it be constantly repeated, and so far as possible in the same terms. It was Napoleon, I believe, who said that there is only one figure in rhetoric of serious importance, namely, repetition. The thing affirmed comes by repetition to fix itself in the mind in such a way that it is accepted in the end as a demonstrated truth.

The influence of repetition on crowds is comprehensible when the power is seen which it exercises on the most enlightened minds. This power is due to the fact that the repeated statement is embedded in the long run in those profound regions of our unconscious selves in which the motives of our actions are forged. At the end of a certain time we have forgotten who is the author of the repeated assertion, and we finish by believing it. To this circumstance is due the astonishing power of advertisements. When we have read a hundred, a thousand, times that X's chocolate is the best, we imagine we have heard it said in many quarters, and we end by acquiring the certitude that such is the fact. When we have read a thousand times that Y's flour has cured the most illustrious persons of the most obstinate maladies, we are tempted at last to try it when suffering from an illness of a similar kind. If we always read in the same papers that A is an arrant scamp and B a most honest man we finish by being convinced that this is the truth, unless, indeed, we are given to reading another paper of the contrary opinion, in which the two qualifications are reversed. Affirmation and repetition are alone powerful enough to combat each other.

When an affirmation has been sufficiently repeated and there is unanimity in this repetition—as has occurred in the case of certain famous financial undertakings rich enough to purchase every assistance—what is called a current of opinion is formed and the powerful mechanism of contagion intervenes. Ideas, sentiments, emotions, and beliefs possess in crowds a contagious power as intense as that of microbes. This phenomenon is very natural, since it is observed even in animals when they are together in number. Should a horse in a stable take to biting his manger the other horses in the stable will imitate him. A panic that has seized on a few sheep will soon extend to the whole flock. In the case of men collected in a crowd all emotions are very rapidly contagious, which explains the suddenness of panics.

Brain disorders, like madness, are themselves contagious. The frequency of madness among doctors who are specialists for the mad is notorious. Indeed, forms of madness have recently been cited—agoraphobia, for instance—which are communicable from men to animals. [. . .]

Contagion is so powerful that it forces upon individuals not only certain opinions, but certain modes of feeling as well. Contagion is the cause of the contempt in which, at a given period, certain works are held—the example of "Tannhauser" may be cited—which, a few years later, for the same reason are admired by those who were foremost in criticising them.

The opinions and beliefs of crowds are specially propagated by contagion, but never by reasoning. The conceptions at present rife among the working classes have been acquired at the public-house as the result of affirmation, repetition, and contagion, and indeed the mode of creation of the beliefs of crowds of every age has scarcely been different. Renan justly institutes a comparison between the first founders of Christianity and "the socialist working men spreading their ideas from public-house to public-house"; while Voltaire had already observed in connection with the Christian religion that "for more than a hundred years it was only embraced by the vilest riff-raff." [...]

Prestige

Great power is given to ideas propagated by affirmation, repetition, and contagion by the circumstance that they acquire in time that mysterious force known as prestige.

Whatever has been a ruling power in the world, whether it be ideas or men, has in the main enforced its authority by means of that irresistible force expressed by the word "prestige." The term is one whose meaning is grasped by everybody, but the word is employed in ways too different for it to be easy to define it. Prestige may involve such sentiments as admiration or fear. Occasionally even these sentiments are its basis, but it can perfectly well exist without them. The greatest measure of prestige is possessed by the dead, by beings, that is, of whom we do not stand in fear—by Alexander, Caesar, Mahomet, and Buddha, for example. On the other hand, there are fictive beings whom we do not admire—the monstrous divinities of the subterranean temples of India, for instance—but who strike us nevertheless as endowed with a great prestige.

Prestige in reality is a sort of domination exercised on our mind by an individual, a work, or an idea. This domination entirely paralyses our critical faculty, and fills our soul with astonishment and respect. The sentiment provoked is inexplicable, like all sentiments, but it would appear to be of the same kind as the fascination to which a magnetised person is subjected. Prestige is the mainspring of all authority. Neither gods, kings, nor women have ever reigned without it.

The various kinds of prestige may be grouped under two principal heads: acquired prestige and personal prestige. Acquired prestige is that resulting from name, fortune, and reputation. It may be independent of personal prestige. Personal prestige, on the contrary, is something essentially peculiar to the individual; it may coexist with reputation, glory, and fortune, or be strengthened by them, but it is perfectly capable of existing in their absence.

Acquired or artificial prestige is much the most common. The mere fact that an individual occupies a certain position, possesses a certain fortune, or bears certain titles, endows him with prestige, however slight his own personal worth. A soldier in uniform, a judge in his robes, always enjoys prestige. Pascal has very properly noted the necessity for judges of robes and wigs. Without them they would be stripped of half their authority. The most unbending socialist is always somewhat impressed by the sight of a prince or a marquis; and the assumption of such titles makes the robbing of tradesmen an easy matter.

The prestige of which I have just spoken is exercised by persons; side by side with it may be placed that exercised by opinions, literary and artistic works, etc. Prestige of the latter kind is most often merely the result of accumulated repetitions. History, literary and artistic history especially, being nothing more than the repetition of identical judgments, which nobody endeavours to verify, every one ends by repeating what he learnt at school, till there come to be names and things which nobody would venture to meddle with. For a modern reader the perusal of Homer results incontestably in immense boredom; but who would venture to say so? The Parthenon, in its present state, is a wretched ruin, utterly destitute of interest, but it is endowed with such prestige that it does not appear to us as it really is, but with all its accompaniment of historic memories. The special characteristic of prestige is to prevent us seeing things as they are and to entirely paralyse our judgment. Crowds always, and individuals as a rule, stand in need of ready-made opinions on all subjects. The popularity of these opinions is independent of the measure of truth or error they contain, and is solely regulated by their prestige.

I now come to personal prestige. Its nature is very different from that of artificial or acquired prestige, with which I have just been concerned. It is a faculty independent of all titles, of all authority, and possessed by a small number of persons whom it enables to exercise a veritably magnetic fascination on those around them, although they are socially their equals, and lack all ordinary means of domination. They force the acceptance of their ideas and sentiments on those about them, and they are obeyed as is the tamer of wild beasts by the animal that could easily devour him.

The great leaders of crowds, such as Buddha, Jesus, Mahomet, Joan of Arc, and Napoleon, have possessed this form of prestige in a high degree, and to this endowment is more particularly due the position they attained. Gods, heroes, and dogmas win their way in the world of their own inward strength. They are not to be discussed: they disappear, indeed, as soon as discussed. [...]

Still, the various examples that have just been cited represent extreme cases. To fix in detail the psychology of prestige, it would be necessary to place them at the extremity of a series, which would range from the founders of religions and empires to the private individual who endeavours to dazzle his neighbours by a new coat or a decoration.

Between the extreme limits of this series would find a place all the forms of prestige resulting from the different elements composing a civilisation—sciences, arts, literature, &c.—and it would be seen that prestige constitutes the fundamental element of persuasion. Consciously or not, the being, the idea, or the thing possessing prestige is immediately imitated in consequence of contagion, and forces an entire generation to adopt certain modes of feeling and of giving expression to its thought. This imitation, moreover, is, as a rule, unconscious, which accounts for the fact that it is perfect. The modern painters who copy the pale colouring and the stiff attitudes of some of the Primitives are scarcely alive to the source of their inspiration. They believe in their own sincerity, whereas, if an eminent master had not revived this form of art, people would have continued blind to all but its naive and inferior sides. Those artists who, after the manner of another illustrious master, inundate their canvasses with violet shades do not see in nature more violet than was detected there fifty years ago; but they are influenced, "suggestioned," by the personal and special impressions of a painter who, in spite of this eccentricity, was successful in acquiring great prestige. Similar examples might be brought forward in connection with all the elements of civilisation.

CHAPTER TWO

The Laws of Imitation (1903)

Gabriel Tarde

Translated by Elsie Clews Parsons, New York: Henry Holt, pp. 74–87 [with elisions]. Originally published in French in 1890.

EDITOR'S INTRODUCTION

Gabriel Tarde (1843–1904), along with Le Bon, has been credited as one of the founders of social psychology (Martindale 1981, 282; Murphy and Newcomb 1937, 4). Born in southern France and schooled in Paris, he studied law with an emphasis on criminal behavior. He became a professor at College de France and, with a strong penchant for quantitative analysis, the head of the Bureau of Statistics at the French Ministry of Justice.

His major scholarly works included *Les Lois de L'imitation* (1890) and *L'Opinion et la Foule* [*Opinion and the Crowd*] (1901) and focused on the maintenance and transmission of social norms, laws, and customs. At the heart of his explanation for social cohesion was the act of imitation, or as it was often expressed, suggestion-imitation.

As with Le Bon's use of suggestion, numerous commentators have noted that Tarde's treatment of imitation was not novel (Martindale 1981; Karpf 1932). Its role as a force in social interaction had been noted as early as David Hume, examined by Walter Bagehot and applied by William James and Josiah Royce (see below), among others. But, as noted by Karpf, "Instead of giving imitation *a* place in his thought . . . Tarde gave it *the* place" (1932, 95). It was, for him, "the elementary social phenomenon" (Ellwood 1901, 722) and the mechanism for the transmission of all social forms. Or, as Tarde himself declared, "The unvarying characteristic of every social fact whatsoever is that it is imitative" (1891, 41).

In *L'Opinion et la Foule* [*Opinion and the Crowd*], Tarde explored the role of suggestion-imitation in various collective settings. Presaging Herbert Blumer and others, he distinguished "crowds"—individuals in a local, specific congregation—from "publics"—individuals united not spatially but in senti-ment or belief. Publics, moreover, were the creations of modern mass media, specifically the press (Martindale 1981, 284). For Tarde, public opinion, or the "public mind," was the product of the interaction of the press with the geographically disaggregated audience which, by virtue of the spatial and temporal distance, was more capable than the crowd of thoughtful political or social deliberation.

In the following excerpt from *The Laws of Imitation*, Tarde begins with a physiologically oriented consideration of memory and habit that constituted for him "self-imitation" and "suggestion." He expands his analysis to the social, invoking the contemporaneous language of hypnotism—the "magnetizer," the "magnetized," and the "somnambulist"—to explain the maintenance and evolution of social structure. Here again, the power of authority, or social prestige, is of central importance: "Since the somnambulist is for the time being deprived of this power of resistance, he can illustrate for us the imitative quiescence of the social being in so far as he is social." He notes, succinctly, "Society is imitation and imitation is a kind of somnambulism."

Along with Le Bon, Tarde's ideas percolated through early social psychol-ogy and into the work of leading US social scientists such as Ross, Baldwin, Giddings, and Ellwood.

References

Ellwood, Charles. 1901. "The Theory of Imitation in Social Psychology." *American Journal of Sociology* 6, no. 6: 721–41.

Karpf, Fay Berger. 1932. *American Social Psychology: Its Origins, Development and European Background.* New York: McGraw Hill.

Martindale, Don. 1981. *The Nature and Types of Sociological Theory.* 2nd ed. Boston: Houghton Mifflin.

Murphy, Gardner, and Theodore Newcomb. 1937. *Experimental Social Psychology*. Rev. ed. New York: Harper.

Tarde, Gabriel. 1890. *Les Lois de L'imitation*. Paris: F. Alcan. Translated by Elsie C. Parsons as The Laws of Imitation (New York: Henry Holt, 1903).

Tarde, Gabriel. 1899. *Social Laws: An Outline of Sociology*. Translated by Howard Warren. New York: MacMillan.

Tarde, Gabriel. 1901. *L'Opinion* et la Foule. Paris: F. Alcan.

The Laws of Imitation (1903)

IV

1. Taine sums up the thought of the most eminent physiologists when he happily remarks that the brain is a repeating organ for the senses and is itself made up of elements which repeat one another. In fact, the sight of such a congery of like cells and fibres makes any other idea impossible. Moreover, direct proof is at hand in the numerous observations and experiments which show that the cutting away of one hemisphere of the brain, and even the removal of much of the substance of the other, affects only the intensity, without at all changing the integrity, of the intellectual functions. The part that was removed, therefore, did not collaborate with the part that remained; both parts could only copy and reinforce each other. Their relation was not economic and utilitarian, but imitative and social in the sense that I use that term. Whatever may be the cellular function which calls forth thought (a highly complex vibration, perhaps?), there is no doubt that it is reproduced and multiplied in the interior of the brain every moment of our mental life and that to every distinct perception a distinct cellular function corresponds. The indefinite and inexhaustible continuation of these intricate and richly intersecting radiations constitutes memory and habit. When the multiplying repetition in question is confined to the nervous system, we have memory; when it spreads out into the muscular system, we have habit. Memory, so to speak, is a purely nervous habit; habit is both a nervous and a muscular memory.

Thus every act of perception, in as much as it involves an act of memory, which it always does, implies a kind of habit, an unconscious imitation of self by self. There is, evidently, nothing social in this. When the nervous system is sufficiently excited to set in motion a certain set of muscles, habit, properly speaking, appears. It is another case of non-social, or, as I might better say, of presocial or subsocial self-imitation. This does not mean that, as alleged, an idea is an abortive act. Action is only the following up of an idea, the acquisition of a steadfast faith. Muscle works only for the enrichment of nerves and brain.

But if the remembered idea or image was originally lodged in the mind through conversation or reading, if the habitual act originated in the view or knowledge of a similar act on the part of others, these acts of memory and habit are social as well as psychological facts, and they show us the kind of imitation of which I have already spoken at such length. Here we have memory and habit which are not individual, but collective. Just as a man does not see, listen, walk, stand, write, play the flute, or, what is more, invent or imagine, except by means of many co-ordinated muscular memories, so a society could not exist or change or advance a single step unless it possessed an untold store of blind routine and slavish imitation which was constantly being added to by successive generations.

2. What is the essential nature of the suggestion which passes from one cerebral cell to another and which constitutes mental life? We do not know.[1] Do we know anything more about the essence of the suggestion which passes from one person to another and which constitutes social life? We do not; for if we take this phenomenon in itself, in its higher state of purity and intensity, we find it related to one of the most mysterious of facts, a fact which is being studied with intense curiosity by the baffled philosophic alienists of the day, i.e., somnambulism.[2] If you re-read contemporaneous works on this subject, especially those of Richet, Binet and Féré, Beaunis, Bernheim, Delboeuf, I shall not seem fanciful in thinking of the social man as a veritable somnambulist. I think, on the contrary, that I am conforming to the most rigorous scientific method in endeavouring to explain the complex by the simple, the compound by the element, and to throw light upon the mixed and complicated social tie, as we know it, by means of a social tie which is very pure, which is reduced to its simplest expression, and which is so happily realised for the edification of the sociologist in a state of somnambulism. Let

---

[1] At the time when the foregoing and the following considerations first appeared in print, in November, 1884, in thᴇ *Revue philosophique*, hypnotic suggestion was but barely spoken of and the idea of universal social suggestion, an idea which has since been so strongly emphasised by Bernheim and others, was cast up against me as an untenable paradox. Nothing could be commoner than this view at present.

[2] This old-fashioned term shows that at the time of the first publication of this passage the word hypnotism had not as yet been altogether substituted for somnambulism.

us take the hypothetical case of a man who has been removed from every extra-social influence, from the direct view of natural objects, and from the instinctive obsessions of his different senses, and who has communication only with those like himself or, more especially, to simplify the question, with one person like himself. Is not such an ideal subject the proper one through which to study by experiment and observation the really essential characteristics of social relations, set free in this way from all complicating influences of a natural or physical order? But are not hypnotism and somnambulism the exact realisation of this hypothesis? Then I shall not excite surprise if I briefly review the principal phenomena of these singular states and if I find both magnified and diminutised, both overt and covert, forms of them in social phenomena. Through such a comparison, we may perhaps come to a better understanding of the fact that is called abnormal by showing to what extent it is general, and of the fact that is general by perceiving its distinctive traits in high relief in the apparent anomaly.

The social like the hypnotic state is only a form of dream, a dream of command and a dream of action. Both the somnambulist and the social man are possessed by the illusion that their ideas, all of which have been suggested to them, are spontaneous. To appreciate the truth of this sociological point of view, we must not take ourselves into consideration, for should we admit this truth about ourselves, we would then be escaping from the blindness which it affirms; and in this way a counter argument might be made out. Let us call to mind some ancient people whose civilisation differs widely from our own, the Egyptians, or Spartans, or Hebrews. Did not that people think, like us, that they were autonomous, although, in reality, they were but the unconscious puppets whose strings were pulled by their ancestors or political leaders or prophets, when they were not being pulled by their own contemporaries? What distinguishes us modern Europeans from these alien and primitive societies is the fact that the magnetisation has become mutual, so to speak, at least to a certain extent; and because we, in our democratic pride, a little exaggerate this reciprocity, because, moreover, forgetting that in becoming mutual, this magnetisation, the source of all faith and obedience, has become general, we err in flattering ourselves that we have become less credulous and docile, less imitative, in short, than our ancestors. This is a fallacy, and we shall have to rid ourselves of it. But even if the aforesaid notion were true, it would nevertheless be clear that before the relations of model and copyist, of master and subject, of apostle and neophyte, had become reciprocal or alternative, as we ordinarily see them in our democratic society, they must of necessity have begun by being one-sided and irreversible. Hence castes. Even in the most democratic societies, the one-sidedness and irreversibility in question always exist at the basis of social imitations, i.e., in the family. For the father is and always will be his son's first master, priest, and model. Every society, even at present, begins in this way.

Therefore, in the beginning of every old society, there must have been, *a fortiori*, a great display of authority exercised by certain supremely imperious and positive individuals. Did they rule through terror and imposture, as alleged? This explanation is obviously inadequate. They ruled through their *prestige*. The example of the magnetiser alone can make us realise the profound meaning of this word. The magnetiser does not need to lie or terrorise to secure the blind belief and the passive obedience of his magnetised subject. He has prestige—that tells the story. That means, I think, that there is in the magnetised subject a certain potential force of belief and desire which is anchored in all kinds of sleeping but unforgotten memories, and that this force seeks expression just as the water of a lake seeks an outlet. The magnetiser alone is able through a chain of singular circumstances to open the necessary outlet to this force. All forms of prestige are alike; they differ only in degree. We have prestige in the eyes of anyone in so far as we answer his need of affirming or of willing some given thing. Nor is it necessary for the magnetiser to speak in order to be believed and obeyed. He need only act; an almost imperceptible gesture is sufficient.

This movement, together with the thought and feeling which it expresses, is immediately reproduced. Maudsley says that he is not sure that the somnambulist is not enabled to read unconsciously what is in the mind through "an *unconscious* imitation of the attitude and expression of the person whose *exact* muscular contradictions are *instinctively copied*."[3] Let us observe that the magnetised subjects imitates the magnetiser, but that the latter does not imitate the former. *Mutual imitation*, mutual prestige or *sympathy*, in the meaning of Adam Smith, is produced only in our so-called waking life and among people who seem to exercise no magnetic influence over one another. If, then, I have put prestige, and not sympathy, at the foundation and origin of society, it is because, as I have said before, the unilateral must have preceded the reciprocal.[4] Without an age of authority, however sur-

---

[3] *The Pathology of Mind* [p. 69. Henry Maudsley, M. D., New York, 1890. The italics are the author's.-Tr.].

[4] On this point I need correction. Sympathy is certainly the primary source of sociability and the hidden or overt soul of every kind of imitation, even of imitation which is envious and calculating, even of imitation of an enemy. Only, it is certain that sympathy itself

prising this fact may be, an age of comparative fraternity would never have existed. But, to return, why should we really marvel at the one-sided, passive imitation of the somnambulist? Any act of any one of our fellows inspires us who are lookers-on with the more or less irrational idea of imitation. If we at times resist this tendency, it is because it is neutralised by some antagonistic suggestions of memory or perception. Since the somnambulist is for the time being deprived of this power of resistance, he can illustrate for us the imitative quiescence of the social being in so far as he is social, i.e., in so far as he has relations exclusively with his fellows and, especially, with one of his fellows.

If the social man were not at the same time a natural being, open and sensitive to the impressions of external nature and of alien societies, he would never be capable of change. Like associates would remain forever incapable of changing spontaneously the type of traditional ideas and desires which had been impressed upon them by the conventional teaching of their parents, priests, or leaders. Certain peoples have been known to approach singularly close to this condition. Nascent communities, like young children, are, in general, indifferent and insensible to all which does not concern man or the kind of man whom they resemble, the man of their own race or tribe. "The somnambulist sees and hears," says A. Maury, "only what enters into the preoccupations of his dream." In other words, all his power of belief and desire is concentrated on a single point. Is not this the exact effect of obedience and imitation through fascination? Is not fascination a genuine neurosis, a kind of unconscious polarisation of love and faith? [...]

But I must not dwell any longer upon the above comparison. At any rate, I hope that I have at least made my reader feel that to thoroughly understand the essential social fact, as I perceive it, knowledge of the infinitely subtle facts of mind is necessary, and that the roots of even what seems to be the simplest and most superficial kind of sociology strike far down into the depths of the most inward and hidden parts of psychology and physiology. Society is imitation and imitation is a kind of somnambulism. This is the epitome of this chapter. As for the second part of the proposition, I beg the reader's indulgence for any exaggeration I may have been guilty of. I must also remove a possible objection. It may be urged that submission to some ascendency does not always mean following the example of the person whom we trust and obey. But does not belief in anyone always mean belief in that which he believes or seems to believe? Does not obedience to someone mean

---

begins by being one-sided instead of mutual.

that we will that which he wills or seems to will? Inventions are not made to order, nor are discoveries undertaken as a result of persuasive suggestion. Consequently, to be credulous and docile, and to be so as pre-eminently as the somnambulist and the social man, is to be, primarily, imitative. To innovate, to discover, to awake for an instant from his dream of home and country, the individual must escape, for the time being, from his social surroundings. Such unusual audacity makes him super-social rather than social.

CHAPTER THREE

The Imitative Functions and Their Place in Human Nature (1894)

Josiah Royce

Century Illustrated Magazine *48, no. 1: pp. 137–42.*

EDITOR'S INTRODUCTION

In an age when US scholars frequently received training at the major universities of Europe, the impact of Le Bon and Tarde, and concern about the potential social power of suggestion-imitation, was felt domestically even before their works were translated into English. Josiah Royce (1855–1916) offers an early example. Royce was a major figure in American philosophical thought and a leading proponent of Hegelian Idealism. He took a BA in Classics at the University of California in Oakland (1875) and a PhD at Johns Hopkins University (1878). He studied for a year in Germany and, following his doctorate, taught English composition and literature at the University of California at Berkeley before moving to Harvard University in 1882. There he befriended William James, his long-time intellectual sparring partner, and eventually took over as chair of the Department of Philosophy.

While known primarily as a philosopher, Royce also studied psychology and integrated it into his larger work, writing a textbook on the subject in

1903 (*Outlines of Psychology*, New York: Macmillan) and serving as president of the American Psychological Association in 1902. Tarde's conception of the role of imitation in human interaction was central to Royce's psychology, as demonstrated in the following article from *Century Illustrated Magazine*. It is included here as one of the earliest published English language pieces on suggestion-imitation (along with the Sidis excerpt below). And it provides a reminder that this view of communicative influence was gaining academic speed in the United States even before the turn of the century. Published in the popular press, it is, further, an example of suggestion-imitation as a popular, as well as academic, topic. In fact, over the following decades, suggestion theory as an explanation for communication influence would come to exert significant sway over public thinking, and public policy, with respect to both state and commercial propaganda.

The excerpt below, then, is to some extent a heralding review of Tarde's *Laws of Imitation*. While Royce takes as common knowledge the human tendency to imitate, especially in children, he enters a long list of early research questions: is imitation an instinctive or a learned behavior?; "how, in the growth of the individual, do these imitative functions arise?"; and "when and in what order do [the imitative functions] appear" in child development?

Following Tarde, he examines the importance of, and prior research on, hypnotism as a tool in psychology, extending the process to the influence of existing social belief systems on the "waking man," who "usually believes, concerning politics, concerning the state of business, concerning religion, whatever the people of his party, or set, or faction, or profession, or sect, declares to be the truth; and he supposes, nevertheless, that his mind is his own." Here we also see, for one of the first times in the published record, the use of the term "social suggestion" to describe the operation of various social forces on the formation and alteration of attitudes and perceptions.

Royce notes, at the same time, that the effect of the imitative functions and social suggestion is as complex as it is fascinating and may work as much to the benefit of society and the individual as to its detriment. "It is on these accounts," declares Royce, "that I deem the study of the imitative functions probably the most important task in the psychology of the immediate future."—*P.P.*

The Imitative Functions and Their Place in Human Nature (1894)

I HAVE been led of late, in connection with certain philosophical inquiries, to begin the study of a subject the general interest of which, for teachers, for students of any region of art, and for lovers of human nature at large, seems to me so considerable, that I am now disposed to ask for the cooperation of a larger public in the pursuit of the research. At the same time, I may as well take the opportunity which this paper affords to explain, as well as I can, why I have begun this task, and why I see so much reason to hope for good results from the further consideration of the matter.

I.

THE object of this study is, directly speaking psychological, and relates to the nature, the scope, and the significance of what may be called, in general, the imitative functions of mankind. No functions are, in one sense, more familiar. None are more frequently interesting. We all are aware that children are imitative, that both among children and among adults virtue and vice alike are, under favorable circumstances, "catching"; that fashion has, in certain matters, an irresistible sway; that not only commercial panics, and mobs, and "fads," but also great reform movements, and disciplined armies, and such historical events as the conversion of nations in the old days from heathenism to Christianity, all illustrate, in their several ways, the potency of imitative tendencies; and that art itself, at least according to Aristotle's famous definition, is essentially imitation. We know that there are sometimes epidemics of crime or of suicide. We know that the doleful prevalence of the current popular melody is due, not to a love of music, but to the insistent force of the imitative tendency. Turn thus, which way we will, the familiar presence of the imitative functions in human life impresses itself upon us.

"Verily," says M. Tarde, an eminent French sociologist, in his remarkable book, "Les Lois d'Imitation"—verily, "*La societe, c'est l'imitation,*" or as one may freely translate, "Imitation of imitations," saith the professor, "in society all is imitation." In this extreme form, of course, the assertion does indeed remind us of many qualifications; but of these we shall speak further on.

Were I anxious, then, for mere illustrations of the frequency of the imitative functions in the life of man, I should indeed have no trouble in getting my fill of them, without other aid than that of my own eyes. But with the mere confirmation of their frequency, the question of their real significance is first brought really to the front. And along with this question there come before us a vast number of others, all interesting to the student of human nature. How, in the growth of the individual, do these imitative functions arise? Are any of them truly instinctive, or are all of them, as Alexander Bain has contended, acquired functions, due to experience? Or, in other words, does man learn to imitate because he is brought up in a social environment; or, on the contrary, is he capable of life in a social environment only because he is first, by nature and instinct, an imitative animal? What is the history of the imitative functions in childhood? When, and in what order, do they appear? How are they related to the growth of the childish reason, conscience, imagination, insight, skill? Of what use can the imitative functions, at any age, be made for the development of the child's intellect and will? Such are the first psychological questions that come to one's mind in this connection. It may already, in general, be clear how serviceable the study of such problems can become both to teachers and to all others interested in the psychology of childhood.

II.

BUT a wider scope still has of late been given to the psychological study of the imitative functions by the results of research in the domain of hypnotism. How deep-seated the imitative functions are, it has needed hypnotic research not so much to demonstrate as to illustrate, and to bring, through illustration, to our clearer scientific consciousness. The principal positive value of hypnotism for psychology, up to the present time, has consisted in the fact that the apparently marvelous, and, at first sight, even miraculous-seeming, phenomena of the hypnotic state have served to make the familiar facts of the prevalence of imitation in human life look, for the time, in these singular illustrations, unfamiliar; so that, in consequence, the attention of psychologists has been attracted to the matter in a new way and from a new side. That this is the principal service rendered by hypnotism to psychology was first pointed out at some length by the aforesaid M. Tarde, who herein, I believe, followed up a suggestion of Taine's. In a paper first published in 1884, early in the history of hypnotic research,—a paper which was later incorporated into the book called "Les Lois d'Imitation,"—M. Tarde asserted and developed the interesting formula that what the individual hypnotizer is to his sleeping and abnormally plastic subject, such, almost precisely, is society to the waking and normally plastic man.

The hypnotized subject believes what the hypnotizer says, and supposes this belief to be his own conviction; does what his hypnotizer suggests, and believes, or may believe, that he does this of his own freewill; has suggested hallucinations of taste, sight, smell, or suggested emotions, and believes these to be his own independent and individual experiences. Well, just so the waking man usually believes, concerning politics, concerning the state of business, concerning religion, whatever the people of his party, or set, or faction, or profession, or sect, declares to be the truth; and he supposes, nevertheless, that his mind is his own. The waking man, moreover, as to all the endlessly numerous deeds of convention and custom, does what his portion of society declares to be the proper thing, and fancies all the while that he is choosing of his own free will. Finally, the waking man's emotions—as, for example, his esthetic emotions—are usually at the mercy, or, at all events, deeply under the influence, of social suggestion; and even his sensations and perceptions are not exempt from this influence.

Illustrations are here easy. What is beautiful in decorative art the community at large learns by social suggestion. Esthetic tastes as to domestic interiors, and as to the architecture of private dwellings, are subject in every generation to changes which work upon individuals in almost precisely the same way as hypnotic suggestions made to sleeping subjects work during experiments in hypnotism. One hears that this or this is admirable in the way of house-building or of decoration. Society declares the fact; and forthwith one perceives with one's own eyes, if one is but an average man, that this is indeed beautiful, just as the people say; and one is naively unaware that if all the people had said that it was ugly, one would equally have observed that fact instead. Even so, too, as to our sensations, or, at all events, as to our immediate reaction of liking or of dislike in presence of our sensations. Everybody has many acquired tastes. Some people, to be sure, have liked olives from the first taste of them; but many have not. Yet, as the saying goes, if you eat in succession seven olives, you will henceforth like them. It would be more psychological to say that after you have received seven quasi-hypnotic social suggestions from your neighbors, each suggestion being strong enough to make you try to behave toward olives as the rest do, then, at length, your immediate sensations may yield, and henceforth the olives will taste as the other men say that they taste—namely, good. It is in such a fashion that one becomes a connoisseur in the world of mere sensations of taste and of smell, just as before in the world of art. The connoisseur as to wines, teas, perfumes, dinners, and other such sensory experiences, is a person of fairly keen native sensory discrimination, whose actual discriminations, and expressions of like and dislike, have been subjected to a long course of quasi-hypnotic social training. His tastes are never purely, or even largely, his own, although it is his game, as connoisseur, to pretend, and often his fate, as social bondman, to believe, that they are his own. Were they, however, original, he would not be reckoned as a connoisseur, but as a barbarian.

Such are some of the possible illustrations of M. Tarde's interesting thesis. In bringing them forward here in my own way, and with my own choice determining their selection, I am of course well aware that there are other factors at work besides the conventional or suggested factors, and that, too, even in the most conventional regions of life—factors which, despite all our imitativeness, determine our individual varieties of taste. We never reach perfect agreement with our neighbors as to these things of convention. A certain stubborn variety of individual caprice consciously forms a pleasant social contrast to our more imitative judgments. And so for the rest, despite all conformity, there are many social conventions which themselves require of the individual, within certain limits, a certain degree of individuality and of nonconformity.

But here is only one of the many cases where the imitative functions become, as we shall later more fully see, beautifully, and almost inextricably, entangled with the "temperamental" varieties of function in the individual. And it is this entanglement, as we shall find, that constitutes the very soul of the significance of the imitative functions, which, when properly developed, do not lead at all to the suppression of originality, but may actually form the condition of the growth of individuality, and of the only true independence of opinion and of ideals that is possible to man. But of this hereafter. Moreover, it is this same endless entanglement of imitative or "suggested" factors in taste and in belief with individual factors that makes the psychology of the imitative functions of man so complex and fascinating a problem for the student of human nature.

If the social phenomena in themselves, considered thus, serve to indicate by their universality, as it were, the breadth, the extent, of the imitative functions of humanity, certain of the well-known phenomena of hypnotism, viewed apart, tend especially to bring to mind the depth, the inner potency, of these functions in the life of each individual. It is true, as we have seen, that, viewed on the whole, the plasticity of the hypnotic subject is not something essentially novel, but insubstantially the normal social plasticity of a man set at work under somewhat abnormal conditions. It is, however, also true that, under these abnormal conditions, there appear some unexpected special consequences of the general imitativeness of man—consequences that startle us by the indications which they give of the depth to which the imitative tendency reaches in its influence upon our unconscious, yes, upon even our lower physiological, life.

That by suggestion you can make a man notice what he would otherwise overlook is a strictly normal and familiar fact. Much, if not all, of that marvelous acuteness of senses which is often shown by hypnotic subjects seems, in the opinion of many observers, to be only a case of this directly or indirectly suggested concentration of attention upon his own fainter experiences on the part of the hypnotized subject. And so far the anomalies of hypnotism would seem to be related only to the peculiar conditions under which the hypnotic subject is influenced, and to the extraordinary source of the influence, which is here not, as normally, the authority of society in general, but the voice of his hypnotizer. Yet, in addition, it is indeed true that, in case of hypnotism, there also appear certain other aspects of the imitative functions aspects which, in the case of the normal social influences, may also be present, and which probably are present, but which are there masked by their more obvious and conscious accompaniments; while, in case of the hypnotic subject, these other aspects come to light. Hypnotic suggestion, namely, is found to influence not only the acuteness of one's perceptions and the course of one's conscious habits, but the performance of a good many bodily functions that usually seem to have small relation to the will. Circulation, digestion, and general functional nervous conditions of a decidedly manifold sort, have been found to be more or less subject to hypnotic suggestion. To be sure, this sort of influence is seldom without very decided limits, which vary endlessly from person to person. But the fact remains that, in a given person, the imitative plasticity which leads him to follow out so faithfully the ideas which his hypnotizer suggests may lead him also to alter relatively deep and unconscious organic functions, such as he has never explicitly learned to influence by his will, and such as, normally, neither he nor his fellows would be aware of influencing. Yet, as many considerations make probable, what the hypnotic experiment thus brings to light cannot well be anything new in kind. Doubtless our organisms are at all times deeply plastic to suggestions; only this plasticity, on account of the complexity of our normal functions, remains masked until the hypnotic experiment, working upon a much simplified state of affairs, brings it to light.

But if our imitativeness thus actually extends far beyond the region of our conscious and voluntary life, one sees at once that one has to do with functions the basis of which probably lies deep down among the inborn and instinctive tendencies of our nature. And of such probably instinctive and original imitativeness childhood gives us many indications. For children often appear to sympathize imitatively with the expressed emotions of their elders even when there is no adequate basis in the previous childish experience for the emotions in question. A young child, taken unkindly to a funeral, or forced by unhappy fortune to witness one in the family, has suggested to him, in the faces and behavior of his elders, emotions of a depth and intensity for which his own experience can give no basis. These elders themselves know why they sorrow. The young child knows very dimly, or perhaps realizes not yet at all, why death is what it is, and means what it does. Yet sometimes he shows on such occasions an overwhelming sense of the horror of the situation, a sense which people usually refer to his direct and inborn dread of death and of his surroundings. There is, in fact, probably present some such original instinct concerning death; but very likely this instinct does not account for the whole of the child's horror, or yet perhaps for the larger part of it. This larger part is probably due rather to a contagion of emotion, the origin of which lies in another instinct—that of imitation. The child, without consciousness of the reason, assumes, by instinctive imitation, the expressive bodily states and attitudes of his elders, and accordingly, since our emotions are, in part at least, the results rather than the causes of our bodily states of emotional expression,[1] the child, having imitated the organic expression, consequently in some measure imitates the emotion, without at all well comprehending why the emotion ought to be felt. If everybody else at the funeral conspired with his fellows to seem gay and to talk merrily, it is unlikely that the child's own original instincts about death would be enough to terrify him. He would then very likely look at the corpse rather with wonder than with horror.

Just so, too, it is in youth, or even throughout life, so long as we retain any freshness of sympathetic experience. With the aid of certain deep and instinctive tendencies to assume imitatively the bodily attitudes or the other expressive functions of our fellows, functions which may be in part internal as well as external, we are able to share the emotions of others even when these

---

[1] To this fact Professor James has recently given an expression in his now well-known theory of the emotions—a theory according to which "we do not cry because we feel sorry, but feel sorry because we cry." This theory, in its extreme form, may be inadequate. There can be little doubt that it expresses an important part of the truth.

emotions relate to matters that lie far beyond our own previous experience. When one first witnesses a serious accident, or attends another through a painful illness, or sees a friend suffering from some tremendous personal grief, one gets a sense of what this calamity means—a sense which may far transcend one's power to recall similar experiences in one's own life. There are some people, to be sure, who sympathize, like the maids of Andromache when she parted from Hector, or like the comforters of Gudrun when she sat tearless over Sigurd's body, or like Polonius himself, only by recalling, in the sufferer's presence, their own present or past griefs. "Truly, I in youth suffered many things of love—very near this." But such sympathy is not the only sort or the most spontaneous. The emotions of the theater carry the sensitive spectator, especially when he is young, far beyond any memory of his own experiences. Notice such a spectator, and you will see him imitating unconsciously, by play of feature, or possibly even by gestures of hands, arms, or body, the actor whose skill absorbs him. But meanwhile, through this imitation, he is experiencing something of emotions before unknown to him—the sorrows of *Lear,* the remorse of *Macbeth,* the agony of *Othello.* To him these experiences seem as novel as if they had been original happenings in his own life. Such are the quasi-hypnotic suggestions of the stage. They often give us, as we say, wholly new insights into life.

As for other instances of the depth of such imitative emotions, there will be known to many of us cases of sensitive young women who, at the sight of accidents, or bodily ailments (say in elder women), misfortunes the causes of which they themselves have never yet experienced, are quite capable of feeling suggested internal pangs, or serious, if temporary, physical derangements, of the imitative, and at the same time partly instinctive, character of which there can be little reason to doubt. Nor are women alone in such imitative sufferings. Many men have felt such, and have been surprised at their vigor. The emotions of mobs, moreover, have the same character of imitative contagion, going much beyond the previous personal experiences of many, or perhaps, most members of the mob. In an important sociological monograph, entitled (in its French translation) "La Foule Criminelle," an Italian criminologist, Signor Scipio Sighele, has recently treated at length the problem of the psychology of mobs, and has dwelt much on the analogy between these phenomena, and those of hypnotic suggestion. It seems impossible to interpret such cases without supposing that the imitative functions of man have a very profound instinctive basis, and are by no means as purely secondary and acquired functions as Alexander Bain has supposed.

So much, then, for the lessons derived from hypnotism, and from daily life, concerning the depth and significance of imitation in man.

III.

But now, as regards the uses and the results of the imitative functions in human life, the foregoing general indication of their breadth and their depth is only the merest beginning of a comprehension of the part they play in our education and in our consciousness. It is not because they are common, or because they are, in deepest origin, partly instinctive, that I lay such stress upon them. It is because they are, in their proper and almost inextricable entanglement with our individual or temperamental functions, absolutely essential elements of all our rationality, of all our mental development, of all our worth as thinkers, as workers, or as producers; it is, too, because this value of imitation as the necessary concomitant, and condition and instrument, of all sound originality is still so inadequately understood by teachers, by critics of art, by students of human nature generally—it is on these accounts that I deem the study of the imitative functions probably the most important task in the psychology of the immediate future. The mental relations of the imitative functions are what I therefore have, next, briefly to indicate. This I may here do in the most summary form, thus:

It is a commonplace that most of our rational thinking (some psychologists incorrectly say, *all* of our rational thinking) is done in language. Well, language is very obviously a product of social imitation; is, therefore, a case of human imitativeness in every individual who learns it. So, then, without imitativeness, no higher development of rational thought in any of us. Only the imitative animal can become rational. So much for a beginning. But the fruitfulness of the imitative functions does not cease here. It is, in the second place, well recognized that our social morality, whatever else within or without us it implies, is in one direction dependent upon our regard for the will, the interest, the precepts, or the welfare of our fellows. Now such regard is, in its turn, dependent upon our power, by imitation, to experience and to comprehend the suggested will, interest, authority, and desires of those about us. So, then, without imitativeness, no chance for the development of the social conscience. The imitative functions, in combination of course with other functions, but still with essential significance, as factors in the whole process, are thus at the basis of the development of both reason and conscience. Nor yet is this all. Reason not only uses language as an instrument, but it aims at a certain well known goal; it aims at the imitation in conscious terms of the truth of things beyond us. Reason thus not only depends upon imitative functions; it is explicitly imitative in its purposes. Just so, too, conscience is not only based, as to its origin, upon social imitations, so that you educate the childish conscience through obedience and through authority; but conscience, too, is in its goal explicitly imitative. It sets before us ideals of character, and then bids us imitate them. These ideals are, in general, personal. Conscience says: Such and such a self, thus and thus employed in reasonable service, is the right sort of self for you. You conceive such an ideal self. Now, in your practical life, imitate this conception. One imitates the ideal—precisely as, in childhood, the little boys imitate the big boys. Man the imitative animal is thus at the very heart of man the rational and man the moral animal, no matter how high in the scale the developed man may rise.

Yet the psychological importance of the imitative functions is not even thus to be exhausted. It is an odd fact, and one of vast significance, that all of us come by our developed personal self-consciousness through very decidedly imitative processes. Of this fact a later discussion may give a fuller account. It is enough now to remind observers of children how full of proud self-consciousness is the little boy who drives horse, or who plays soldier, or who is himself a horse, or a bird, or other creature, in his play. To be what we call his real self is, for his still chaotic and planless inner consciousness, so long as it is not set in order by his imitativeness, the same as to be nobody in particular. But to be a horse, or a coachman, or a soldier, or the hero of a favorite story, or a fairy, that is to be somebody, for that sort of self one first witnesses from without, or finds portrayed in the fascinating tale, and then imitatively assimilates, so that one thereupon conceives this new self from within, and rejoices in one's prowess as one does so.

Nor does this process of acquiring one's selfhood vicariously, as it were, cease with childhood. My various present social functions I have, in the first place, imitatively learned. Others, my guides and advisers, first showed me the way to these functions; for it was thus that I learned to move in company, to speak, to assume the outward forms of my calling, to conduct myself as just this particular kind of social organ. Now I myself, as what the psychologist calls an "empirical ego," am just now, for myself as well as for my fellows, the man who possesses, among other things, such and such a calling, position, office, rights, and aptitudes. Of all these things I had no knowledge in childhood. I had to learn my whole social trade; I learned it by imitations. But now that I have got such a calling and place, my knowledge of it determines for me, all the while, my current notion of who I am. I am what my profession and my social relations define me to be. Thus it is actually true that just as my social guides—my parents, teachers, advisers, friends, critics—together gave me, through my love of imitating them and of being influenced by their characters, by their conduct, and by their ideals—just as they, I say, gave me a knowledge of my calling, so too they have furnished me with the very material of my present self-consciousness. Self-consciousness itself, in each one of us, is a product of imitation.

Reason, conscience, self-consciousness—these are significant possessions. Yet without imitativeness we should never have come by any one of them. They are results, and, as they stand, are even now embodiments of imitation. Such is my present thesis. Nor is this statement itself more than the beginning. As a fact, I hold that far more specific mental products than have yet been named—for instance, specific beliefs of reason, such as the so-called "axioms" at the basis of science—can be explained as determined in their nature by the special conditions under which the imitative functions of mankind have been developed. But herewith, indeed, I reach topics that lie far beyond the scope of the present paper, and within the domain of the deepest problems of philosophy. [...]

CHAPTER FOUR

Mental Development of the Child and the Race (1911)

James Mark Baldwin

3rd ed. New York: Macmillan, pp. 100–27, 332–39 [with elisions].

EDITOR'S INTRODUCTION

While Royce offered an early example of US interest in suggestion and imitation, it was James Mark Baldwin (1861–1934) who influenced a generation of psychologists and social psychologists. He was a pioneer in the field and his work became a ritual touchstone in US writing on the topic. Earning a BA (1884) and PhD (1898) from Princeton University, he initially taught in theology (his undergraduate degree) before transitioning to philosophy and eventually psychology. In 1893 he joined the faculty at his alma mater, where he helped found the university's Psychology Department. Active across the young discipline, he also co-founded *Psychological Review* and *Psychological Monographs* and was founding editor of *Psychological Bulletin*.

His 1896 treatise, *The Mental Development in the Child and the Race*, was a groundbreaking work in developmental and social psychology. Among other things, it helped nudge early US social thought away from the European collectivism of Durkheim and Herbert Spencer and toward a toward a stronger focus on the individual and social groups. The study had the novel component of employing his own two young children as research subjects, chronicling their personality development over two years.

The conceptual core of the study was Baldwin's reliance on the Le Bon–Tarde formulation of suggestion and imitation as the chief driver of personality development. According to Martindale, "Baldwin's importance lay in the extension of the ideas of imitation and suggestion to the problems of personality and the relation between self and society. . . suggestion [for Baldwin] represents all the processes which mold psychic life" (Martindale 1981, 288–89). Stated Baldwin, "Suggestion by idea, or through consciousness, must be recognized to be as fundamental a kind of motor stimulus as the direct excitation of a sense organ."

In the following excerpt from the 1911 third revised edition, Baldwin, as did the previous authors, starts with an exposition on hypnotism as "an entirely new method of mental study," and, borrowing from James, couches it in terms of "ideo-motor suggestion." He advances the consideration of imitation and suggestion by breaking each into multiple sub-categories, such as "psychological suggestion" and "deliberative suggestion." Ultimately (beyond the excerpt), he categorizes suggestion into nine discrete types.

In addition, where Tarde and Le Bon commonly used suggestion and imitation as a combined phrase and failed to clearly distinguish between the two, we see in Baldwin an early effort to disentangle them. For him, suggestion was the environmental *stimulus* and imitation the *response* to the suggestion. As will be seen, ultimately the two concepts were cleaved, with each following a distinct evolutionary path. In the excerpt, Baldwin additionally offers one of the first uses of the term "suggestibility" to describe an individual's susceptibility to suggestion.

This early text would become, again, a major influence on subsequent turn-of-the-century social scientists as social psychology delved more deeply into suggestion theory.—*P.P.*

References

Martindale, Don. 1981. *The Nature and Types of Sociological Theory.* 2nd ed. Boston: Houghton Mifflin.

Mental Development in the Child and the Race (1911)

CHAPTER VI: SUGGESTION

§ 1. General Definition

THE rise of hypnotism in late years has opened the way to an entirely new method of mental study. The doctrine of reflexes was before largely physiological, and only pathological cases could be cited in evidence of a mechanism in certain forms of consciousness as well as out of it; and even pathological cases of extreme sensitiveness to casual suggestion from the environment or from other men did not receive the interpretation which the phenomena of hypnotic suggestion are now making possible, *i.e.* that suggestion by idea, or through consciousness, must be recognized to be as fundamental a kind of motor stimulus as the direct excitation of a sense organ. Nervous reflexes may work directly through states of consciousness, or be stimulated by them; these states of consciousness may be integral portions of such reflexes; and, further, a large part of our mental life is made up of a mass of such ideo-motor 'suggestions,' which are normally in a state of subconscious inhibition.

Without discussing the nature of the hypnotic state in the first instance, nor venturing to pass judgment in this connection upon the question whether the suggestion theory is sufficient to explain all the facts, we may yet isolate the aspect spoken of above, and discuss its general bearings in the normal life, especially of children. Of course, the question at once occurs, is the normal life a life to any degree of ideo-motor or suggestive reactions, or is the hypnotic sleep in this aspect of it, quite an artificial thing? Further, if such suggestion is normal or typical in the mental life, what is the nature of the inhibition by which it is ordinarily kept under—in other words, what is its relation to what we call will? Leaving this second question altogether unanswered for the present,[1] it has occurred to me to observe children, especially my own H. and E., during their first two years, to see if light could be thrown upon the first inquiry above. If it be true that ideo-motor suggestion is a normal thing, then early child life should present the most striking analogies to the hypnotic state in this essential respect. This is a field that has hitherto, as far as I know, been largely unexplored by workers in the psychology of suggestion.

---

[1] See, however, Chap. XIII., below.

It is not necessary, I think, to discuss in detail the meaning of this much-abused but, in the main, very well defined word, 'suggestion.' The general conception may be sufficiently well indicated for the present by the following quotations from authorities. They all agree on the main phenomenon, their definitions differing in the place of emphasis, according as one aspect rather than another supplies ground for a theory. I may gather them up in my own definition, which aims to describe the fundamental fact apart from theory, and is therefore better suited to our preliminary exposition. I have myself defined suggestion as "from the side of consciousness ... the tendency of a sensory or an ideal state to be followed by a motor state,[2] in the manner typified by the abrupt entrance from without into consciousness of an idea or image, or a vaguely conscious stimulation, which tends to bring about the muscular or volitional effects which ordinarily follow upon its presence."[3]

Janet defines suggestion as "a motor reaction brought about by language or perception."[4] This narrows the field to certain classes of stimulations, well defined in consciousness, and overlooks the more subtle suggestive influences emphasized by the Nancy school of theorizers. Schmidkunz makes it: "die Herbeirufung eines Ereignisses durch die Erweckung seines psychischen Bildes."[5] This again makes a mental picture of the suggested 'event' in consciousness necessary, and, besides, does not rule out ordinary complex associations. It neglects the requirement insisted upon by Janet, *i.e.* that the stimulus be from without, as from hearing words, seeing actions, objects, etc. Wundt says: "Suggestion ist Association mit gleichzeitiger Verengerung des Bewusstseins auf die durch die Association angeregten Vorstellungen."[6] In this definition Wundt meets the objection urged against the definition of suggestion in terms of complex association, by holding down the association to a 'narrowed consciousness'; but he, again, neglects the outward nature of the stimulus, and does not give an adequate account of how this narrowing of consciousness upon one or two associated terms, usually a sensori-motor association, is brought about. Ziehen: "In der Beibringung der Vorstellung liegt das Wesen der Suggestion."[7] Here we have the sufficient recognition of the artificial and external source of the stimulation, but yet we surely

---

[2] *Science*, Feb. 27, 1891, where many of the observations given in this chapter were first recorded.

[3] Cf. also *Handbook of Psychology*, II., 297.

[4] *Aut. Psych.*, p. 218.

[5] *Hypnotism u. Suggestion*, II. Abs.

[6] *Psych. der Suggestion.*

[7] *Philos. Monatshefte*, XXIX., 1893, p. 489.

cannot say that all such stimulations succeed in getting suggestive force. A thousand things suggested to us are rejected, scorned, laughed at. This is so marked a fact in current theory, especially on the pathological side, that I have found it convenient to use a special phrase for consciousness when in the purely suggestible condition, *i.e.* 'reactive consciousness.'[8] The phrase 'conscious reflex' is sometimes used, but is not good as applied to these suggestive reactions; for they are cortical in their brain seat, and are not as definite as ordinary reflexes.

For our present purposes, the definition just given from my earlier work is sufficient, since it emphasizes the *movement side* of suggestion. The fundamental fact about all suggestion,—not hypnotic suggestion alone, which some of the definitions which I have cited have exclusive reference to[9]—is, in my view, the removal of inhibitions to movement brought about by a certain condition of consciousness which may be called 'suggestibility.' The further question, what makes consciousness suggestible, is open to some debate. There are two general statements—not to elaborate a theory here, however—which are not done justice to by any of the current theories. We may say, first, that a suggestible consciousness is one in which the ordinary *criteria of belief* are in abeyance; the coefficients of reality, to use the terms of an earlier discussion of belief,[10] are no longer apprehended. Consciousness finds all presentations of equal value, in terms of uncritical reality-feeling. It accordingly responds to them all, each in turn, readily and equally. Second: this state of things is due primarily to a violent reaction or fixation of attention, resulting in its usual monoideism, or 'narrowing of consciousness.' For belief is a motor attitude resting upon complexity of presentation and representation. Just as soon as this mature complexity is destroyed, belief disappears, and all ideas 'become free and equal' in doing their executive work. Each presentation streams out in action by suggestion; and stands itself fully in the possession of consciousness, with none of the pros and cons of its usual claim to be accepted as real, gaining also the still greater establishment which comes from the return wave upon itself of its own motor discharge. The question of suggestion becomes then that of the mechanism of attention in working three results: (1) the narrowing of consciousness upon the suggested idea, (2) the consequent narrowing of

---

[8] *Handbook of Psychology, Feeling and Will*, pp. 60 ff., and Chap. XII.

[9] See the section below in this chapter in which the main facts of hypnosis are briefly stated, and the further references to the theory of hypnotism in sect.3 of the chapter on Volition, below.

[10] *Handbook*, II., Chap. VII.

the motor impulses to simpler lines of discharge, and (3) the consequent inhibition of the discriminating and selective attitude which constitutes belief in reality.

The truth of these general statements is thoroughly confirmed by the observation of children, in whom the general system of adjustments, which constitute the 'worlds of reality' of us adults, are not yet effected. Little children are credulous, in an unreflective sense, even to illusion. Tastes, colours, sensations generally, pains, pleasures, may be suggested to them, as is shown by the instances given in later pages.

It is, however, to the truth of the fundamental fact of normal motor suggestion found in children, that I wish to devote a large part of this chapter; and observations of reactions clearly due to such suggestion, either under natural conditions or by experiment, lead me to distinguish the varying sorts of suggestion mentioned in the following paragraphs, in what I find to be about the order of their appearance in child-life. [...]

Surveying the ground that we have gone over so far in this chapter, the progress of suggestion may be seen by the following brief definitions:

1. *Physiological suggestion* is the tendency of a reflex or secondary automatic process to get itself associated with and influenced by stimulating processes of a physiological and vaguely sensory sort. Perhaps the plainest case of it, on a large scale in animal life, is seen in the decay of instincts when no longer suited to the creature's needs and environment.

2. *Sensori-motor and ideo-motor suggestion* is the tendency of all nervous reactions to adapt themselves to new stimulations, both sensory and ideal, in such a way as to be more ready for the repetition or continuance of these stimulations.

3. *Deliberative suggestion* is the tendency of different competing sensory processes to merge in a single conscious state with a single motor reaction, illustrating the principles of nervous summation and arrest.

4. *Imitative suggestion* is the tendency of a sensory or ideal process to maintain itself by such an adaptation of its discharges that they reinstate in turn new stimulations of the same kind. [...]

CHAPTER XII: CONSCIOUS IMITATION (CONCLUDED)

§ 1. Classification

IT is possible, on the basis of the preceding developments, to lay out a scheme of notions and terms to govern the discussion of the whole matter of imitation. This has been the 'loose joint' in many discussions; the utter lack of any well defined limits set to the phenomena in question. Tarde practically claims all cases of organic or social resemblance as instances of imitation, overlooking the truth, as one of his critics takes pains to point out, that two things which resemble each other may be common effects of the same cause! Others are disposed to consider the voluntary imitation of an action as the only legitimate case of imitation. This, we have seen, has given rise to great confusion among psychologists. We have reason to think that volition requires a finely complex system of copy elements, whose very presence can be accounted for only on the basis of earlier organic, or certainly ideo-motor, imitations. Further, it is the lower, less volitional types of mind that simple imitation characterizes, the undeveloped child, the parrot, the idiot, the hypnotic, the hysterical. If again we say, with yet others, that imitation always involves a presentation or image of the situation or object imitated,—a position very near the popular use of the term,—then we have great difficulty in accounting for the absorption and reproduction of sub-conscious, vaguely present stimulations; as, for example, the acquisition of facial expression, the contagion of emotion, the growth of style in dress and institutions—what may be called the influence of the 'psychic atmosphere.'

I think we have found reason from the analysis above, to hold that our provisional definition of imitation is just; an imitative reaction is one which tends normally to maintain or repeat its own stimulating process. This is what we find the nervous and muscular mechanism suited to, and this is what we find the organism doing in a progressive way in all the types of function which we have passed in review. If this is too broad a definition, then what we have traced must be given some other name, and imitation applied to any more restricted function that can be clearly and finally marked out. But let us give no rein to the fanciful and strained analogies which have exercised the minds of certain writers on imitation.

Adhering, then, to the definition which makes of imitation a 'circular' process, we may point out its various 'kinds,' according to the degree in which a reaction of the general type has, by complication, abbreviation, substitution, inhibition, or what not, departed in the development of consciousness from its typical simplicity. We find, in fact, three great instances of function, all of which conform to the imitative type. Two of these have already been put in evidence in detail; the third I am going on to characterize briefly in the following section under the phrase 'plastic imitation.'

First: the organic reaction which tends to maintain, repeat, reproduce, its own stimulation, be it simple contractility, muscular contraction, or selected reactions which have become habitual. This may be called *biological* or *organic imitation.* Under this head fall all cases lower down than the conscious picturing of copies; lower down in the sense of not involving, and never having involved, for their execution, a conscious sensory or intellectual suggesting stimulus, with the possibility of its revival as a memory. On the nervous side, such imitations may be called *subcortical;* and in view of another class mentioned below, they may be further qualified as *primarily subcortical.*

These 'biological' imitations are evidently first in order of development, and represent the gains or accommodations of the organism made independently of the conscious picturing of stimulations and adaptation to them. They serve for the accumulation of material for conscious and voluntary actions. In the young of the animals, their scope is very limited, because of the complete instinctive equipment which young animals bring into the world; but in human infants they play an important part, as the means of the gradual reduction to order and utility of the diffused motor discharges of the new-born. I have noted its presence under the phrase 'physiological' suggestion in another place. It is under this head that the so-called 'selective' function of the nervous system finds its first illustration.

Second: we pass to *psychological, conscious,* or *cortical* imitations. The criterion of imitation—the presence of a copy to be aimed at—is here fulfilled in the form of conscious presentations and images. The copy becomes consciously available in two ways: first, as presentation, which the imitative reaction seeks to continue or reproduce (as the imitation of words heard, movements seen, etc.); and second, as memory. In this latter case there arises complexity in the 'copy system,' with desire, in which there is consciousness of the imitative tendency as respects an agreeable memory copy; and with the persistence of such a copy, and its partial repression by other elements of memory, comes volition. We find, accordingly, two kinds of psychological or cortical imitation, which I have called respectively 'simple' and 'persistent' imitation. Simple imitation is the sensori-motor or ideo-motor suggestion which tends to keep itself going by reinstating its own stimulation; and persistent imitation is the 'try-try-again,' experience of early volition, to be taken up in more detail below.

Third: a great class of facts which we may well designate by the term 'plastic' or 'secondarily subcortical' imitations, to which more particular attention may now be given.

§ 2. Plastic Imitation

This phrase is used to cover all the cases of reaction or attitude, toward the doings, customs, opinions of others, which once represented more or less conscious adaptations either in race or in personal history, but which have become what is ordinarily called 'secondary automatic' and subconscious. With them are all the less well-defined kinds of response which we make to the actions, suggestions, etc., of others, simply from the habit we are in, by heredity and experience, or conforming to social 'copy.' Plastic imitation represents the general fact of that normal *suggestibility* which is, as regards personal *rapport,* the very soul of our social relationships with one another.

These cases come up for detailed discussion in the later volume. They serve to put in evidence the foundation facts of a possible psychology of masses, crowds, organized bodies generally. They may be readily explained by one or both of two principles—both really one, that of Habit. The principle of 'lapsed links,' already explained, applies to cases of conventional conformity, or custom, which is but an expression for abbreviated processes of social imitation. This accounts for the influence of the old, the venerated, the antique, upon mankind. The other principle is the application of habit itself to imitation, whereby absorption by imitation has become the great means, the first resort of consciousness, in the presence of new kinds of experience. We have become used to getting new accommodations, fine outlets for action and avenues of happiness, by taking up new thoughts, beliefs, fashions, etc. This accounts for the tyranny of novelty in all social affairs. So in these two principles, both exhibitions of the one law of imitation, we reach the two great forces of social life, conservatism and liberalism. So we find under this heading such fundamental facts as the social phenomena of contagion, fashion, mob-law, which Tarde and Sighele so well emphasize, the imitation of facial and emotional expression, moral influence, organic sympathy, personal *rapport,* etc., all matters set aside for later treatment. The term 'plastic' serves to point out the rather helpless condition of the person who imitates, and so interprets in his own action the more intangible influences of his estate in life.

The general character of plastic imitation may be made clearer if we give attention to some of its more obscure instances, and assign them places in the general scheme of development.

The social instances noticed at length by Tarde, and summarized under so-called 'laws,' are easily reduced to the more general principles now stated. Tarde enunciated a law based on the fact that people imitate one another in thoughts and opinions before they do so in dress and customs, his inference being that 'imitation proceeds from the internal to the external.' So far as this is true it is only partially imitation. Thoughts and opinions are imitated because they are most important, and most difficult to maintain for one self. And it is only a result of similar thought that action should be similar, without in all cases resorting to imitation to account for this last similarity. But the so-called facts are not true. The relatively trivial and external things are most liable to be seized upon. A child imitates persons, and what he copies most largely are the personal points of evidence, so to speak; the boldest, most external manifestations, the things that he with his capacity is most likely to see, not the inner essential mental things. It is only as he grows to make a conscious distinction between thought and action that he gets to giving the former a higher valuation. And so it is in the different strata of society. The relative force of convention, imitation of externals, worship of custom, seems to have an inverse relation to the degree of development of a people.

Again, Tarde's laws relative to *imitation mode* and *imitation coutume*—the former having in its eye the new, fashionable, popular, the fad; the latter, the old, venerable, customary—are so clearly partial statements of the principles of accommodation and habit, as they get application in the broader genetic ways already briefly pointed out, that it is not necessary to dwell further upon them. [11]

The phenomena of hypnotism illustrate most strikingly the reality of this kind of imitation at a certain stage of mental life. Delbreuf makes it probable [12] that the characteristic peculiarities of the 'stages' of the Paris school are due to this influence; and the wider question may well be opened, whether suggestion generally, as understood in hypnotic work, might not be better expressed by some formula which recognizes the fundamental sameness of all reactions—normal, pathological, hypnotic, degenerative—which exhibit the form of stimulus-repeating or 'circular' process characteristic of simple imitation. In normal, personal, and social suggestion the copy elements

---

[11] Tarde's other principle, that 'inferiors imitate superiors,' is clearly a corollary from the view that the progressive sense of personality arises through social suggestion.

[12] *Revua Philosophique*, XXII., pp. 146 ff.

are, in part, unrecognized; and their reactions are subject to inhibition and blocking-off by the various voluntary and complicated tendencies which have the floor. In sleep, on the other hand, the copy elements are largely spontaneous images, thrown up by the play of association, or stimulated by outside trivialities, and all so weak that while action follows in the dream persons, it does not generally follow in the dreamer's own muscles. But in hypnotic somnambulism, the copy elements are from the outside, thrown in; the inner fountains are blocked; action tends to follow upon idea, whatever it is. Even the idea of no action is acted out by the lethargic, and the idea of fixed self-sustaining action by the cataleptic. [13]

Further, in certain cases of madness (*jolie a deux*, etc.) the patient responds to the copy which has been learned from a single person only, and which has aided in the production of the disease. [14] In all these cases, the peculiar character of which is the performance, under conditions commonly called those of aboulia, of reactions which require the muscular co-ordinations usually employed by voluntary action, we have illustrations of 'plastic' imitation. On the pathological side, we find, in aphasic patients who cannot write or speak spontaneously, but who still can copy handwriting and speak after another, cases which illustrate the same kind of defect, yet in which the defect is not general, but rather confined to a particular group of reactions, by reason of a circumscribed lesion.

In this form of imitative suggestion, it is now clear, we have a second kind of subcortical reaction. It is 'secondarily subcortical,' in contrast with the organic or 'primarily subcortical' imitations. When looked at from the point of view of race history, it gives us further reason for finding in imitation a native impulse.

---

[13] It may be well to quote Janet's summary of his determinations of the characteristic features of general catalepsy, all of which indicate a purely imitative condition of consciousness, *Aut. Psych.*, p. 55: "The different phenomena which we have described are these; i.e. the continuation of an attitude or a movement, the repetition of movements which have been seen and of sounds which have been heard, the harmonious association of the members and of their movements." Cf. Janet on hysteria, *Arch. de Neurologie*, June, July, 1893.

[14] Cf. Falret, *Eludes cliniques sur les maladies et nerveuses*, p. 547.

CHAPTER FIVE

The Psychology of Suggestion (1898)

Boris Sidis

New York: D. Appleton, pp. 5–18, 29–34, 297–311 [with elisions].

EDITOR'S INTRODUCTION

Where scholars like Le Bon and Baldwin employed suggestion and imitation in their larger analyses, Boris Sidis (1867–1923) focused on suggestion exclusively, writing the first book-length treatment of the subject. Sidis was born in the Ukraine and emigrated to the US in 1887 to escape Czarist political persecution. He earned an AB (1894), PhD (1897), and MD (1908) from Harvard University, where he studied under William James and specialized in abnormal psychology. He founded the *Journal of Abnormal Psychology* but spent most of his professional career as a practicing psychopathologist, also founding the New York State Psychopathic Institute.

As with Le Bon, his research interests were colored by his early experience with real-world mob behavior, in his case the witnessing of and escape from the violent Czarist pogroms of the 1880s. But while suggestion theory was the subject of Sidis's analyses, he did not, interestingly, cite the work of Le Bon or Tarde. Instead, he built on then-popular research in hypnotic suggestion, especially Charcot, with whom he briefly studied, and added a few citations to Baldwin.

In February 1895, he published a popularized version of his views in the *Atlantic Monthly*, titled "A Study of the Mob." With heavy reliance on research in hypnotism, the article attempted to explain mob behavior as a form of social hypnotism, with special attention to examples from, and conditions in, Czarist Russia.

Four years later, he released his scholarly examination of the subject, *The Psychology of Suggestion*, with an introduction by James. Notable again as the first book dedicated to suggestion theory, Sidis begins with an explanation of the basic concept as a process in which "the subject accepts *uncritically* the idea suggested to him, and carries it out almost *automatically*" (italics in the original). "Social suggestion" was the mechanism, either direct or indirect, which mobilizes the mob or the crowd. "Social life," he declared, "presupposes suggestion…. Man is a social animal, no doubt: but he is social because he is suggestible."

In the following excerpt, Sidis further distinguishes between normal and abnormal states of hypnosis and between individual "suggestibility" (one-on-one hypnosis) and "social suggestibility," both with implications for theories of attitude change. Foreshadowing future studies in persuasion, he also offers observations on the impact, in practice, of the frequency of a suggestion and on what would later be called order effects: *"Of all the modes of suggestion, however, the most powerful, the most effective, and the most successful is a skillful combination of frequency and last impression"*(italics in the original). Relevant as well in today's world of social media, he wrote in some detail about the nature of suggestion-driven social manias and public panics.

Like many of the Progressives who came after him, Sidis nonetheless retained optimism in the fundamental nature of people's critical ability, especially when properly schooled. "In the spirit of his adoptive country, Sidis believed in the power of education in preparing the masses for more informed, rational decision making" (Prislin and Crano 2012, 322).—*P.P.*

References

Prislin, Radmila, and William Crano. 2012. "A History of Social Influence Research." In *Handbook of the History of Social Psychology*, edited by Arie Kruglanski and Wolfgang Stroebe, 321–40. New York: Psychological Press

The Psychology of Suggestion (1898)

PART I. SUGGESTIBILITY.

CHAPTER I. SUGGESTION AND SUGGESTIBILITY.

PSYCHOLOGICAL investigators employ the term "suggestion" in such a careless and loose fashion that the reader is often puzzled as to its actual meaning. Suggestion is sometimes used for an idea bringing in its train another idea, and is thus identified with association. Some extend the province of suggestion and make it so broad as to coincide with any influence man exerts on his fellow-beings. Others narrow down suggestion and suggestibility to mere symptoms of hysterical neurosis. This is done by the adherents of the Salpêtrière school. Suggestion, again, is used by the Nancy school to indicate the cause which produces that peculiar state of mind in which the phenomena of suggestibility become especially prominent.

This vague and hazy condition of the subject of suggestion causes much confusion in psychological discussions. To free the subject from this confusion of tongues, we must endeavour in some way or other to give a strict definition of suggestion, and rigorously study the phenomena contained within the limited field of our investigation. We must not follow in the way of those writers who employ the terms suggestion and suggestibility in all possible meanings. Such carelessness can not but lead into a tangle of words. In order to give a full description of suggestion and make its boundary lines clear, distinct, and definite, let us take a few concrete cases and inspect them closely. [...]

A stump orator mounts a log or a car and begins to harangue the crowd. In the grossest way he praises the great intelligence, the brave spirit of the people, the virtue of the citizens, glibly telling his audience that with such genius as they possess they must clearly see that the prosperity of the country depends on the politics he favours, on the party whose valiant champion he now is. His argumentation is absurd, his motive is contemptible, and still, as a rule, he carries the body of the crowd, unless another stump orator interferes and turns stream of sentiment in another direction. The speech of Antony in Julius Cæsar is an excellent example of suggestion.

All examples undoubtedly belong to the province suggestion. Now what are their characteristic traits? What are the elements common to all these cases of suggestion? We find in all these instances a stream of consciousness that goes on flowing in its peculiar, individual, idiosyncratic way; suddenly from the depths of the stream a wave rises to the surface, swamps the rest of the waves, overflows the banks, deflects for a while the course of the current, and then suddenly subsides, disappears, and the stream resumes its natural course, flowing once more in its former bed. On tracing the cause of this disturbance, we invariably find it is due to some external source, to some other stream running alongside the one disturbed. Stating the same in the language of Baldwin, we may say that "by suggestion is meant a great class of phenomena typified by the abrupt entrance from without into consciousness—of an idea or image which becomes a part of the stream of thought, and tends to produce the muscular and volitional efforts which ordinarily follow upon its presence."[1]

Is this our last say of suggestion? Far from being the case. On closer inspection of our examples we find traits which are of the utmost importance. The subject accepts *uncritically* the idea suggested to him, and carries it out almost *automatically*. [...]

By suggestion is meant the intrusion into the mind of an idea; met with more or less opposition by the person; accepted uncritically at last; and realized unreflectively, almost automatically.

By suggestibility is meant that peculiar state of mind which is favourable to suggestion.

CHAPTER II. THE CLASSIFICATION OF SUGGESTION AND SUGGESTIBILITY.

ONCE the subject-matter under investigation is defined, we must proceed to a further subdivision of it; we must define and classify the different species of suggestion and suggestibility. Already in our last chapter, in adducing different cases of suggestion, suggestibility in the normal state was tacitly implied. We have reached a stage in our discussion in which we must state this fact more explicitly. The soil favourable for seeds of suggestion exists also in what we call the individual. Suggestibility is present in what we call the normal state, and in order to reveal it we only know how to tap it. The suggestible element is a constituent of our nature; it never leaves us; it is always present in us. Before Janet, Binet, and other investigators undertook the study of hysterical subjects, no one suspected the existence of those remarkable phenomena of double consciousness that opened for us new regions in the psychical life of man. Phenomena were merely not noticed,

---

[1] *Psychology*, vol. ii.

although all the while; and when at times they rose from their obscurity, came to light, and obtruded themselves on the attention of people, they were either put down as sorcery, witchcraft, or classed contemptuously with lying, cheating and deception. The same is true with regard to normal suggestibility. It rarely attracts our attention, as it manifests itself in but trifling things. When, however, it rises to the surface and with the savage fury of a hurricane cripples and maims on its way everything it can not destroy, menaces life, and throws social order into the wildest confusion possible, we put it down as mobs. We do not in the least suspect that the awful, destructive, automatic spirit of the mob moves in the bosom of the peaceful crowd, reposes in the heart of the quiet assembly, and slumbers in the breast of the law-abiding citizen. We do not suspect that the spirit of suggestibility lies hidden even in the best of men; like the evil jinnee of the Arabian tales is corked up in the innocent-looking bottle. Deep down in the nature of man we find hidden the spirit of suggestibility. Every one of us is more or less suggestible. Man is often defined as a social animal. This definition is no doubt true, but it conveys little information as to the psychical state of each individual within society. There exists another definition which claims to give an insight into the nature of man, and that is the well-known ancient view that man is a rational animal; but this definition breaks down as soon as we come to test it by facts of life, for it scarcely holds true of the vast multitudes of mankind. Not sociality, not rationality, but suggestibility is what characterizes the average specimen of humanity, for *man is a suggestible animal.*

The fact of suggestibility existing in the normal individual is of the highest importance in the theoretical field of knowledge, in psychology, sociology, ethics, history, as well as in practical life, in education, politics, and economics; and since this fact of suggestibility may be subject to doubt on account of its seeming paradoxicalness, it must therefore be established on a firm basis by a rigorous experimentation, and I have taken great pains to prove this fact satisfactorily. The evidence for the existence of normal suggestibility I shall adduce later on in our discussion; meanwhile I ask the reader to take it on trust, sincerely hoping that he will at the end be perfectly satisfied with the demonstration of its truth.

The presence of suggestibility in such states as the hysterical and the hypnotic is a fact well proved and attested, and I think there is no need to say a word in its defence. Since the hysterical, the hypnotic, the somnambulic states do not belong to the routine of our experience; since they are but rare and occur under special peculiar conditions; since they unfit one for social life, disable in the struggle for existence, I think the reader will not quarrel with me for naming such states abnormal.

Thus it becomes quite clear that suggestibility must be classed under two heads: (1) Suggestibility in the normal state, or normal suggestibility, and (2) suggestibility in the abnormal state, or abnormal suggestibility. [...]

While looking for evidence for normal suggestibility, an opportunity was also taken to arrange the experiments according to different factors, so that should it be proved that suggestion in the normal state is an indubitable fact, we should be enabled to know what kind of factors are the more impressive and suggestive.

The series of letters and figures were arranged according to the following factors and their combinations: 1. Repetition. 2. Frequency 3. Coexistence. 4. Last impression. [...]

On the whole, we may say that in the normal state temporal or spatial repetition is the most unfortunate mode of suggestion, while the best, the most successful of all the particular factors, is that of the last impression— that is, the mode of bringing the idea intended for suggestion at the very end. This rule is observed by influential orators and widely read popular writers; it is known in rhetoric as bringing the composition to a climax. *Of all the modes of suggestion, however, the most powerful, the most effective, and the most successful is a skillful combination of frequency and last impression.* This rule is observed by Shakespeare in the speech of Antony. Be these rules of the particular factors what they may, one thing is clear and sure: these experiments unquestionably prove the reality of normal suggestibility; they prove the presence of suggestibility in the average normal individual. [...]

PART III. SOCIETY.

CHAPTER XXVII. SOCIAL SUGGESTIBILITY.

SUGGESTIBILITY is a fundamental attribute of man's nature. We must therefore expect that man, in his social capacity, will display this general property; and so do we actually find the case to be. What is required is only the condition to bring about a disaggregation in the social consciousness. This disaggregation may either be fleeting, unstable—then the type of suggestibility is that of the normal one; or it may become stable—then the suggestibility is of the abnormal type. *The one is the suggestibility of the crowd, the other that of the mob.* In the mob direct suggestion is effective, in the crowd indirect suggestion. The clever stump orator, the politician, the preacher, fix the attention of their listeners on themselves, interesting them in the subject. They as a rule distract the attention of the crowd by their stories, frequently giving the suggestion in some indirect and striking way, winding up the long yarn by a climax requiring the immediate execution of the suggested act. Out of the infinite number of cases, I take the first that comes to my hand:

In August 11, 1895, at Old Orchard, Me., a camp meeting was held. The purpose was to raise a collection for the evangelization of the world. The preacher gave his suggestions in the following way: "The most impressive memory I have of foreign lands is the crowds, the billows of lost humanity dashing ceaselessly on the shores of eternity.... How desperate and unloved they are—no joy, no spring, no song in their religion! I once heard a China-man tell why he was a Christian. It seemed to him that he was down in a deep pit, with no means to get out. [Story.] Have you wept on a lost world as Jesus wept? If not, woe unto you. Your religion is but a dream and a fancy. We find Christ testing his disciples. Shall he make them his partners ? Be-loved, he is testing you to-day. [Indirect suggestion.] He could convert one thousand millionaires, but he is giving us a chance. [Suggestion more direct than before.] Have we faith enough? [A discourse on faith follows here.] God can not bring about great things without faith. I believe the coming of Jesus will be brought about by one who believes strongly in it.... Beloved, if you are going to give grandly for God you have got faith. [The suggestion is still more direct.] The lad with the five loaves and the two small fishes [story]—when it was over the little fellow did not lose his buns; there were twelve baskets over.... Oh, beloved, how it will come back!... Some day the King of kings will call you and give you a kingdom of glory, and just for trusting him a little! What you give to-day is a great investment.... Some day God will let us know how much better he can invest our treasures than we ourselves." The suggestion was effective. Money poured in from all sides, contributions ran from hundreds into thousands, into tens of thousands. The crowd contributed as much as seventy thousand dollars.

A disaggregation of consciousness is easily effected in the crowd. Some of the conditions of suggestibility work in the crowd with great power and on a large scale. The social psychical scalpels are big, powerful; their edges are extremely keen, and they cut sure and deep. If anything gives us a strong sense of our individuality, it is surely our voluntary movements. We may say that the individual self grows and expands with the increase of variety and intensity of its voluntary activity; and conversely, the life of the individual self sinks, shrinks with the decrease of variety and intensity of voluntary movements. We find, accordingly, that the condition of limitation of voluntary movements is of great importance in suggestibility in general, and this condition is of the more importance since it, in fact, can bring about a narrowing down of the field of consciousness with the conditions consequent on that contraction—all favourable to suggestibility. [...]

Besides limitation of voluntary movements and contraction of the field of consciousness, there are also present in the crowd, the matrix of the mob, the conditions of monotony and inhibition. When the preacher, the politician, the stump orator, the ringleader, the hero, gains the ear of the crowd, an ominous silence sets in, a silence frequently characterized as "awful." The crowd is in a state of overstrained expectation; with suspended breath it watches the hero or the interesting, all-absorbing object. Disturbing impressions are excluded, put down, driven away by main force. So great is the silence induced in the fascinated crowd, that very frequently the buzzing of a fly, or even the drop of a pin, can be distinctly heard. All interfering impressions and ideas are inhibited. The crowd is entranced, and rapidly merges into the mob-state. [...]

The given suggestion reverberates from individual to individual, gathers strength, and becomes so overwhelming as to drive the crowd into a fury of activity, into a frenzy of excitement. As the suggestions are taken by the mob and executed the wave of excitement rises higher and higher. Each fulfilled suggestion increases the emotion of the mob in volume and intensity. Each new attack is followed by a more violent paroxysm of furious demoniac frenzy. The mob is like an avalanche: the more it rolls the more menacing and dangerous it grows. The suggestion given by the hero, by the ringleader, by the master of the moment, is taken up by the crowd and is reflected and reverberated from man to man, until every soul is dizzied and every person is stunned. In the entranced crowd, in the mob; every one influences and is influenced in his turn; every one suggests and is suggested to, and the surging billow of suggestion swells and rises until it reaches a formidable height. [...]

The consciousness of the mob is reflex in its nature. In the entranced crowd, in the mob, social consciousness is disaggregated, thus exposing to the direct influence of the environment the reflex consciousness of the social subwaking self. The subwaking mob self slumbers within the bosom of society.

CHAPTER XXVIII. SOCIETY AND EPIDEMICS.

When animals, on account of the great dangers that threaten them, begin to rove about in groups, in companies, in herds, and thus become social, such animals, on pain of extinction, must vary in the direction of suggestibility; they must become more and more susceptible to the emotional expression of their comrades, and reproduce it instantaneously at the first impression. When danger is drawing near, and one of the herd detects it and gives vent to his muscular expression of fear, attempting to escape, those of his comrades who are most susceptible reproduce the movements, experience the same emotions that agitate their companion, and are thus alone able to survive in the struggle for existence. A delicate susceptibility to the movements of his fellows is a question of life and death to the individual in the herd. Suggestibility is of vital importance to the group, to society, for it is the only way of rapid communication social brutes can possibly possess. Natural selection seizes on this variation and develops it to its highest degree. Individuals having a more delicate susceptibility to suggestions survive, and leave a greater progeny which more or less inherit the characteristics of their parents. In the new generation, again, natural selection resumes its merciless work, making the useful trait of suggestibility still more prominent, and the sifting process goes on thus for generations, endlessly. A highly developed suggestibility, an extreme, keen susceptibility to the sensori-motor suggestions, coming from its companions, and immediately realizing those suggestions by passing through the motor processes it witnesses, is the only way by which the social brute can become conscious of the emotions that agitate its fellows. The sentinel posted by the wasps becomes agitated at the sight of danger, flies into the interior of the nest buzzing violently, the whole nestful of wasps raises a buzzing, and is thus put into the same state of emotion which the sentinel experiences.

Suggestibility is the cement of the herd, the very soul of the primitive social group. A herd of sheep stands packed close together, looking abstractedly, stupidly, into vacant space. Frighten one of them; if the animal begins to run, frantic with terror, a stampede ensues. Each sheep passes through the movements of its neighbour. The herd acts like one body animated by one soul. Social life presupposes suggestion. No society without suggestibility. Man is a social animal, no doubt; but *he is social because he is suggestible*. Suggestibility, however, requires disaggregation of consciousness; hence, society presupposes a cleavage of the mind, it presupposes a plane of cleavage between the differentiated individuality and the undifferentiated reflex consciousness, the indifferent subwaking self. *Society and mental epidemics are intimately related; for the social gregarious self is the suggestible subconsciates self.*

The very organization of society keeps up the disaggregation of consciousness. The rules, the customs, the laws of society are categorical, imperative, absolute. One must obey them on pain of death. Blind obedience is a social virtue. But blind obedience is the very essence of suggestibility, the constitution of the disaggregated subwaking self. Society by its nature, by its organization, tends to run riot in mobs, manias, crazes, and all kinds of mental epidemics.

With the development of society the economical, political, and religious institutions become more and more differentiated; their rules, laws, by-laws, and regulations become more and more detailed, and tend to cramp the individual, to limit, to constrain his voluntary movements, to contract his field of consciousness, to inhibit all extraneous ideas—in short, to create conditions requisite for a disaggregation of consciousness. If, now, something striking fixes the attention of the public—a brilliant campaign, a glittering holy image, or a bright "silver dollar"—the subwaking social self, the demon of the demos, emerges, and society is agitated with crazes, manias, panics, and mental plagues of all sorts.

CHAPTER SIX

Social Psychology: An Outline and Sourcebook (1908)

Edward Alsworth Ross

New York: Macmillan, pp. 11–47, 63–65, 346–48 [with elisions].

EDITOR'S INTRODUCTION

Edward Alsworth Ross (1866–1951) was born in Illinois and received his AB (1886) from Coe College in Iowa. He studied in Germany, returning to the US to earn a PhD in political economy at Johns Hopkins University in 1891. He taught for several years at Stanford University but was fired because of his outspoken support of eugenics. After a few years at the University of Nebraska, he moved to the University of Wisconsin-Madison, where he spent the rest of his career as professor of sociology and founding chair of the department.

Despite his early political views, Ross was a leading US sociologist, the president of the American Sociological Association in 1914, and a prominent Progressive. In his theorizing, he was among the roster of early intellectual stars to come under the spell of French crowd theory. He authored *Social Psychology: An Outline and Sourcebook*, one of the two founding textbooks in the field, both published in 1908 (the other by William McDougall).

Ross was particularly concerned with the problem of social order in the transition to modernity and in the forms of control by which social stability was maintained in the process. His first book, *Social Control* (1901), dealt entirely with this problem. For Ross, social control could be coercive or non-coercive, and included law, religion, public opinion, custom, and even art.

Broadening his focus in *Social Psychology*, he engaged Tarde and Le Bon to consider the process and consequences of an array of forms of social interaction. The book was, for one commentator, "essentially a treatise on the suggestion-imitation theory of the social processes as made famous by Tarde and others" (Karpf 1932, 309). Along with Baldwin's *Mental Development*, the text was also important in introducing suggestion theory to US audiences.

The following excerpt from *Social Psychology* offers Ross's view of suggestion, which he finds to be inherent in human nature and the psychological foundation for social control. "Many a man thinks he makes up his mind, whereas, in truth, it is made up for him by some masterful associate or by the man who talked with him last." Following Baldwin, he also distinguishes suggestion, the "cause," from imitation, the "effect." He examines the importance of speaker "prestige" in crowd behavior and "the mass mind," and even delves into the power of mass media. "Space-annihilating devices," the telegraph, the mails, and the daily press are "able to assail the individual with a mass of suggestion almost as vivid as if he actually stood in the midst of an immense crowd"—and the results can be "rage, alarm, enthusiasm, or horror."

In stark contrast to mid-century articulations of a uniform effects "Magic Bullet" model of media impact, suggestion theory always included wide space for variability. That is, levels of suggestibility ranged across defined groups and individuals. Ross examines this, describing levels of susceptibility to suggestion based on, among other things, ethnicity, gender, and age. The analysis here is starkly misogynistic and racist, but not untypical for this period. Ross also anticipates the role of cognitive selectivity in the formation and manipulation of public opinion, with an acknowledgement of the important role of individual pre-existing beliefs in the process of attitude change.

Finally, it's important to note that while Ross was concerned with the irrational suggestibility of the public, as a Progressive he, like Sidis, placed great hope in the efficacy of education and educated leaders to help overcome its darker implications. —*P.P.*

References

Karpf, Fay Berger. 1932. *American Social Psychology: Its Origins, Development and European Background*. New York: McGraw Hill.

Ross, Edward A. 1901. *Social Control*. New York: Macmillan.

Social Psychology: An Outline and Sourcebook (1908)

CHAPTER II: SUGGESTIBILITY

The older psychology was individualistic in its interpretations. The contents of the mind were looked upon as elaborations out of personal experience. It sought to show how from the primary sense perceptions are built up ideas, at first simple, then more and more complex—ideas of space, time, number, cause, etc. The upper stories of personality, framed on beliefs, standards, valuations, and ideals, were comparatively neglected. The psychologist failed to note that for these highly elaborated products we are more indebted to our fellow-men than to our individual experience, that they are wrought out, as it were, collectively, and not by each for himself.

The newer psychology in accounting for the contents of the mind gives great prominence to the social factor. It insists that without interaction with other minds the psychic development of the child would be arrested at a stage not far above idiocy. Such interaction arises necessarily from the suggestibility of human nature. A person cannot unswervingly follow the orbit prescribed by his heredity or his private experience. He does not sit serene at the centre of things and coolly decide which of the examples and ideas that present themselves he shall adopt. Much of what impinges on his consciousness comes with some force. It has momentum, and if he does not yield to it, it is because his mind resists with a greater force. The weak mind, like Sir James Brooke in "Middlemarch," "takes shape easily, but won't keep shape." Many a man thinks he makes up his mind, whereas, in truth, it is made up for him by some masterful associate or by the man who talked with him last.

Stimuli welling up from within may be termed impulses, whereas those reaching us directly from without may be termed suggestions. The latter may be defined as "the abrupt entrance from without into consciousness of an idea or image which becomes a part of the stream of thought and tends to produce the muscular and volitional effects which ordinarily follow upon its presence." [1] Examples of the working of suggestion are legion. Persons accustomed to being put under the influence of anaesthetics have "gone off" as soon as the familiar chloroform mask was laid on the face, but before any chloroform had been poured on it. [...]

Suggestions are true forces and enact themselves unless they meet resistance. The power to withstand, ignore, or throw off suggestions is one form of *inhibition, i.e.,* will power. Suggestion and imitation are merely two aspects of the same thing, the one being cause, the other effect.

Suggestibility varies according to,—

1. *Species.*—It appears to be more marked in gregarious than in solitary creatures. Not all simians are imitative, but the gregarious simians, the monkeys, are proverbially so. Sheep are so imitative that if a file of them be driven through a narrow passage and the leader be made to jump over a stick held across the passage, every one of the file will jump at that place, even if the stick be withdrawn. Only high suggestibility could produce the wonderful instantaneous concert of action seen in the herd of deer or buffalo, the band of wild horses or elephants.

2. *Race.* — Suggestibility is not a weakness produced by civilization [...] The American Indian, far from being impassive, is an extremely susceptible type. The ghost-dance religion that spread among the Indians, 1889–1892, took possession of probably sixty thousand souls. Its central feature was a sacred dance, reënforced by hypnotizing operations by the medicine man upon dancers who began to show signs of ecstasy. Under the power of the emotion and of the passes employed by the medicine man, first one and then another would break from the ring, stagger, and fall down. "They kept up dancing until fully one hundred persons were lying unconscious. Then they stopped and seated themselves in a circle, and as each one recovered from his trance, he was brought to the centre of the ring to relate his experience." [2]

Among the civilized races the Celto-Slavs seem to be more suggestive than the English or the Scandinavians. The demonstrativeness of French and Italian audiences is in high contrast to the "phlegm" of English and German audiences. Nothing surpasses the fire and dash of a French cavalry charge. The English are at their best in individualistic fighting, such as defence or retreat. The French and Irish orators hold the palm, while it is the mobs of Frenchmen and of Russians that yield the best material for crowd psychology. Mesmerism and, later, hypnotism originated in France. Politeness and the

---

[1] Baldwin, "Handbook of Psychology," II, 297.
[2] Fourteenth Annual Report of the Bureau of Ethnology, 917.

refinements of intercourse are well-nigh spontaneous with the Irish and the French, owing to their quick susceptibility to slight indications of feeling in the other person. The rudeness so often complained of in the English seems due to an insensitiveness to certain ranges of suggestion.

3. *Age.*—Suggestibility is at its maximum in young children, and it is said that most children above the age of seven are hypnotizable.[3] Here is the secret of childhood's "plasticity." The adult may be progressive, *i.e.,* open to new ideas, but he ought not to be plastic, *i.e.,* shaped readily by whatever happens to impinge on him. Juvenile testimony is very untrustworthy, seeing that by a series of skillful leading questions a child may be led to give almost any desired story on the witness-stand. It is the suggestibility of the young that prompts us to segregate youthful offenders, institute juvenile courts, keep vicious women off the street, penalize the dissemination of obscene literature, outlaw "treating," and eliminate the commercial motive from the sale of liquor.

4. *Temperament.*—Coe[4] finds those of the sanguine or the melancholic temperament decidedly more suggestible than the choleric. [...]

5. *Sex.*—Among the Indian ghost-dancers, "young women are usually the first to be affected, then older women, and lastly men." Coe finds that among those who definitely seek for a striking religious transformation, the proportion of those whose expectation is completely satisfied is decidedly greater among the women. Starbuck's figures,[5] showing six times as many women as men converted at the regular church services, indicates the greater response of women to external suggestion. In conversion "men display more friction against surroundings, more difficulty with points of belief, more doubt arising from educational influences, more readiness to question traditional beliefs and customs, more pronounced tendency to resist conviction, to pray, to call on God, to lose sleep and appetite." For them the period of doubt and struggle is longer than for women. Ellis[6] points out that women are more hypnotizable than men. [...]

The mob susceptibilities in woman cause many strongly to oppose granting women more power in our social or political organization. But women are more than a sex. They are, in a sense, a social class shut out from many of the bracing and individualizing experiences that come to men. "Nowhere

---

[3]Binet, "La Suggestibilite," sets forth investigations showing a marked normal suggestibility in school children.

[4]"The Spiritual Life," 120.

[5]*American Journal of Psychology*, VIII, 271.

[6]"Man and Woman," ch. XII.

in the world," declares Professor Thomas,[7] "do women as a class lead a perfectly free intellectual life in common with the men of the group unless it be in restricted and artificial groups like the modern revolutionary party in Russia." Hence *woman* is by no means synonymous with *human female*. Almost everywhere propriety and conventionality press more mercilessly on woman than on man, thereby lessening her freedom and range of choice and dwarfing her will. Individuality develops through practice in choosing. If women are mobbish, it is largely for the same reason that monks, soldiers, peasants, *moujiks*, and other rigidly regulated types are mobbish. Much of woman's exaggerated impressionability disappears once she enjoys equal access with men to such individualizing influences as higher education, travel, self-direction, professional pursuits, participation in intellectual and public life.

6. *Mental Condition.*—In the normal mental state indirect distraction, *i.e.*, absence of mind, is favorable to the uncritical acceptance of suggestion. The mind must be "caught napping," as it were, in order that an uncongenial suggestion may find lodgment. [...]

By one in the normal state, then, slantwise suggestion is far more likely to be accepted than direct suggestion, on the principle that a flank movement succeeds when a frontal attack fails. [...]

7. *Source of Suggestion.*—One is most susceptible to suggestions from certain quarters or from certain people—from those clothed with *prestige*. Prestige is that which excites such wonder or admiration as to paralyze the critical faculty. It is not the same at all stages. The boy, trying constantly to do things, admires most those who can do things better than he can or things he cannot do at all. Says Cooley: "His father sitting at his desk probably seems an inert and unattractive phenomenon, but the man who can make shavings or dig a deep hole is a hero; and the seemingly perverse admiration which children at a later age show for circus men and for the pirates and desperadoes they read about, is to be explained in a similar manner. What they want is *evident* power."[8] [...]

The born leader is one whose superiority seems boundless. If it is only relative, if we can measure it, if we can fathom the secret of it and can see how we can finally attain to it ourselves, he is no longer our hero. In every crisis he must appear to be master of the situation, not perplexed, dubious, or vacillating. His faith in himself and in his undertaking must appear

---

[7] "Sex and Society," 311.
[8] "Human Nature and the Social Order," 290–293.

tremorless. He must bear up when others despair, remain serene when they are agitated. His intelligence must overarch and reach beyond that of his followers. Not unbroken success, not measurable excellence, but the gift of striking and stirring the imagination of others is, perhaps, the essential thing in natural leadership. Cooley[9] remarks: "A sense of power in others seems to involve a sense of their inscrutability; and, on the other hand, so soon as a person becomes plain he ceases to stimulate the imagination; we have seen all around him, so that he no longer appears an open door to new life." "The power of mere inscrutability arises from the fact that it gives a vague stimulus to thought and then leaves it to work out the details to suit itself."[...]

8. *Duration of Suggestion.*—Reiteration of the same idea in various forms is essential to the production of an effect upon people in a normal state of mind. It takes time for the orator to weave his spell. It is in the closing weeks of the legislative session that the tireless lobbyist registers his triumph over the scruples of the legislators. Advertising, to bring in returns, must be persevered in; it may be months after heavy advertising is begun before the sales swell noticeably. The insurance solicitor knows the efficacy of "follow up" letters and conversations. The reiterated phrases of a church liturgy gradually inspire in the hearer the mood of worship. It is a trick of balladists to call up a certain emotional tone by a recurring phrase at the close of each stanza. [...]

9. *Volume of Suggestion.*—What strikes us from all directions at almost the same instant has a tremendous effect. [...]

Men who easily throw off the thousand successive suggestions of every-day life are carried off their feet by the volume of suggestion that emanates from great numbers. This is the secret of the power of public opinion. [...]

CHAPTER III: THE CROWD

THE strength of multiplied suggestion is at its maximum when the individual is in the midst of a throng, helpless to control his position or movements. The same pressure on the body that prevents voluntary movement conveys promptly to him all the electrifying swayings and tremors that betray the emotions of the mass. This squeeze of the crowd tends to depress the self-sense. [...]

An excited throng easily turns mob because excitement weakens the reasoning power and predisposes to suggestions in line with the master emotion. Thus, frightened persons are peculiarly susceptible to warnings,

---

[9] "Human Nature and the Social Order," 313–315.

angry persons to denunciations, expectant persons to promises, anxious persons to rumors. An agitated gathering is tinder, and the throngs that form in times of public tension are very liable to become mobs.

Although crowding, fixation of attention, and excitement exalt suggestibility, all members of the crowd do not experience this in the same degree. There are at least two descriptions of people who, in the give-and-take of the throng, are more likely to impose suggestions than to accept them. The *intelligent* are able to criticise and appraise the suggestions that impinge upon them. They are quick to react if a suggestion clashes with their interests or their convictions, whereas the ignorant are at the mercy of the leader or the claque, and may be stampeded into a course of action quite at variance with their real desires. The *fanatical and impassioned* are little responsive to impressions from without, because of their inner tension. Being determined from within, they emit powerful suggestions, but are hard to influence. There is thus a tendency for the warped and inflamed members to impart their passion to the rest and to sweep along with them the neutral and indifferent. This is why, as the crowd comes under the hypnotic spell, the extremists gain the upper hand of the moderates.

Feelings, having more means of vivid expression, run through the crowd more readily than ideas. Masked by their anonymity, people feel free to give rein to the expression of their feelings. To be heard, one does not speak; one shouts. To be seen, one does not simply show one's self; one gesticulates. Boisterous laughter, frenzied objurgations, frantic cheers, are needed to express the merriment or wrath or enthusiasm of the crowd. Such exaggerated signs of emotion cannot but produce in suggestible beholders exaggerated states of mind. The mental temperature rises, so that what seemed hot now seems lukewarm, what felt tepid now feels cold. The intensifying of the feelings in consequence of reciprocal suggestion will be most rapid when the crowd meets under agitating circumstances. In this case the unbridled manifestation of feeling prevails from the first, and the psychic fermentation proceeds at a great rate.

To the degree that feeling is intensified, reason is paralyzed. In general, strong emotion inhibits the intellectual processes. In a sudden crisis we expect the sane act from the man who is "cool," who has not "lost his head." Now, the very hurly-burly of the crowd tends to distraction. Then, the high pitch of feeling to which the crowd gradually works up checks thinking and results in a temporary imbecility. There is no question that, taken herdwise, people are less sane and sensible than they are dispersed.

In a real deliberative assembly there is a possibility that the best thought, the soundest opinion, the shrewdest plan advanced from any quarter will prevail. Where there is cool discussion and leisurely reflection, ideas struggle with one another, and the fittest are accepted by all. In the fugitive, structure-less crowd, however, there can be no fruitful debate. Under a wise leader the crowd may act sagaciously. But there is no guarantee that the master of the crowd shall be wiser than his followers. The man of biggest voice or wildest language, the aggressive person who first leaps upon a table, raises aloft a symbol, or utters a catching phrase, is likely to become the bell-wether. [...]

CHAPTER IV: MOB MIND

PRESENCE is not essential to mass suggestion. Mental touch is no longer bound up with physical proximity. With the telegraph to collect and transmit the expressions and signs of the ruling mood, and the fast mail to hurry to the eager clutch of waiting thousands the still damp sheets of the morning daily, remote people are brought, as it were, into one another's presence. Through its organs the excited public is able to assail the individual with a mass of suggestion almost as vivid as if he actually stood in the midst of an immense crowd.

Formerly, within a day, a shock might throw into a fever all within a hundred miles. The next day it might agitate the zone beyond, but mean-while the first body of people would have cooled down and become ready to listen to reason. And so, while a wave of excitement passed slowly over the country, the entire folk was at no moment in a state of agitation. Now, however, our space-annihilating devices make a shock well-nigh simultane-ous. A vast public shares the same rage, alarm, enthusiasm, or horror. Then, as each part of the mass becomes acquainted with the sentiment of all the rest, the feeling is generalized and intensified. In the end the public swallows up the individuality of the ordinary man in much the same way the crowd swallows up the individuality of its members.

Nevertheless, public and crowd are not identical in their characteristics. If by the aid of a telephonic news service—as in Budapest—people were brought into immediate touch, there would still be lacking certain conditions of the mob state. The hurly-burly, the press and heave of the crowd are avoided when contact is purely mental. As we have seen, in the throng the means of expressing feeling are much more effective than the facilities for expressing thought. But in a dispersed group feeling enjoys no such advantage. Both are confined to the same vehicle the printed word and so ideas and opinions run as rapidly through the public as emotions.

One is member of but one crowd at a time, but by reading a number of newspapers, one can belong to several publics with, perhaps, different planes of vibration. So far as these various unanimities cross and neutralize one another, the suction of the public will be weakened. The crowd may be stampeded into folly or crime by accidental leaders. The public can receive suggestions only through the columns of its journal, the editor of which is like the chairman of a mass-meeting, for no one can be heard without his recognition. For all these reasons the psychology of the public, though similar to that of the crowd, is more normal.

Ours is not the era of hereditary rulers, oligarchies, era of publics hierarchies, or close corporations. But neither is it, as some insist, "the era of crowds." It is, in fact, *the era of publics.* Those who perceive that to-day under the influence of universal discussion the old fixed groupings which held their members so tenaciously—sects, parties, castes, and the like—are liquefying, that allegiances sit lightly, and that men are endlessly passing into new combinations, seek to stigmatize these loose associations as "crowds." The true crowd is, however, in a declining rôle. Universal contact by means of print ushers in "the rule of public opinion," which is a totally different thing from "government by the mob."

The principal manifestations of mob mind in vast bodies of dispersed individuals are the craze and the fad. These may be defined as *that irrational unanimity of mob mind interest, feeling, opinion, or deed in a body of communicating individuals, which results from suggestion and imitation.* In the chorus of execration over a sensational crime, in the clamor for the blood of an assassin, in waves of national feeling, in political "land-slides," in passionate "sympathetic" strikes, in cholera scares, in popular delusions, in religious crazes, in migration manias, in "booms" and panics, in agitations and insurrections, we witness contagion on a gigantic scale, favored in some cases by popular hysteria. […]

CHAPTER XXII: PUBLIC OPINION

A DISCUSSION that attracts general attention finds its natural issue in a state of *public (or social) opinion.* The formation of this may best be observed during a discussion that must close at a certain date, i.e., a campaign. A campaign is a social deliberation. This does not necessarily mean general individual irresolution. If nobody had made up his mind, there could be no conflict whatever in the social mind. [...]

In a campaign the public is like a more or less inert substance placed between two chambers containing different active acids. The acid that eats into and assimilates this substance the more rapidly is the propaganda of the winning party. Sometimes there is a simple acid acting on a homogeneous substance—the communion cup agitation in a certain church, or the policy of withdrawal from the state militia mooted in a labor organization. Usually, however, the substance is heterogeneous, and each acid has a number of ingredients,—arguments, appeals, proposals, planks, each of which is presumed to be effective with some section of the public. The acid must be complex when, as in a political campaign, the entire public is being acted upon.

The affinities individuals develop are by no means determined simply by the rational balancing of opposing considerations. There is first the factor of prepossession and prejudice. Says Bryce [10]: "Every one is, of course, predisposed to see things in some one particular light by his previous education, habits of mind, accepted dogmas, religious or social affinities, notions of his own personal interest. No event, no speech or article ever falls upon a perfectly virgin soil; the reader or listener is always more or less biased already. When some important event happens, which calls for the formation of a view, these preëxisting habits, dogmas, affinities, help to determine the impression which each man experiences, and so are factors in the view he forms."

This original impression is soon overlaid by a variety of influences of social origin. Nearly every man looks for guidance to certain quarters, bows to the example of trusted leaders, of persons of influence or authority. Every editor, politician, banker, capitalist, railroad president, employer, clergyman, or judge has a following with whom his opinion has weight. He, in turn, is likely to have his authorities. The anatomy of collective opinion shows it to be organized from centres and subcentres, forming a kind of intellectual feudal system. The average man responds to several such centres of influence, and when they are in accord on a particular question he is almost sure to acquiesce. But when his authorities disagree, there results either confusion or else independence of judgment.

---

[10] "The American Commonwealth," II, ch. LXXVI.

"A Sociological Definition of Suggestion" (1921), "Definition of Imitation" (1921), & "Attention, Interest, and Imitation" (1921)

W. V. Bechterew, Charles Judd, & George Stout

In Introduction to Science of Sociology, *edited by Robert Park and Ernest Burgess. Chicago: University of Chicago Press, pp. 391–94, 408–20 [with elisions].*

EDITOR'S INTRODUCTION

In 1921, Robert Park and Ernest Burgess published an anthology of over one thousand pages that aggregated scholarly articles from across the young field of sociology. With more than two hundred fifty individual entries, the *Introduction to the Science of Sociology* represented an exhaustive survey of topics from "Human Nature" to "Progress." It was to become a landmark work in the discipline. To graduate students (and faculty) in universities across the country, it was known as "the green bible."

Nested in that volume, between "Social Contacts" and "Social Forces," was a section on "Social Interaction" that included more than a half dozen entries on suggestion and imitation. Even more articles examined "social contagion," "the crowd," and "types of mass movements" in the section on "Collective Behavior." Foundational theorists from Darwin to Le Bon were included in the volume along with younger scholars who offered the latest in summary and evaluation of the relevant theories and topics.

Two samples from the anthology are presented here. They illustrate, first, the established place the theories had acquired in the scholarship of the period, not just in social psychology but in sociology as well. They also provide a descriptive snapshot of the then-current definitions, processes, and implications at issue. Finally, they show the ways in which imitation and suggestion had begun to conceptually separate themselves in the literature and start to mix with other theoretical camps.

Vladimir Bechterew (1857–1927) was a Russian psychologist and neurologist with academic and medical degrees from the Medical and Surgery Academy of St. Petersburg (1881), where he later taught and conducted research. He founded the Psychoneurological Institute at the Academy and made significant contributions in the field of neurology. Bechterew was an exponent of "objective psychology," or "reflexology," a forerunner of behaviorism. In 1905, he wrote a short book on *The Importance of Suggestion in Social Life*, which he drew from for his contribution to the Park and Burgess collection.

In the following entry, he offers first "A Sociological Definition of Suggestion" and then a description of "Social Suggestion and Mass or 'Corporate' Action." (In the original they are listed as separate entries in the anthology, combined here for convenience.) It is interesting, in part, as an example of a blending of the doctrine of suggestion with concepts and language drawn from Freudian psychology. Suggestion is divided into conditions of active versus passive perception, the distinction being the involvement of the ego. External impressions that enter the mind without the participation of the ego—as when we are distracted—"make their way into the sphere of personal consciousness" passively and without awareness of their origin. They sneak "so to speak—up the back steps" of consciousness and "directly into the inner rooms of the soul."

In reviewing social suggestion in the context of mass action, Bechterew considers the interaction between the powerful leader and "the multitudes," considered as crowds and publics. Offering historical examples of the use of suggestive influence to marshal groups large and small to frequently problematic action (e.g., war), he declares it "the art of manipulating the masses." In the end, it is a potential social problem that "should be the object of the most attentive study for the historians and the sociologists."

Bechterew does not discuss imitation. That is reserved for separate treatments by Judd and by Stout. Charles Judd (1873–1946) spent his career in educational psychology. With a BA from the University of Connecticut (1894), he studied under Wilhelm Wundt at the University of Leipzig, earning his PhD in 1896. From 1909 to 1938 he was director of the Department of Education at the University of Chicago. George Stout (1869–1944) was a prominent English psychologist and philosopher. On the faculty at Oxford, he advanced a complex theory of psychology that he labeled "analytic psychology" (not to be confused with Carl Jung's analytical psychology).

Unlike Bechterew, who does not explicitly mention Le Bon or Tarde in his article, Judd draws directly from the earlier major statements of Tarde, Royce, and Baldwin. His short chapter highlights the role of imitation in providing long-term continuity, and therefore stability, to social practice, as well as introducing a source of social conflict when varying social practices and fashions collide.

Stout similarly notes the role of generational imitation in the maintenance of cultural practices and traditions. His focus, however, is more psychological, and he discusses the influence of personal interest and attention in the processes of imitation, especially as they affect learning.—*P.P.*

"A Sociological Definition of Suggestion" (1921)

Vladimir Bechterew

The nature of suggestion manifestly consists not in any external peculiarities whatever. It is based upon the peculiar kind of relation of the person making the suggestion to the "ego" of the subject during the reception and realization of the suggestion.

Suggestion, is, in general, one of many means of influence of man on man that is exercised with or without intention on persons, who respond either consciously or unconsciously.

For a closer acquaintance with what we call "suggestion," it may be observed that our perceptive activities are divided into (*a*) active, and (*b*) passive.

a) Active perception.—In the first case the "ego" of the subject necessarily takes a part, and according to the trend of our thinking or to the environmental circumstances directs the attention to these or those external impressions. These, since they enter the mind through the participation of attention and will and through reflection and judgment, are assimilated and permanently incorporated in the personal consciousness or in our "ego." This type of perception leads to an enrichment of our personal consciousness and lies at the bottom of our points of view and convictions. The organization of more or less definite convictions is the product of the process of reflection instituted by active perception. These convictions, before they become the possession of our personal consciousness, may conceal themselves awhile in the so-called subconsciousness. They are capable of being aroused at any moment at the desire of the "ego" whenever certain experienced representations are reproduced.

b) Passive perception.—In contrast to active perception we perceive much from the environment in a passive manner without that participation of the "ego." This occurs when our attention is diverted in any particular direction or concentrated on a certain thought, and when its continuity for one or another reason is broken up, which, for instance, occurs in cases of so-called distraction. In these cases the object of the perception does not enter into the personal consciousness, but it makes its way into other spheres of our mind, which we call the general consciousness. The general consciousness is to a certain degree independent of the personal consciousness. For this reason everything that enters into the general consciousness cannot be introduced at will into the personal consciousness. Nevertheless products of the general consciousness make their way into the sphere of the personal consciousness, without awareness by it of their original derivation.

In passive perception, without any participation of attention, a whole series of varied impressions flow in upon us and press in past our "ego" directly to the general consciousness. These impressions are the sources of those influences from the outer world so unintelligible even to ourselves, which determine our emotional attitudes and those obscure motives and impulses which often possess us in certain situations.

The general consciousness, in this way, plays a permanent role in the spiritual life of the individual. Now and then an impression passively received in the train of an accidental chain of ideas makes its way into the sphere of the personal consciousness as a mental image, whose novelty astounds us. In specific cases this image or illusion takes the form of a peculiar voice, a vision, or even a hallucination, whose origin undoubtedly lies in the general consciousness. When the personal consciousness is in abeyance, as in sleep or in profound hypnosis, the activity of the general consciousness comes into the foreground. The activity of the general consciousness is limited neither by our ways of viewing things nor by the conditions under which the personal consciousness operates. On this account, in a dream and in profound hypnosis acts appear feasible and possible which with our full personal consciousness we would not dare to contemplate.

This division of our mind into a personal and a general consciousness affords a basis for a clear understanding of the principles of suggestion. The personal consciousness, the so-called "ego," aided by the will and attention, largely controls the reception of external impressions, influences the trend of our ideas, and determines the execution of our voluntary behavior. Every impression that the personal consciousness transmits to the mind is usually subject to a definite criticism and remodeling which results in the development of our points of view and of our convictions.

This mode of influence from the outer world upon our mind is that of "logical conviction." As the final result of that inner reconstruction of impressions appears always the conviction: "This is true, that useful, inevitable, etc." We can say this inwardly when any reconstruction of the impressions has been affected in us through the activity of the personal consciousness. Many impressions get into our mind without our remarking them. In case of distraction, when our voluntary attention is in abeyance, the impression from without evades our personal consciousness and enters the mind without coming into contact with the "ego." Not through the front door, but—so to speak—up the back steps, it gets, in this case, directly into the inner rooms of the soul.

Suggestion may now be defined as the direct infection of one person by another of certain mental states. In other words, suggestion is the penetration or inoculation of a strange idea into the consciousness, without direct immediate participation of the "ego" of the subject. Moreover, the personal consciousness in general appears quite incapable of rejecting the suggestion, even when the "ego" detects its irrationality. Since the suggestion enters the mind without the active aid of the "ego," it remains outside the borders of the personal consciousness. All further effects of the suggestion, therefore, take place without the control of the "ego."

By the term suggestion we do not usually understand the effect upon the mind of the totality of external stimuli, but the influence of person upon person which takes place through passive perception and is therefore independent of the activity of the personal consciousness. Suggestion is, moreover, to be distinguished from the other type of influences operating through mental processes of attention and the participation of the personal consciousness, which result in logical convictions and the development of definite points of view.

Lowenfeld emphasized a distinction between the actual process of "suggesting" and its result, which one simply calls "suggestion." It is self-evident that these are two different processes, which should not be mistaken for each other. A more adequate definition might be accepted, which embraces at once the characteristic manner of the "suggesting," and the result of its activity.

Therefore for suggestion it is not alone the process itself that is characteristic, or the kind of psychic influence, but also the result of this reaction. For that reason I do not understand under "suggesting" alone a definite sort and manner of influence upon man but at the same time the eventual result of it; and under "suggestion" not only a definite psychical result but to a certain degree also the manner in which this result was obtained.

An essential element of the concept of suggestion is, first of all, a pronounced directness of action. Whether a suggestion takes place through words or through attitudes, impressions, or acts, whether it is a case of a verbal or of a concrete suggestion, makes no difference here so long as its effect is never obtained through logical conviction. On the other hand, the suggestion is always immediately directed to the mind by evading the personal consciousness, or at least without previous recasting by the "ego" of the subject. This process represents a real infection of ideas, feelings, emotions, or other psychophysical states.

In the same manner there arise somewhat similar mental states known as auto-suggestion. These do not require an external influence for their appearance but originate immediately in the mind itself. Such is the case, for instance, when any sort of an image forces itself into the consciousness as something complete, whether it is in the form of an idea that suddenly emerges and dominates consciousness, or a vision, a premonition, or the like.

In all these cases psychic influences which have arisen without external stimulus have directly inoculated the mind, thereby evading the criticism of the "ego" or of personal consciousness.

"Suggesting" signifies, therefore, to inoculate the mind of a person more or less directly with ideas, feelings, emotions, and other psychical states, in order that no opportunity is left for criticism and consideration. Under "suggestion," on the other hand, is to be understood that sort of direct inoculation of the mind of an individual with ideas, feelings, emotions, and other psychophysical states which evade his "ego," his personal self-consciousness, and his critical attitude.

Now and then, especially in the French writers, one will find besides "suggestion" the term "psychic contagion," under which, however, nothing further than involuntary imitation is to be understood (compare A. Vigouroux and P. Juquelier, *La contagion mentale*, Paris, 1905). If one takes up the conception of suggestion in a wider sense, and considers by it the possibility of involuntary suggestion in the way of example and imitation, one will find that the conceptions of suggestion and of psychic contagion depend upon each other most intimately, and to a great extent are not definitely to be distinguished from each other. In any case, it is to be maintained that a strict boundary between psychic contagion and suggestion does not always exist, a fact which Vigouroux and Juquelier in their paper have rightly emphasized. [...]

3. Social Suggestion and Mass or "Corporate" Action

In most cases the crowd naturally is under leaders, who, with an instinctive consciousness of the importance and strength of the crowd, seek to direct it much more through the power of suggestion than by sound conviction.

It is conceivable, therefore, that anyone who understands how to arrest the attention of the crowd, may always influence it to do great deeds, as history, indeed, sufficiently witnesses. One may recall from the history of Russia Minin, who with a slogan saved his native land from the gravest danger. His "Pawn your wife and child, and free your fatherland" necessarily acted as a powerful suggestion on the already intense crowd. [...]

Of analogous importance are the factors of suggestions in wars, where the armies go to brilliant victories. Discipline and the sense of duty unite the troops into a single mighty giant's body. To develop its full strength, however, this body needs some inspiration through a suggested idea, which finds an active echo in the hearts of the soldiers. Maintenance of the warlike spirit in decisive moments is one of the most important problems for the ingenious general.

Even when the last ray of hope for victory seems to have disappeared, the call of an honored war chief, like a suggestive spark, may fire the hosts to self-sacrifice and heroism. A trumpet signal, a cry "hurrah," the melody of the national hymn, can here at the decisive moment have incalculable effects. There is no need to recall the rôle of the "Marsellaise" in the days of the French Revolution. The agencies of suggestion in such cases make possible, provided that they are only able to remove the feeling of hopelessness, results which a moment before are neither to be anticipated nor expected. Where will and the sense of duty alone seem powerless, the mechanisms of suggestion may develop surprising effects.

Excited masses are, it is well known, capable of the most inhuman behavior, and indeed for the very reason that, instead of sound logic, automatism and impulsiveness have entered in as direct results of suggestion. The modern barbarities of the Americans in the shape of lynch law for criminals or those who are only under a suspicion of a crime redound to the shame of the land of freedom, but find their full explanation in that impulsiveness of the crowd which knows no mercy.

The multitude can, therefore, ever be led according to the content of the ideas suggested to it, as well to sublime and noble deeds as, on the other hand, to expressions of the lower and barbaric instincts. That is the art of manipulating the masses.

It is a mistake to regard popular assemblies who have adopted a certain uniform idea simply as a sum of single elements, as is now and then attempted. For one is dealing in such cases, not with accidental, but with actual psychical, processes of fusion, which reciprocal suggestion is to a high degree effective in establishing and maintaining. The aggressiveness of the single elements of the mass arrives in this at their high point at one and the same time, and with complete spiritual unanimity the mass can now act as *one man;* it moves, then, like one enormous social body, which unites in itself the thoughts and feelings of all by the very fact that there is a temper of mind common to all. Easily, however, as the crowd is to excite to the highest degrees of activity, as quickly—indeed, much more quickly—does it allow itself, as we have already seen, to be dispersed by a panic. Here too the panic rests entirely on suggestion, contra-suggestion, and the instinct of imitation, not on logic and conviction. Automatism, not intelligence, is the moving factor therein.

Other, but quite generally favorable, conditions for suggestions are universally at hand in the human society, whose individual members in contrast to the crowd are physically separated from each other but stand in a spiritual alliance to each other. Here obviously those preliminary conditions for the dissemination of psychical infections are lacking as they exist in the crowd, and the instruments of the voice, of mimicry, of gestures, which often fire the passions with lightning rapidity, are not allowed to assert themselves. There exists much rather a certain spiritual cohesion on the ground perhaps of common impressions (theatrical representations), a similar direction of thoughts (articles in periodicals, etc.). These conditions are quite sufficient to prepare the foundation on which similar feelings propagate themselves from individual to individual by the method of suggestion and auto-suggestion, and similar decisions for many are matured.

Things occur here more slowly, more peacefully, without those passionate outbreaks to which the crowd is subjected; but this slow infection establishes itself all the more surely in the feelings, while the infection of the crowd often only continues for a time until the latter is broken up.

Moreover, such contagious examples in the public do not usually lead to such unexpected movements as they easily induce in the crowd. But here, too, the infection frequently acts in defiance of a man's sound intelligence; complete points of view are accepted upon trust and faith, without further discussion, and frequently immature resolutions are formed. On the boards representing the stage of the world there are ever moving idols, who after the first storm of admiration which they call out, sink back into oblivion. The fame of the people's leaders maintains itself in quite the same way by means of psychical infection through the similar national interest of a unified group. It has often happened that their brightness was extinguished with the first opposition which the masses saw setting its face against their wishes and ideals. What we, however, see in close popular masses recurs to a certain degree in every social milieu, in every larger society.

Between the single elements of such social spheres there occur uninterrupted psychical infections and contra-infections. Ever according to the nature of the material of the infection that has been received, the individual feels himself attracted to the sublime and the noble, or to the lower and bestial. Is, then, the intercourse between teacher and pupil, between friends, between lovers, uninfluenced by reciprocal suggestion? Suicide pacts and other mutual acts present a certain participation of interacting suggestion. Yet more. Hardly a single deed whatever occurs that stands out over the everyday, hardly a crime is committed, without the concurrence of third persons, direct or indirect, not unseldom bearing a likeness to the effects of suggestion.

We must here admit that Tarde was right when he said that it is less difficult to find crimes of the crowd than to discover crimes which were not such and which would indicate no sort of promotion or participation of the environment. That is true to such a degree that one may ask whether there are any individual crimes at all, as the question is also conceivable whether there are any works of genius which do not have a collective character.

Many believe that crimes are always pondered. A closer insight into the behavior of criminals testifies, however, in many cases that even when there is a long period of indecision, a single encouraging word from the environment, an example with a suggestive effect, is quite sufficient to scatter all considerations and to bring the criminal intention to the deed. In organized societies, too, a mere nod from the chief may often lead with magic power to a crime.

The ideas, efforts, and behavior of the individual may by no means be looked on as something sharply distinct, individually peculiar, since from the form and manner of these ideas, efforts, and behavior, there shines forth ever, more or less, the influence of the milieu.

In close connection with this fact there stands also the so-called astringent effect of the milieu upon the individuals who are incapable of rising out of their environment, of stepping out of it. In society that bacillus for which one has found the name "suggestion" appears certainly as a leveling element, and, accordingly, whether the individual stands higher or lower than his environment, whether he becomes worse or better under its influence, he always loses or gains something from the contact with others. This is the basis of the great importance of suggestion as a factor in imposing a social uniformity upon individuals.

The power of suggestion and contra-suggestion, however, extends yet further. It enhances sentiments and aims and enkindles the activity of the masses to an unusual degree.

Many historical personages who knew how to embody in themselves the emotions and the desires of the masses—we may think of Jeanne d'Arc, Mahomet, Peter the Great, Napoleon I—were surrounded with a nimbus by the more or less blind belief of the people in their genius; this frequently acted with suggestive power upon the surrounding company which it carried away with a magic force to its leaders, and supported and aided the mission historically vested in the latter by means of their spiritual superiority. A nod from a beloved leader of any army is sufficient to enkindle anew the courage of the regiment and to lead them irresistibly into sure death.

Many, it is well known, are still inclined to deny the individual personality any influence upon the course of historic events. The individual is to them only an expression of the views of the mass, an embodiment of the epoch, something, therefore, that cannot actively strike at the course of history; he is much rather himself heaved up out of the mass by historic events, which, unaffected by the individual, proceed in the courses they have themselves chosen.

We forget in such a theory the influences of the suggestive factors which, independently of endowments and of energy, appear as a mighty lever in the hands of the fortunately situated nature and of those created to be the rulers of the masses. That the individual reflects his environment and his time, that the events of world-history only take their course upon an appropriately prepared basis and under appropriately favorable circumstances, no one will deny. There rests, however, in the masters of speech and writing, in the demagogues and the favorites of the people, in the great generals and statesmen, an inner power which welds together the masses for battle for an ideal, sweeps them away to heroism, and fires them to do deeds which leave enduring impressions in the history of humanity.

I believe, therefore, that suggestion as an active agent should be the object of the most attentive study for the historians and the sociologists. Where this factor is not reckoned with, a whole series of historical and social phenomena is threatened with the danger of incomplete, insufficient, and perhaps even incorrect elucidation.

"Definition of Imitation" (1921)

Charles Judd

The term "imitation" is used in ordinary language to designate any repetition of any act or thought which has been noted by an observer. Thus one imitates the facial expression of another, or his mode of speech. The term has been brought into prominence in scientific discussions through the work of Gabriel Tarde, who in his *Les lois de l'imitation* points out that imitation is a fundamental fact underlying all social development. The customs of society are imitated from generation to generation. The fashions of the day are imitated by large groups of people without any consciousness of the social solidarity which is derived from this common mode of behavior. There is developed through these various forms of imitation a body of experiences which is common to all of the members of a given social group. In complex society the various imitations which tend to set themselves up are frequently found to be in conflict; thus the tendency toward elaborate fashions in dress is constantly limited by the counter-tendency toward simpler fashions. The conflict of tendencies leads to individual variations from the example offered at any given time, and, as a result, there are new examples to be followed. Complex social examples are thus products of conflict.

This general doctrine of Tarde has been elaborated by a number of recent writers. Royce calls attention to the fundamental importance of imitation as a means of social inheritance. The same doctrine is taken up by Baldwin in his *Mental Development in the Child and Race*, and in *Social and Ethical Interpretations*. With these later writers, imitation takes on a significance which is somewhat technical and broader than the significance which it has either with Tarde or in the ordinary use of the term. Baldwin uses the term to cover that case in which an individual repeats an act because he has himself gone through the act. In such a case one imitates himself and sets up what Baldwin terms a circular reaction. The principle of imitation is thus introduced into individual psychology as well as into general social psychology, and the relation between the individual's acts and his own imagery is brought under the same general principle as the individual's responses to his social environment. The term "imitation" in this broader sense is closely related to the processes of sympathy.

The term "social heredity" has very frequently been used in connection with all of the processes here under discussion. Society tends to perpetuate itself in the new individual in a fashion analogous to that in which the physical characteristics of the earlier generation tend to perpetuate themselves in the physical characteristics of the new generation. Since modes of behavior, such as acts of courtesy, cannot be transmitted through physical structure, they would tend to lapse if they were not maintained through imitation from generation to generation. Thus imitation gives uniformity to social practices and consequently is to be treated as a form of supplementary inheritance extending beyond physical inheritance and making effective the established forms of social practice.

"Attention, Interest, and Imitation" (1921)

George Stout

Imitation is a process of very great importance for the development of mental life in both men and animals. In its more complex forms it presupposes trains of ideas; but in its essential features it is present and operative at the perceptual level. It is largely through imitation that the results of the experience of one generation are transmitted to the next, so as to form the basis for further development. Where trains of ideas play a relatively unimportant part, as in the case of animals, imitation may be said to be the sole form of social tradition. In the case of human beings, the thought of past generations is embodied in language, institutions, machinery, and the like. This distinctively human tradition presupposes trains of ideas in past generations, which so mold the environment of a new generation that in apprehending and adapting itself to this environment it must re-think the old trains of thought. Tradition of this kind is not found in animal life, because the animal mind does not proceed by way of trains of ideas. None the less, the more intelligent animals depend largely on tradition. This tradition consists essentially in imitation by the young of the actions of their parents, or of other members of the community in which they are born. The same directly imitative process, though it is very far from forming the whole of social tradition in human beings, forms a very important part of it.

a) *The imitative impulse.*—We must distinguish between ability to imitate and impulse to imitate. We may be already fully able to perform an action, and the sight of it as performed by another may merely prompt us to reproduce it. But the sight of an act performed by another may also have an educational influence; it may not only stimulate us to do what we are already able to do without its aid; it may also enable us to do what we could not do without having an example to follow. When the cough of one man sets another coughing, it is evident that imitation here consists only in the impulse to follow suit. The second man does not learn how to cough from the example of the first. He is simply prompted to do on this particular occasion what he is otherwise quite capable of doing. But if I am learning billiards and someone shows me by his own example how to make a particular stroke, the case is different. It is not his example which in the first instance prompts me to the action. He merely shows the way to do what I already desire to do.

We have then first to discuss the nature of the imitative impulse—the impulse to perform an action which arises from the perception of it as performed by another.

This impulse is an affair of attentive consciousness. The perception of an action prompts us to reproduce it when and so far as it excites interest or is at least intimately connected with what does excite interest. Further, the interest must be of such a nature that it is more fully gratified by partially or wholly repeating the interesting action. Thus imitation is a special development of attention. Attention is always striving after a more vivid, more definite, and more complete apprehension of its object. Imitation is a way in which this endeavor may gratify itself when the interest in the object is of a certain kind. It is obvious that we do not try to imitate all manner of actions, without distinction, merely because they take place under our eyes. What is familiar and commonplace or what for any other reason is unexciting or insipid fails to stir us to re-enact it. It is otherwise with what is strikingly novel or in any way impressive, so that our attention dwells on it with relish or fascination. It is, of course, not true that whatever act fixes attention prompts to imitation. This is only the case where imitation helps attention, where it is, in fact, a special development of attention. This is so when interest is directly concentrated on the activity itself for its own sake rather than for the sake of its possible consequences and the like ulterior motives. But it is not necessary that the act in itself should be interesting; in a most important class of cases the interest centers, not directly in the external act imitated, but in something else with which this act is so intimately connected as virtually to form a part of it. Thus there is a tendency to imitate not only interesting acts but also the acts of interesting persons. Men are apt to imitate the gestures and modes of speech of those who excite their admiration or affection or some other personal interest. Children imitate their parents or their leaders in the playground. Even the mannerisms and tricks of a great man are often unconsciously copied by those who regard him as a hero. In such instances the primary interest is in the whole personality of the model; but this is more vividly and distinctly brought before consciousness by reproducing his external peculiarities. Our result, then, is that interest in an action prompts to imitation in proportion to its intensity, provided the interest is of a kind which will be gratified or sustained by imitative activity.

b) *Learning by imitation.*—Let us now turn to the other side of the question. Let us consider the case in which the power of performing an action is acquired in and by the process of imitation itself. Here there is a general rule which is obvious when once it is pointed out. It is part of the still more general rule that "to him that hath shall be given." Our power of imitating the activity of another is strictly proportioned to our pre-existing power of performing the same general kind of action independently. For instance, one devoid of musical faculty has practically no power of imitating the violin playing of Joachim. Imitation may develop and improve a power which already exists, but it cannot create it. Consider the child beginning for the first time to write in a copybook. He learns by imitation; but it is only because he has already some rudimentary ability to make such simple figures as pothooks that the imitative process can get a start. At the outset, his pothooks are very unlike the model set before him. Gradually he improves; increased power of independent production gives step by step increased power of imitation, until he approaches too closely the limits of his capacity in this direction to make any further progress of an appreciable kind.

But this is an incomplete account of the matter. The power of learning by imitation is part of the general power of learning by experience; it involves mental plasticity. An animal which starts life with congenital tendencies and aptitudes of a fixed and stereotyped kind, so that they admit of but little modification in the course of individual development, has correspondingly little power of learning by imitation.

At higher levels of mental development the imitative impulse is far less conspicuous because impulsive activity in general is checked and overruled by activity organized in a unified system. Civilized men imitate not so much because of immediate interest in the action imitated as with a view to the attainment of desirable results.

CHAPTER EIGHT

"The Need for Social Psychology" (1927)

John Dewey

Psychological Review *24: pp. 266–72.*

EDITOR'S INTRODUCTION

John Dewey (1859–1952), was one of the intellectual giants of the twentieth century, a philosopher, psychologist, and educational reformer with a boundless faith in the public's capacity for democratic self-governance. He helped shape early pragmatism and was a leading voice in the Progressive movement. Starting his academic career at the University of Michigan, he later moved to the University of Chicago and then to Columbia. In 1899 he was elected president of the American Psychological Association and seventeen years later gave an address before the meeting of the twenty-fifth anniversary of that organization, from which the following excerpt is taken.

His address speaks to a paradigmatic turning point in social psychology. Dewey directs his comments to the discipline's recent past and what he saw as the exciting theoretical evolution being brought about by the emergence of new models. The past, in this case, was embodied in the work of French crowd theory. Dewey noted the dominance of that perspective through the turn of the twentieth century and, for him at least, the paucity of the intellectual argument it represented. "For more than a decade [Tarde's] work and that of his followers in France and in the United States—among whom we may cite in diverse directions Baldwin and Ross—dominated social psychology and almost sociology." But it was time, he declared, to recall "social psychology from the wrong track in which the Imitation and Suggestibility schools had set it going." The problem, for Dewey, was an indefensible separation of the individual from the social and the postulation of a "mythical" crowd mind.

The future, he believed, belonged to the emerging theories of instinct, of which he was especially fond, and behaviorism, along with objective methods based on quantitative analysis. He pointed in particular to the work of McDougall and Thorndike as examples of "the next great force in social psychology." And he saw great promise in the application of statistical analysis to social problems, lauding Condorcet's then-recently introduced science of probabilities, which Dewey described as "fraught with infinite potentiality for control of social progress."

Dewey was not alone in his criticism of crowd theory, which was in fact being displaced during this period by instinct theory and behaviorism. What he did not foresee, however, was the tenacity of the concepts of suggestion and imitation set apart from the broader French social thinking. It turned out that suggestion and imitation, as specific psychological processes, could be cleanly extracted from their European social moorings and neatly inserted into the new US models.

The following section considers the evolution of suggestion, as it migrated into the dominant paradigms of social psychology in the early decades of the new century.—*P.P.*

"The Need for Social Psychology" (1917)

On the surface it is just coincidence that the foundation of this association and the publication of the 'Principles of Psychology' of William James were so nearly contemporaneous, their respective dates being, as you know, 1891 and 1890. In view, however, of the depth and breadth of the influence of James, we who are celebrating today our twentyfifth anniversary are at liberty, I think, to consider the coincidence as more than chronological, and to date back by one year the gestation of our association. At all events, it would be ungrateful to engage in any discussion of the past and future of social psychology without recalling the few rich pages of the 'Principles' which are devoted to the social self, and, in the discussion of instincts, to the native reactions of human beings in the presence of one another. Big books have been written since which are hardly more than an amplification of suggestions found in these few pages. When, for example, a few years later, the *Socius* became the hero of a psychological drama, not many recalled that he had already been introduced under that very name in the pages of James.

Again it is outwardly a mere coincidence that the work of Tarde on the 'Laws of Imitation' was published in the year in which the 'Principles' saw the light of day, and that practically all of Tarde's work fell within the decade lying between 1890 and 1900. But behind the pure coincidence there was the recognition of the need for social ends of a more scientific treatment of collective human nature, and the important role of psychology in building up the new social science. While James confined himself to pregnant suggestions concerning the new forms which human experience and selfhood take on because of the presence of other human selves, Tarde attempted an ambitious interpretation of almost all facts of social organization, progress and degeneration in terms of certain rubrics to which he gave a psychological quality. For more than a decade his work and that of his followers in France and in the United States—among whom we may cite in diverse directions Baldwin and Ross—dominated social psychology and almost sociology. I shall not rehearse the old discussions about Imitation as a psychological fact and a social force. I shall assume with most of contemporary psychological critics that as a descriptive and explanatory conception it misplaced emphasis and tended to distort facts. But nevertheless we cannot minimize the immense power of this stage of social science in popularizing the idea of social psychology, and in bringing into recognition many facts, such as the importance of prestige, fashion, sensitiveness to the beliefs of others, the difficulties which innovation, no matter how reasonable, has to meet, etc., facts which are permanently imbedded in social science. Tarde himself was certainly one of the most stimulating and varied of writers, and I do not think we shall ever outgrow some of his contributions, although to my mind they are found rather in logic than in psychology—such as the necessity for reducing the gross phenomena of social life into minute events which may then be analyzed one by one. The most fruitful of his psychological conceptions was ahead of his time and went almost unnoted. It was that all psychological phenomena can be divided into the physiological and the social, and that when we have relegated elementary sensation and appetite to the former head, all that is left of our mental life, our beliefs, ideas and desires, falls within the scope of social psychology.

I hope I may find general agreement in pointing to the work of McDougall and Thorndike respectively as indicative of the next great force in social psychology, together with such writings as those, upon the social side, of Graham Wallas. Aside from valuable contributions in detail, the significance of these contributions lies, to my mind, in recalling social psychology from the wrong track in which the Imitation and Suggestibility schools had set it going. For those schools gave the dawning science a wrong twist in carrying over into science the old popular and practical antithesis of the individual and the social, and thus setting up two independent and even contrary sciences—individual and social psychology. As a concrete illustration of the absurd results to which this antithesis led, it is perhaps sufficient to refer to those bizarre writings on the psychology of the crowd in which it was assumed that the psychology of the individual left to himself is reflective and rational, while man's emotional obsessions and irrationalities are to be accounted for by the psychology of association with others. From the root of all such aberrations we were recalled the very moment the problem was presented not as one of the relationship of a mythical psychology of an isolated individual mind to the even more mythical psychology of a mass or crowd or public mind, but as the problem of the relationship of original or native activities to acquired capacities and habits. Henceforth our social psychology is placed upon the sure ground of observation of instinctive behavior; it can develop upon the basis of fact undistorted by the requirement of meeting preconceived notions imported from without. The whole question of imitation, for example, reduces itself to one of fact: Is imitativeness one of the original tendencies of human nature. If so, what is its intensity and mode of working in conjunction with the other unlearned activities?

The popularizers of science will doubtless remain half a generation behind this as well as other scientific advances, but for those who have learned the lesson of recourse to fund mental responses, the way is opened for emancipation from the greatest foe with which social science has had to contend—which I shall take the liberty of calling the monistic. How often have we been invited to build up our social, political, and ethical explanations in terms of some single and supposedly dominant mental constituent! How often discussions and disputes have been, at bottom, only a question as to which of rival single claimants we shall yield allegiance. Instincts to power, to control of others, fear of authority, sex, love of pleasure, of ease, all have been appealed to, and explanations constructed in terms of one or another exclusively. Hence forth it is, I submit, pure wilfulness if anyone pretending to a scientific treatment starts from any other than a pluralistic basis: the complexity and specific variety of the factors of human nature, each operating in response to its own highly specific stimulus, and each subject to almost infinite shadings and modulations as it enters into combination and competition with others. The conception of social psychology resulting from this mode of approach becomes essentially one with that set forth by Professor W. I. Thomas in his paper on the province of social psychology at the St. Louis Congress of Arts and Science in 1904. On the one hand our problem is to know the modifications wrought in the native constitution of man by the fact that the elements of his endowment operate in this or that social medium; on the other hand, we want to know how control of the environment may be better secured by means of the operation of this or that native capacity. Under these general heads are summed up the infinity of special and difficult problems relating to education on the one hand and to constructive modification of our social institutions on the other. To form a mind out of certain native instincts by selecting an environment which evokes them and directs their course; to reform social institutions by breaking up habits and giving peculiar intensity and scope to some impulse is the problem of social control in its two phases. To describe how such changes take place is the task of social psychology stated in generalized terms.

I hope I do not need to disclaim an attempt to give in even the barest summary the history of social psychology during the past twenty-five years. My object has been quite other. I have only wanted to refer to some salients in the intellectual fortifications constructed during this period for the sake of pointing out, in equally general terms, something of what now confronts us, waiting, nay demanding, to be done. Before passing on to this point, I feel I must avert possible misunderstanding by mentioning two allied factors which have also influenced the development of which I have spoken. One is the application of statistical methods to psychological research; the other, the behavioristic movement. Neither was devised primarily in the interests of social psychology. The requirements of education have, however, been a powerful agency in promoting the former, while education presents, of course, one phase of the problem of social control. Speaking more broadly, social phenomena are of a kind which demand statistical mathematics rather than the type of mathematics which has been evolved especially for use in dealing with physical facts. Condorcet's great essay on 'The Progress of the Human Mind' forecasts a future in which human arrangements would be regulated by science. In dealing with the influence of mathematical science he points to the newly developing theory of probabilities as that branch of mathematics which is fraught with infinite potentiality for control of social progress. I think it is only fair to see in statistical psychology a step forward, short and halting though it be for the immediate present, in the realization of Condorcet's prophecy.

The behavioristic movement inevitably tends to confirm the tendency of which I have already spoken in connection with the writings of James, McDougall, and Thorndike. It transfers attention from vague generalities regarding social consciousness and social mind to the specific processes of interaction which take place among human beings, and to the details of group-behavior. It emphasizes the importance of knowledge of the primary activities of human nature, and of the modifications and reorganizations they undergo in association with the activities of others. It radically simplifies the whole problem by making it clear that social institutions and arrangements, including the whole apparatus of tradition and transmission, represent simply the acquired transformations of original human endowments.

This provides the possibility of a positive method for analyzing social phenomena. I shall avoid engaging in passing in the disputed question of the value of an introspective psychology. But it seems almost self-evident that even if introspection were a valid method in individual psychology, so called, it could not be of use in the investigation of social facts, even though those facts be labelled social mind or consciousness. Yet one has only to look at the writings of the Austrian and German school of "folk-psychologists" (say of Wundt, obviously the most important) to see how this treatment has been affected by an assumed need of making the method and results of social psychology conform to the received categories of introspective psychology. From such deforming of facts the behavioristic outlook immediately redeems us; it represents not an improvement in detail but a different mode of attack. It is not as yet possible to estimate the significance of this alteration. In my opinion, however, the chief cause of the backwardness of social psychology has resided in the artificiality of the endeavor to adapt the rubrics of introspective psychology to the facts of objective associated life. The opening of another road of approach may therefore be expected to emancipate inquiry.

I thus come to the explicit statement of the purpose of my reminiscent sketch. The aim was to justify the presentation of the conviction that the quarter century in which this Association has existed marks just the emancipation of social psychology from influences which prevented its development on its own feet and its own merits, while the work done on lines which (as it seems to me) must be abandoned, have nevertheless done the great service of enforcing the vast field open to a social psychology, and the great need it has to serve. I turn accordingly from the past to the future, or if *you* will from prophecy taking the guise of history to prophecy frankly avowing itself as such.

I foresee, then, a great reflex wave from social psychology back into general psychology. An important conclusion in the psychology of native activities does not seem to have been drawn as yet by those who would base a scientific psychology upon this foundation. The conclusion seems inevitable that since 'mind' does not appear in the original list of instincts, it represents something acquired. It represents a reorganization of original activities through their operation in a given environment. It is a formation, not a datum; a product, and a cause only after it has been produced. Now theoretically it is possible that the reorganization of native activities which constitute mind may occur through their exercise within a purely physical medium. Empirically, however, this is highly improbable. A consideration of the dependence in infancy of the organization of the native activities into intelligence upon the presence of others, upon sharing in joint activities and upon language, make it obvious that the sort of mind capable of development through the operation of native endowment in a non-social environment is of the moron order, and is practically, if not theoretically, negligible.

The net outcome of the newer type of psychological method is thus an unexpected confirmation of the insight of Tarde that what we call 'mind' means essentially the working of certain beliefs and desires; and that these in the concrete—in the only sense in which mind may be said to *exist*—are functions of associated behavior, varying with the structure and operation of social groups. Speaking in general terms, there is no more a problem of the origin of society than there is of the origin of chemical reactions; things are made that way. But a certain kind of associated or joint life when brought into being has an unexpected by-product—the formation of those peculiar acquired dispositions, sets, attitudes, which are termed mind. This by-product continually gains in relative importance. It increasingly becomes the significant acquisition among all the varied reorganizations of native tendencies. That anything which may properly be called mind or intelligence is not an original possession but is a consequence of the manifestation of instincts under the conditions supplied by associated life in the family, the school, the market place and the forum, is no remote inference from a speculative reconstruction of the mind of primitive man; it is a conclusion confirmed by the development of specific beliefs, ideas and purposes in the life of every infant now observable.

PART TWO

Evolutions & Evaluations

CHAPTER NINE

An Introduction to Social Psychology (1913)

William McDougall

7th ed., London: Methuen, pp. 90–106 [with elisions].

EDITOR'S INTRODUCTION

Ross, as previously noted, wrote one of the two founding texts in social psychology in 1908. The other was written by William McDougall (1871–1938). Historians of social psychology often note that other than their titles, there were few similarities in the two books. While Ross drew his theoretical inspiration from Tarde and Le Bon, McDougall went to Darwin. His was a theory of individual and group behavior based on evolutionary biology.

McDougall was born and educated in Great Britain. He studied medicine and psychology at Cambridge University and taught at Oxford and University College London before accepting the William James Chair of Psychology at Harvard in 1920. He taught there until 1927 when he moved to Duke University.

For him, biologically innate or inherited human tendencies were "the essential springs or motive powers of all thought and action." Human "instincts," he said, were at the core of all human behavior. In the 1910s, his evolutionary psychology swept through the discipline, inspiring work such as Thorndike's *The Original Nature of Man* (1913) and Wallas's *Human Nature and Politics* (1908). "The decade following the appearance of McDougall's *Introduction to Social Psychology* was," according to Allport, "almost wholly dominated by instinct theory" (1968, 57).

McDougall identified a dozen or more instincts (the number varied over time), many aligned with a particular emotion, and assigned to them roles in driving specific kinds of behavior. Among the instincts were reproduction, parenting, curiosity, flight, pugnacity, and acquisition. The instinct to flight was accompanied, by example, with the emotion of fear; the instinct of curiosity with the emotion of wonder.

Suggestibility and imitation were not among the primary instincts but were assigned roles "of great importance for social life" in a set of secondary "general or non-specific innate tendencies." They were, along with sympathy, "the three most important of these pseudo-instincts."

The following excerpt is McDougall's Darwinian elucidation of suggestion and imitation as they affected social behavior. Noting that psychologists had "only in recent years begun to realise the vast scope and importance of suggestion and suggestibility in social life," he offers a definition of suggestion that, because of the relatively early publication of the text and its importance in the field, became a standard formulation, repeated frequently in the literature over the following twenty or more years: "*Suggestion,*" he stated, "*is the process of communication resulting in the acceptance with conviction of the communicated proposition in the absence of logically adequate grounds for its acceptance*" (italics in the original).

Ross and McDougall were in alignment in their view of the suggestion process as variable across individuals and groups, with McDougall perhaps going further than Ross. Suggestibility, he proposed, varies "not only according to the topic and according to the source from which the proposition is communicated, but also with the condition of the subject's brain from hour to hour." The major factors he identified as modifiers of the suggestive process also became frequently cited and often studied subjects in experimental research over the following years. They included, again, source "prestige" or credibility (an impulse of McDougall's "submissive instinct"), along with "deficiency of knowledge or conviction" and personal character or "native disposition."

With respect to imitation, he joined Baldwin and Ross to propose that the term be used to describe the "effect" component in the process of suggestion. On the other hand, he went to some length to explain why both James and Baldwin were badly mistaken in their claims that imitation was a basic instinct. There was too much variety in imitative action and "no common affective state and no common impulse seeking satisfaction" in imitation sufficient to satisfy McDougall's definition of instinct.—*P.P.*

References

Allport, Gordon. 1968. "The Historical Background of Modern Social Psychology." In *The Handbook of Social Psychology*, Vol. 1, edited by Gardner Lindzey and Elliot Aronson, 1–80. 2nd ed. Reading, MA: Addison-Wesley.

Thorndike, Edward. 1913. *The Original Nature of Man*. New York: Columbia University Press.

Wallas, Graham. 1908. *Human Nature in Politics* .New York: Alfred A. Knopf.

An Introduction to Social Psychology (1913)

CHAPTER IV: SOME GENERAL OR NON-SPECIFIC INNATE TENDENCIES

IN this chapter we have to consider certain innate tendencies of the human mind of great importance for social life which are sometimes ascribed to special instincts, but which are more properly classed apart from the instinctive tendencies. For we have seen that an instinct, no matter how profoundly modified it may be in the developed human mind as regards the conditions of its excitement and the actions in which it manifests itself, always retains unchanged its essential and permanent nucleus; this nucleus is the central part of the innate disposition, the excitement of which determines an affective state or emotion of specific quality and a native impulse towards some specific end. And the tendencies to be considered in this chapter have no such specific characters, but are rather of a many-sided and general nature. Consider, for example, the tendency to imitate—the modes of action in which this tendency expresses itself and the accompanying subjective states are as various as the things or actions that can be imitated.

Sympathy or the Sympathetic Induction of the Emotions

The three most important of these pseudo-instincts, as they might be called, are suggestion, imitation, and sympathy. They are closely allied as regards their effects, for in each case the process in which the tendency manifests itself involves an interaction between at least two individuals, one of whom is the agent, while the other is the person acted upon or patient; and in each case the result of the process is some degree of assimilation of the actions and mental state of the patient to those of the agent. They are three forms of mental interaction of fundamental importance for all social life, both of men and animals. These processes of mental interaction, of impression and reception, may involve chiefly the cognitive aspect of mental process, or its affective or its conative aspect. In the first case, when some presentation, idea, or belief of the agent directly induces a similar presentation, idea, or belief in the patient, the process is called one of suggestion; when an affective or emotional excitement of the agent induces a similar affective excitement in the patient, the process is one of sympathy or sympathetic induction of emotion or feeling; when the most prominent result of the process of inter-action is the assimilation of the bodily movements of the patient to those of the agent, we speak of imitation.

Now, M. Tarde[1] and Professor Baldwin[2] have singled out imitation as the all-important social process, and Baldwin, like most contemporary writers, attributes it to an instinct of imitation. But careful consideration of the nature of imitative actions shows that they are of many kinds, that they issue from mental processes of a number of different types, and that none are attributable to a specific instinct of imitation, while many are due to sympathy and others to suggestion. [...]

Suggestion and Suggestibility

"Suggestion" is a word that has been taken over from popular speech and been specialised for psychological use. But even among psychologists it has been used in two rather different senses. A generation ago it was used in a sense very similar to that which it has in common speech; one idea was said to suggest another. But this purpose is adequately served by the word "reproduction," and there is a growing tendency to use "suggestion" only in a still more technical and strict manner, and it is in this stricter sense that it is used in these pages. Psychologists have only in recent years begun to realise the vast scope and importance of suggestion and suggestibility in social life. Their attention was directed to the study of suggestion by the recognition that the phenomena of hypnotism, so long disputed and derided, are genuine

---

[1] "Les Lois de l'Imitation." Paris, 1904.

[2] "Mental Development," and "Social and Ethical Interpretations."

expressions of a peculiar abnormal condition of the mind, and that the leading symptom of this condition of hypnosis is the patient's extreme liability to accept with conviction any proposition submitted to him. This peculiar condition was called one of suggestibility, and the process of communication between agent and patient which leads to the latter's acceptance of any proposition was called suggestion. There was for some time a tendency to regard suggestibility as necessarily an abnormal condition and suggestion as a psychological curiosity. But very quickly it was seen that there are many degrees of suggestibility, ranging from the slight degree of the normal educated adult to the extreme degree of the deeply hypnotised subject, and that suggestion is a process constantly at work among us, the understanding of which is of extreme importance for the social sciences.

It is difficult to find a definition of suggestion which will include all varieties and will yet mark it off clearly from other processes of communication; and there is no sharp line to be drawn, for in many processes by which conviction is produced there is a more or less strong element of suggestion co-operating with logical processes. The following definition will, I think, cover all varieties: *Suggestion is a process of communication resulting in the acceptance with conviction of the communicated proposition in the absence of logically adequate grounds for its acceptance.* The measure of the suggestibility of any subject is, then, the readiness with which he thus accepts propositions. Of course, the proposition is not necessarily communicated in formal language, it may be implied by a mere gesture or interjection. The suggestibility of any subject is not of the same degree at all times; it varies not only according to the topic and according to the source from which the proposition is communicated, but also with the condition of the subject's brain from hour to hour. The least degree of suggestibility is that of a wide-awake, self-reliant man of settled convictions, possessing a large store of systematically organised knowledge which he habitually brings to bear in criticism of all statements made to him. Greater degrees of suggestibility are due in the main to conditions of four kinds—(1) abnormal states of the brain, of which the relative dissociation obtaining in hysteria, hypnosis, normal sleep, and fatigue, is the most important; (2) deficiency of knowledge or convictions relating to the topic in regard to which the suggestion is made, and imperfect organisation of knowledge; (3) the impressive character of the source from which the suggested proposition is communicated; (4) peculiarities of the character and native disposition of the subject.

Of these the first need not engage our attention, as it has but little part in normal social life. The operation of the other three conditions may be illustrated by an example. Suppose a man of wide scientific culture to be confronted with the proposition that the bodies of the dead will one day rise from their graves to live a new life. He does not accept it, because he knows that dead bodies buried in graves undergo a rapid and complete decomposition, and because the acceptance of the proposition would involve a shattering of the whole of his strongly and systematically organised knowledge of natural processes. But the same proposition may be readily accepted by a child or a savage for lack of any system of critical belief and knowledge that would conflict with it. Such persons may accept almost any extravagant proposition with primitive credulity. But, for the great majority of civilised adults of little scientific culture, the acceptance or rejection of the proposition will depend upon the third and fourth of the conditions enumerated above. Even a young child or a savage may reject such a proposition with scorn if it is made to him by one of his fellows; but, if the statement is solemnly affirmed by a recognised and honoured teacher, supported by all the prestige and authority of an ancient and powerful Church, not only children and savages, but most civilised adults, will accept it, in spite of a certain opposition offered by other beliefs and knowledge that they possess. Suggestion mainly dependent for its success on this condition may be called *prestige suggestion*.

But not all persons of equal knowledge and culture are equally open to prestige suggestion. Here the fourth factor comes into play, namely, character and native disposition. As regards the latter the most important condition determining individual suggestibility seems to be the relative strengths of the two instincts that were discussed in Chapter III under the names "instincts of self-assertion" and "subjection." Personal contact with any of our fellows seems regularly to bring one or other, or both, of these two instincts into play. The presence of persons whom we regard as our inferiors in the particular situation of the moment evokes the impulse of self-assertion; towards such persons we are but little or not at all suggestible. But, in the presence of persons who make upon us an impression of power or of superiority of any kind, whether merely of size or physical strength, or of social standing, or of intellectual reputation, or, perhaps, even of tailoring, the impulse of submission is brought into play, and we are thrown into a submissive, receptive attitude towards them; or, if the two impulses are simultaneously evoked, there takes place a painful struggle between them and we suffer the complex emotional disturbance known as bashful feeling. In so far as the impulse of submission predominates we are suggestible towards the person whose presence evokes it. Persons in whom this instinct is relatively strong will, other things being the same, be much subject to prestige suggestion; while, on the other hand, persons in whom this impulse is weak and the opposed instinct of self-assertion is strong will be apt to be self-confident, "cocksure" persons, and to be but little subject to prestige suggestion. In the course of character-formation by social intercourse, excessive strength of either of these impulses may be rectified or compensated to some extent; the able, but innately submissive, man may gain a reasonable confidence; the man of self-assertive disposition may, if not stupid, learn to recognise his own weaknesses; and in so far as these compensations are effected liability to prestige suggestion will be diminished or increased.

Children are, then, inevitably suggestible, firstly, because of their lack of knowledge and lack of systematic organisation of such knowledge as they have; secondly, because the superior size, strength, knowledge, and reputation of their elders tend to evoke the impulse of submission and to throw them into the receptive attitude. And it is in virtue largely of their suggestibility that they so rapidly absorb the knowledge, beliefs, and especially the sentiments, of their social environment. But most adults also remain suggestible, especially towards mass-suggestion and towards the propositions which they know to be supported by the whole weight of society or by a long tradition. To the consideration of the social importance of suggestion we must return in a later chapter.

This brief discussion may be concluded by the repudiation of a certain peculiar implication attached to the word "suggestion" by some writers. They speak of "suggestive ideas" and of ideas working suggestively in the mind, implying that such ideas and such working have some peculiar potency, a potency that would seem to be almost of a magical character; but they do not succeed in making clear in what way these ideas and their operations differ from others. The potency of the idea conveyed by suggestion seems to be nothing but the potency of conviction; and convictions produced by logical methods seem to have no less power to determine thought and action, or even to influence the vital processes, than those produced by suggestion; the principal difference is that by suggestion conviction may be produced in regard to propositions that are insusceptible of logical demonstration, or even are opposed to the evidence of perception and inference.

A few words must be said about *contra-suggestion*. By this word it is usual to denote the mode of action of one individual on another which results in the second accepting, in the absence of adequate logical grounds, the contrary of the proposition asserted or implied by the agent. There are persons with whom this result is very liable to be produced by any attempt to exert suggestive influence, or even by the most ordinary and casual utterance. One remarks to such a person that it is a fine day, and, though, up to that moment, he may have formulated no opinion about the weather, and have been quite indifferent to it, he at once replies, "Well, I don't agree with you. I think it is perfectly horrid weather." Or one says to him, "I think you ought to take a holiday," and, though he had himself contemplated this course, he replies, "No, I don't need one," and becomes more immovably fixed in this opinion and the corresponding course of action the more he is urged to adopt their opposites. Some children display this contra-suggestibility very strongly for a period and afterwards return to a normal degree of suggestibility. But in some persons it becomes habitual or chronic; they take a pride in doing and saying nothing like other people, in dressing and eating differently, in defying all the minor social conventions. Commonly, I believe, such persons regard themselves as displaying great strength of character and cherish their peculiarity. In such cases the permanence of the attitude may have very complex mental causes; but in its simpler instances, and probably at its inception in all instances, contra-suggestion seems to be determined by the undue dominance of the impulse of self-assertion over that of submission, owing to the formation of some rudimentary sentiment of dislike for personal influence resulting from an unwise exercise of it—a sentiment which may have for its object the influence of some one person or personal influence in general.

Imitation

This word has been used by M. Tarde in his well-known sociological treatises to cover processes of sympathy and suggestion as well as the processes to which the name is more usually applied, and, since the verb "to suggest" can be applied only to the part of the agent in the process of suggestion, and since we need some verb to describe the part of the patient, it is perhaps legitimate to extend the meaning of the word "imitate" in this way, so as to make it cover the process of accepting a suggestion.

But in the more strict sense of the word "imitation," it is applicable only to the imitation or copying by one individual of the actions, the bodily movements, of another. Imitation and imitativeness in this narrower sense of the words are usually ascribed to an instinct. Thus James writes: "This sort of imitativeness is possessed by man in common with other gregarious animals, and is an instinct in the fullest sense of the term."[3] Baldwin also uses the phrase "instinct of imitation" and its equivalents,[4] but applies the word "imitation" to so great a variety of processes that it can hardly be supposed he means to attribute all of them to the operation of this assumed instinct.

The reasons for refusing to recognise an instinct of imitation may be stated as follows:—Imitative actions are extremely varied, for every kind of action may be imitated; there is therefore nothing specific in the nature of the imitative movements and in the nature of the sense-impressions by which the movements are excited or guided. And this variety of movement and of sense-impression is not due to complication of a congenital disposition, such as takes place in the case of all the true instincts; for this variety characterises imitative movements from the outset. More important is the fact that, underlying the varieties of imitative action, there is no common affective state and no common impulse seeking satisfaction in some particular change of state. And we have seen reason to regard such a specific impulse, prompting to continued action until its satisfaction is secured, as the most essential feature of every truly instinctive process. Further, if we consider the principal varieties of imitative action, we find that all are explicable without the assumption of a special instinct of imitation. Imitative actions of at least three, perhaps of five, distinct classes may be distinguished, according to the kind of mental process of which they are the outcome.

1. The expressive actions that are sympathetically excited in the way discussed under the head of "sympathy" form one class of imitative actions. Thus, when a child responds to a smile with a smile, when he cries on hearing another child cry, or when he runs to hide himself on seeing other children running frightened to shelter, he may be said to be imitating the actions of others. If we were right in our conclusions regarding the responses of primitive sympathy, these outwardly imitative actions are instinctive, and are due, not to an instinct of imitation, but to special adaptations of the principal instinctive dispositions on their sensory sides, and they are secondary to the sympathetic induction of the emotions and feelings they express. Imitative actions of this sort are displayed by all the gregarious animals, and they are the only kind of which most of the animals seem capable. They are displayed

---

[3] "Principles of Psychology," vol. ii., p. 408.
[4] "Mental Development, Methods and Processes," 3rd ed., p. 281. New York, 1906.

on a great scale by crowds of human beings and are the principal source of the wild excesses of which crowds are so often guilty.

2. Imitative actions of a second class are simple ideo-motor actions. The clearest examples are afforded by subjects in hypnosis and in certain other abnormal conditions. Many hypnotised subjects will, if their attention is forcibly drawn to the movements of the hypnotiser, imitate his every action. A certain proportion of the people of the Malay race are afflicted with a disorder known as *latah*, [5] which renders them liable to behave like the hypnotic subject in this respect. And all of us, if our attention is keenly concentrated on the movements of another person, are apt to make, at least in a partial incipient fashion, every movement we observe—*e.g.*, on watching a difficult stroke in billiards, the balancing of a tight-rope walker, the rhythmic swaying of a dancer. In all these cases the imitative movement seems to be due to the fact that the visual presentation of the movement of another is apt to evoke the representation of a similar movement of one's own body, which, like all motor representations, tends to realise itself immediately in movement. Many of the imitative movements of children are of this class. Some person attracts a child's curious attention, by reason perhaps of some unfamiliar trait; the child becomes absorbed in watching him and presently imitates his movements. It seems to be in virtue of this simple ideo-motor imitation that a child so easily picks up, as we say, the peculiarities of gesture, and the facial expressions and deportment generally, of those among whom he lives. This kind of imitation may be in part voluntary and so merges into a third kind—deliberate, voluntary, or self-conscious imitation.

3. Some person, or some kind of skilled action, excites our admiration, and we take the admired person for our model in all things or deliberately set ourselves to imitate the action.

Between the second and third kinds is a fourth kind of imitation allied to both, and affording for the child a transition from the one to the other. In cases of this fourth type the imitator, a child say, observes a certain action, and his attention is concentrated, not on the movements, but on the effects produced by the movements. When the child again finds himself in a situation similar to that of the person he has observed, the idea of the effect observed comes back to mind and perhaps leads directly to action. For example, a child observes an elder person throw a piece of paper on the fire; then, when on a later occasion the child finds himself in the presence

---

[5] An excellent account of this peculiar affliction may be found in Mr. Hugh Clifford's "Studies in Brown Humanity," as also in Sir F. A. Swettenham's "Malay Sketches."

of fire and paper, he is very apt to imitate the action; he produces a similar effect, though he may do so by means of a very different combination of movements. This kind of imitation is perhaps in many cases to be regarded as simple ideo-motor action due to the tendency of the idea to realise itself in action; but in other cases various impulses may be operative.

CHAPTER TEN

Instincts of the Herd in War and Peace (1917)

Wilfred Trotter

New York: MacMillan, pp. 29–40 [with elisions]

EDITOR'S INTRODUCTION

McDougall developed instinct theory and offered it to the community of social scientists. Wilfred Trotter (1872–1939) expanded both the breadth of the theory and the audience. Trotter examined the role of instinct in social behavior broadly writ, tying it to the nature of "the herd" and its biologically innate instincts. Moreover, his *Instincts of the Herd in War and Peace* was read with enthusiasm far beyond the scientific community, impressing social commentators and the general public.

Trotter was a surgeon by vocation. He studied medicine at the University of London's University College Hospital and worked both in private practice and as professor and then chair of surgery at University College Hospital. Such were his accomplishments in both practice and medical research that he was appointed honorary surgeon to King George from 1928 to 1932 and was elected president of Great Britain's Association of Surgeons. He gained greater public prominence, however, from his writings in social psychology, which popularized Le Bon's crowd theories across England.

For Trotter, the herd was more than just a metaphor for social behavior. Gregariousness was an instinct. As certain animals lived and survived in herds, so did humans, and the explanation for all human behavior could be had through an understanding of the dynamics of the herd. Suggestion, or for Trotter "herd suggestion," was the product of the innate instinct toward submission (from McDougall). Recalling Le Bon's "crowd mind" and the manipulative power of the individual speaker, he held that people would, inherently, submit to the will or "the voice of the herd," or what he termed "the acme of the power of herd suggestion" (1917, 115).

He pushed back against proposals that suggestibility existed only as an occasional and abnormal state. It was "a normal quality of the mind." "Man," he declared, "is not, therefore, suggestible by fits and starts, not merely in panics and in mobs, under hypnosis and so forth, but always, everywhere, and under any circumstances."

Going even further, he rejected the arguments of Le Bon, Sidis, and others that suggestibility was variable according to an individual's gender, age, or circumstance. Such variations, insofar as they might exist, were the result of the "extent to which suggestions are identified with the voice of the herd."

He considered differences of opinion and conduct within the social system—specifically referencing class-based divisions—as manifestations of the influence of the smaller "herd within the herd," and in keeping with the underlying tenets of suggestion theory, argued that people were largely irrational. "Direct observation of man reveals at once the fact that a very considerable proportion of his beliefs are non-rational to a degree which is immediately obvious without any special examination and with no special resources other than common knowledge." Social conflict, therefore, was a product of the clash between the sub-herds, each with its own flawed assumptions about the nature of social reality "derived from herd suggestion." "What we need," he concluded hopefully, "is a technique for directing the emotional drive of the herd instinct in the path of rationality" (1917, 200).

A decade later, Edward Bernays, often called the father of modern public relations, would draw heavily on the work of Trotter, along with Le Bon, in both his writing and his practice: "Trotter and Le Bon concluded that the group mind does not *think* in the strict sense of the word. In place of thoughts, it has impulses, habits and emotions. In making up its mind, its first impulse is usually to follow the example of a trusted leader" ([1928] 2005, 73; italics in the original), precepts Bernays used to help forge contemporary public relations and advertising.—*P.P.*

References

Bernays, Edward L. (1928) 2005. *Propaganda*. New York: H. Liveright. Reprint, Brooklyn, NY: IG Publishing. Citations refer to the IG Publishing edition.

Instincts of the Herd in War and Peace (1917)

General Characteristics of the Gregarious Animal.

The cardinal quality of the herd is homogeneity. It is clear that the great advantage of the social habit is to enable large numbers to act as one, whereby in the case of the hunting gregarious animal strength in pursuit and attack is at once increased to beyond that of the creatures preyed upon, and in protective socialism the sensitiveness of the new unit to alarms is greatly in excess of that of the individual member of the flock.

To secure these advantages of homogeneity, it is evident that the members of the herd must possess sensitiveness to the behaviour of their fellows. The individual isolated will be of no meaning, the individual as part of the herd will be capable of transmitting the most potent impulses. Each member of the flock tending to follow its neighbour and in turn to be followed, each is in some sense capable of leadership; but no lead will be followed that departs widely from normal behaviour. A lead will be followed only from its resemblance to the normal. If the leader go so far ahead as definitely to cease to be in the herd, he will necessarily be ignored.

The original in conduct, that is to say resistiveness to the voice of the herd, will be suppressed by natural selection; the wolf which does not follow the impulses of the herd will be starved; the sheep which does not respond to the flock will be eaten.

Again, not only will the individual be responsive to impulses coming from the herd, but he will treat the herd as his normal environment. The impulse to be in and always to remain with the herd will have the strongest instinctive weight. Anything which tends to separate him from his fellows, soon as it becomes perceptible as such, will be strongly resisted.

So far, we have regarded the gregarious animal objectively. We have seen that he behaves as if the herd were the only environment in which he can live, that he is especially sensitive to impulses coming from the herd, and quite differently affected by the behavior of animals not in the herd. Let us now try to estimate the mental aspects of these impulses. Suppose a species in possession of precisely the instinctive endowments which we have been considering, to be also self-conscious, and let us ask what will be the forms under which these phenomena will present themselves in its mind. In the first place, it is quite evident that impulses derived from herd feeling will enter the mind with the value of instincts—they will present themselves as "*a priori* syntheses of the most perfect sort needing no proof but their own evidence." They will not, however, it is important to remember, necessarily always give this quality to the same specific acts but will show this great distinguishing characteristic that they may give to *any opinion, whatever* the characters of instinctive belief, making it into an "*a priori synthesis*"; so that we shall expect to find acts which it would be absurd to look upon as the results of specific instincts carried out with all the enthusiasm of instinct, and displaying all the marks of instinctive behaviour. The failure to recognize this appearance of herd impulse as a tendency, as a power which can confer instinctive sanctions on any part of the field of belief, or action, has prevented the social habit of man from attracting as much of the attention of psychologists as it might profitably have done.

In interpreting into mental terms the consequences of gregariousness, we may conveniently begin with the simplest. The conscious individual will feel an unanalysable primary sense of comfort in the actual presence of his fellows, and a similar sense of discomfort in their absence. It will be obvious truth to him that it is not good for the man to be alone. Loneliness will be a real terror, insurmountable by reason.

Again, certain conditions will become secondarily associated with presence with, or absence from, the herd. For example, take the sensations of heat and cold. The latter is prevented in gregarious animals by close crowding, and experienced in the reverse condition; hence it comes to be connected in the mind with separation, and so acquires altogether unreasonable associations of harmfulness. Similarly, the sensation of warmth is associated with feelings of the secure and salutary. It has taken medicine many thousands of years to begin to doubt the validity of the popular conception of the harmfulness of cold; yet to the psychologist such a doubt is immediately obvious.

Slightly more complex manifestations of the same tendency to homogeneity are seen in the desire for: identification with the herd in matters of opinion. Here we find the biological explanation: of the ineradicable impulse mankind has always displayed towards segregation into classes. Each one of us, in his opinions and his conduct, in matters of dress, amusement, religion, and politics, is compelled to obtain the support of a class, of a herd within the herd. The most eccentric in opinion or conduct is, we may be sure, supported by the agreement of a class, the smallness of which accounts for his apparent eccentricity, and the preciousness of which accounts for his fortitude in defying general opinion. Again, anything which tends to emphasize difference from the herd is unpleasant. In the individual mind there will be an unanalysable dislike of the novel in action or thought. It will be "wrong," "wicked," "foolish," "undesirable," or as we say "bad form," according to varying circumstances which we can already to some extent define.

Manifestations relatively more simple are shown in the dislike of being conspicuous, in shyness and in stage fright. It is, however, sensitiveness to the behaviour of the herd which has the most important effects upon the structure of the mind of the gregarious animal. This sensitiveness is closely associated with the suggestibility of the gregarious animal, and therefore with that of man. The effect of it will clearly be to make acceptable those suggestions which come from the herd, and those only. It is of especial importance to note that this suggestibility is not general, and that it is only herd suggestions which are rendered acceptable by the action of instinct. Man is, for example, notoriously insensitive to the suggestions of experience. The history of what is rather grandiosely called human progress everywhere illustrates this. If we look back upon the development of some such thing as the steam-engine, we cannot fail to be struck by the extreme obviousness of each advance, and how obstinately it was refused assimilation until the machine almost invented itself.

Again, of two suggestions, that which the more perfectly embodies the voice of the herd is the more acceptable. The chances an affirmation has of being accepted could therefore be most satisfactorily expressed in terms of the bulk of the herd by which it is backed.

It follows from the foregoing that anything which dissociates a suggestion from the herd will tend to ensure such a suggestion being rejected. For example, an imperious command from an individual known to be without authority is necessarily disregarded, whereas the same person making the same suggestion in an indirect way so as to link it up with the voice of the herd will meet with success.

It is unfortunate that in discussing these facts it has been necessary to use the word "suggestibility," which has so thorough an implication of the abnormal. If the biological explanation of suggestibility here set forth be accepted, the latter must necessarily be a normal quality of the human mind. To believe must be an ineradicable natural bias of man, or in other words an affirmation, positive or negative, is more readily accepted than rejected, unless its source is definitely dissociated from the herd. Man is not, therefore, suggestible by fits and starts, not merely in panics and in mobs, under hypnosis, and so forth, but always, everywhere, and under any circumstances. The capricious way in which man reacts to different suggestions has been attributed to variations in his suggestibility. This in the opinion of the present writer is an incorrect interpretation of the facts which are more satisfactorily explained by regarding the variations as due to the differing extent to which suggestions are identified with the voice of the herd.

Man's resistiveness to certain suggestions, and especially to experience, as is seen so well in his attitude to the new, becomes therefore but another evidence of his suggestibility, since the new has ways to encounter the opposition of herd tradition.

The apparent diminution in direct suggestibility with advancing years, such as was demonstrated in children by Binet, is in the case of the adult familiar to all, and is there usually regarded as evidence of a gradually advancing organic change in the brain. It can be regarded, at least plausibly, as being due to the fact that increase of years must bring an increase in the accumulations of herd suggestion, and so tend progressively to fix opinion.

In the early days of the human race, the appearance of the faculty of speech must have led to an immediate increase in the extent to which the decrees of the herd could be promulgated, and the field to which they applied. Now the desire for certitude is one of profound depth in the human mind, and possibly a necessary property of any mind, and it is very plausible to suppose that it led in these early days to the whole field of life being covered by pronouncements backed by the instinctive sanction of the herd. The life of the individual would be completely surrounded by sanctions of the most tremendous kind. He would know what he might and might not do, and what would happen if he disobeyed. It would be immaterial if experience confirmed these beliefs or not, because it would have incomparably less weight than the voice of the herd. Such a period is the only trace perceptible by the biologist of the Golden Age fabled by the poet, when things happened as they ought, and hard facts had not begun to vex the soul of man. In some such condition we still find the Central Australian native. His whole life, to its minutest detail, is ordained for him by the voice of the herd, and he must not, under the most dreadful sanctions, step outside its elaborate order. It does not matter to him that an infringement of the code under his very eyes is not followed by judgment, for with tribal suggestion so compactly organized, such cases are in fact no difficulty, and do not trouble his belief, just as in more civilized countries apparent instances of malignity in the reigning deity are not found to be inconsistent with his benevolence.

Such must everywhere have been primitive human conditions, and upon them reason intrudes as an alien and hostile power, disturbing the perfection of life, and causing an unending series of conflicts.

Experience, as is shown by the whole history of man, is met by resistance because it invariably encounters decisions based upon instinctive belief, and nowhere is this fact more dearly to be seen than in the way in which the progress of science has been made.

In matters that really interest him: man cannot support the suspense of judgment which science so often has to enjoin. He is too anxious to feel certain to have time to know.

So that we see of the sciences, mathematics appearing first, then astronomy, then physics, then chemistry, then biology, then psychology, then sociology—but always the new field was grudged to the new method, and we still have the denial to sociology of the name of science. Nowadays, matters of national defence, of politics, of religion, are still too important for knowledge, and remain subjects for certitude; that is to say, in them we still prefer the comfort of instinctive belief, because we have not learnt adequately to value the capacity to foretell.

Direct observation of man reveals at once the fact that a very considerable proportion of his beliefs are non-rational to a degree which is immediately obvious without any special examination and with no special resources other than common knowledge.

If we examine the mental furniture of the average man, we shall find it made up of a vast number of judgments of a very precise kind upon subjects of very great variety, complexity, and difficulty. He will have fairly settled views upon the origin and nature of the universe, and upon what he will probably call its meaning; he will have conclusions as to what is to happen to him at death and after, as to what is and what should be the basis of conduct. He will know how the country should be governed, and why it is going to the dogs, why this piece of legislation is good and that bad. He will have strong views upon military and naval strategy, the principles of taxation, the use of alcohol and vaccination, the treatment of influenza, the prevention of hydrophobia, upon municipal trading, the teaching of Greek, upon what is permissible in art, satisfactory in literature, and hopeful in science.

The bulk of such opinions must necessarily be without rational basis, since many of them are concerned with problems admitted by the expert to be still unsolved, while as to the rest it is clear that the training and experience of no average man can qualify him to have any opinion upon them at all. The rational method adequately used would have told him that on the great majority of these questions there could be for him but one attitude—that of suspended judgment.

In view of the considerations that have been discussed above, this wholesale acceptance of non-rational belief must be looked upon as normal. The mechanism by which it is effected demands some examination, since it cannot be denied that the facts conflict noticeably with popularly current views as to the part taken by reason in the formation of opinion.

It is clear at the outset that these beliefs are invariably regarded by the holder as rational, and defended as such, while the position of one who holds contrary views is held to be obviously unreasonable. The religious man accuses the atheist of being shallow and irrational, and is met by a similar reply; to the Conservative, the amazing thing about the Liberal is his incapacity to see reason and accept the only possible solution of public problems. Examination reveals the fact that the differences are not due to the commission of the mere mechanical fallacies of logic, since these are easily avoided, even by the politician, and since there is no reason to suppose that one party in such controversies is less logical than the other. The difference is due rather to the fundamental assumptions of the antagonists being hostile, and these assumptions are derived from herd suggestion; to the Liberal, certain basal conceptions have acquired the quality of instinctive truth, have become "*a priori* syntheses," because of the accumulated suggestions to which he has been exposed, and a similar explanation applies to the atheist, the Christian, and the Conservative. Each, it is important to remember, finds in consequence the rationality of his position flawless, and is quite incapable of detecting in it the fallacies which are obvious to his opponent, to whom that particular series of assumptions has not been rendered acceptable by herd suggestion.

To continue further the analysis of non-rational opinion, it should be observed that the mind rarely leaves uncriticized the assumptions which are forced on it by herd suggestion, the tendency being for it to find more or less elaborately rationalized justifications of them. This is in accordance with the enormously exaggerated weight which is always ascribed to reason in the formation of opinion and conduct, as is very well seen, for example, in the explanation of the existence of altruism as being due to man seeing that it "pays."

It is of cardinal importance to recognize that in this process of the rationalization of instinctive belief, it is the belief which is the primary thing, while the explanation, although masquerading as the cause of the belief, as the chain of rational evidence on which the belief is founded, is entirely secondary, and but for the belief would never have been thought of. Such rationalizations are often, in the case of intelligent people, of extreme ingenuity, and may be very misleading unless the true instinctive basis of the given opinion or action is thoroughly understood. [...]

The process of rationalization which has just been illustrated by some of its simpler varieties is best seen on the largest scale, and in the most elaborate form, in the pseudosciences of political economy and ethics. Both of these are occupied in deriving from eternal principles justifications for masses of non-rational belief which are assumed to be permanent merely because they exist. Hence the notorious acrobatic feats of both in the face of any considerable variation in herd belief.

It would seem that the obstacles to rational thought which have been pointed out in the foregoing discussion have received much less attention than should have been directed towards them. To maintain an attitude of mind which could be called scientific in any complete sense, it is of cardinal importance to recognize that belief of affirmations sanctioned by, the herd is a normal mechanism of the human mind, and goes on however much such affirmations may be opposed by evidence, that reason cannot enforce belief against herd suggestion, and finally that totally false opinions may appear to the holder of them to possess all the characters of rationally verifiable truth, and may be justified by secondary processes of rationalization which it may be impossible directly to combat by argument.

It should be noticed, however, that verifiable truths may acquire the potency of herd suggestion, so that the suggestibility of man does not necessarily or always act against the advancement of knowledge. For example, to the student of biology the principles of Darwinism may acquire the force of herd suggestion through being held by the class which he most respects, is most in contact with and the class which has therefore acquired suggestionizing power with him. Propositions consistent with these principles will now necessarily be more acceptable to him, whatever the evidence by which they are supported, than they would be to one who had not been exposed to the same influences. The opinion, in fact, may be hazarded that the acceptance of any proposition is invariably the resultant of suggestive influences, whether the proposition be true or false, and that the balance of suggestion is usually on the side of the false, because, education being what it is, the scientific method—the method, that is to say, of experience—has so little chance of acquiring suggestionizing force.

Thus far sensitiveness to the herd has been discussed in relation to its effect upon intellectual processes. Equally important effects are traceable in feeling.

It is obvious that when free communication is possible by speech, the expressed approval or disapproval of the herd will acquire the qualities of identity or dissociation from the herd respectively. To know that he is doing what would arouse the disapproval of the herd will bring to the individual the same profound sense of discomfort which would accompany actual physical separation, while to know that he is doing what the herd would approve will give him the sense of rightness, of gusto, and of stimulus which would accompany physical presence in the herd and response to its mandates. In both cases it is clear that no actual expression by the herd is necessary to arouse the appropriate feelings, which would come from within and have, in fact, the qualities which are recognized in the dictates of conscience. Conscience, then, and the feelings of guilt and of duty are the peculiar possessions of the gregarious animal.

CHAPTER ELEVEN

The Original Nature of Man (1913)

Edward Lee Thorndike

New York: Columbia University, pp. 289–93.

EDITOR'S INTRODUCTION

Real history is messy. The evolution of thinking on attitude formation and change was not unilinear. Lines of thought were multiple,
chronologically overlapping, and frequently intertwined. Edward Thorndike
(1874–1949) offers a good example. Cited by Dewey (above) as one of the
important transitional figures in early social psychology, he mixed elements
of instinct theory and suggestion in a larger context of proto-behaviorism.

Thorndike is known primarily for his pioneering work in educational
psychology and learning theory. He took a BS at Wesleyan (1895) and an
MA at Harvard (1897), where he worked, as did so many others noted here,
with William James. He earned his PhD at Columbia University in 1898 and,
after a short stint at Case Western Reserve, returned to Columbia where he
spent the rest of his career at Columbia's Teachers College.

His earliest work involved animal research (typically cats); he was among
the first to do psychological experiments with non-humans. He sought to
determine whether animals learned most effectively through observation
and imitation or through trial and error. He ultimately found for the latter,
concluding that animals did not acquire new behavior through imitation.

As a consequence, in later work on adult learning, he rejected the efficacy of pure suggestion and imitation. He did, however, maintain a role for suggestion in a larger and more multi-faceted psychological process. Most of the major themes in his thinking about suggestion are evident in the following reading, which he interestingly casts in a very positive light, using examples aimed at promoting pro-social and even heroic behavior.

He starts with the observation that the mental system is a composite of multiple interacting elements, not always acting in concert: "Consciousness is the theatre of an incessant conflict."

He critiques unidimensional suggestion theory, although perhaps unfairly given the appreciation of suggestible variability even by strong proponents, but nonetheless saves for it a role as a trigger that can initiate behavior within a larger psychological context. Here he draws on McDougall's concept of instincts and James's concept of habits. "Successful suggestion toward an act consists in arousing, not the state of mind which is like that act, but the one which that act follows by instinct or habit, and in preventing from being aroused the state of mind or body which some contrary act so follows," he states.

In the last clause above, and throughout the excerpt, we also see Thorndike's reliance on the learned association between an act and its consequent effect. He was, in fact, an important figure in the history of social psychology for laying the early groundwork for behaviorism through his "law of effect." In his animal experiments, he discovered that acts that were found to be successful by the animal (locating food) were more likely to be repeated, and so behavioral associations that led to "a satisfying state of affairs" would be strengthened. Concepts of rewards and punishments, stimulus-response, and behavioral reinforcement were all central to Thorndike's learning theory and to the consequent theoretical paradigm that would dominate social psychology for the following fifty years.—*P.P.*

The Original Nature of Man (1913)

ORIGINAL TENDENCIES AS MEANS: SUGGESTION IN EDUCATION

If there were in human nature an original tendency to act out in conduct any idea present in consciousness, an easy and universal means to moral improvement would be to inoculate the mind with ideas of good acts. If all motor representations tend to realize themselves in movement the most remunerative form of education for skill and morals is to fill the mind with representations of the desirable movements.

Many thinkers about moral education have assumed the truth of the ideo-motor theory and so have trusted that presenting stories of noble acts was such a universal means of ennobling conduct. For example, Thomas says that "An idea always implies, in different degrees, an activity which tends to spread, a power which tends to pass into action and cause bodily movement.... To think of play or of study is truly for them (children) to play and to study." [Thomas, P.F., '07, *La suggestion: son role dans l'education,*' p. 5 f.] Sisson notes that the child "has a distinct tendency to do what he sees done, or hears about, or whatever in any way comes into the range of his perception. All these tendencies which are really summed up in the last sentence, constitute what is called suggestibility, or the tendency to repeat in one's own person any act the image of which enters the mind. The most clearly recognized form of this great tendency is, of course, imitation." [Sisson, E.O., '10. *The Essentials of Character,*' p. 13 f.]

The logical consequence of this doctrine is confidence that tales of heroism, thrift, sacrifice, studiousness and other virtuous deeds will tend to create them in the hearers—will surely create them except for the existence of ideas of contrary acts or strong contrary habits. So Thomas says:

> If the state of perfect monoideism could be realized, the execution of an act would always follow immediately the conception of it, and we have seen that such is frequently the case with children; but in the state of polyideism which is the mind's ordinary condition the case is different. Consciousness is the theatre of an incessant conflict which we take account of only at the moment of deliberation. ['07, p. 13]

Keatinge writes to the same effect:

> A certain portion of the mental content is attended to and becomes the idea which
> fills the focus of consciousness. Suppose it to be the idea of giving the whole of
> one's property for charitable purposes. As an idea this possesses the constant
> energy of all ideas in the tendency to realize itself. But the field is not clear for
> it. It is obstructed (a) by the inherited impulses and tendencies of self-protection,
> which incline one to make certain that one's own welfare is assured; (b) by the
> impulses arising from habit, which look askance at the tendency to give more
> than the small portion of income which is usually assigned to charity; (c) by a
> number of family prudential ideas, such as the duty of educating one's children
> or of assisting poor relatives; (d) by the fear that indiscriminate charity may do
> harm. As a result the incipient tendency to the renunciation of worldly goods is
> strangled at birth, and its only contribution towards the mental system in which
> it occurs is that of initiating a train of association. On the other hand (a) I may be
> the possessor of professional skill which enables me to earn my livelihood with
> ease, and may therefore be in no fear of indigence; (b) I may have inherited the
> fortune suddenly and therefore may have no established habits of dealing with
> money on a large scale; (c) I may dislike my children and my relatives; (d) I may
> be ignorant of the economics of social life. In this case the idea will be operative,
> and yet it is ex hypothesi the same idea as in the former case; the same impulse to
> give combined with the same conception of suffering, and the same anticipation
> of the pleasure to be derived from munificence to others. Stated schematically,
> an idea A introduced into a mental system has a tendency by association to call
> up other ideas and impulses, B, C, D, which may be (1) contrariant, critical, and
> inhibitory; (2) sympathetic and furthering. This is its total association value,
> and it works equally in all directions; it calls up ideas that are friendly to it and
> also ideas that are hostile. *This enumeration does not exhaust its latent powers. It
> possesses also a suggestive energy which may be converted into suggestive force, and
> which overcomes or avoids the resistance offered to it so that action results.* [1]

These two qualities of an idea must be clearly distinguished. The associative
tendency is not necessarily a tendency to action or belief. I may mass together
a number of ideas that deal with a certain line of conduct, but the result may
be no more than a clear understanding of the positions; for increased insight
by no means leads to action if there is in existence a system of opposed ideas
and impulses, and such a system is often called into existence in proportion to
the size of the favoring system; while, on the other hand, an idea in so far as it

---

[1] Italics not in the original.

is suggestive tends to realize itself quite apart from insight or understanding. [Keatinge, M.W., '07, *Suggestion in Education*, p. 30 f.]

This confidence that an idea will be realized in behavior if only we can get it into the mind and keep the opposite ideas out, has as its consequence, in turn, the expectation of vast moral improvement from the study of literary descriptions of virtue, the subservience of the scientific and practical aims to the moral aim in the teaching of history, and in the end the deliberate insertion in the curriculum of subject-matter chosen because it gives impressive ideas of good acts and so, supposedly, creates them.

It is, however, obvious to sagacious observers that ideas of good acts do not always, or even perhaps often, create good acts in this easy way, and that the effect in any case varies greatly with the individual and with the sources of the idea. So the very moralist who has boldly proclaimed that ideo-motor action is a fundamental law of conduct, may accept none of its logical consequences. Mr. Keatinge, for example, though specially interested in ideo-motor action, imitation, and suggestion, is compelled by his sense of fact to limit and encumber their action to such an extent that almost all of the practical advice given in his book, *Suggestion in Education*, might almost, if not quite, as well have appeared under the title *Habit Formation in Education*, or even *The Falsity of the Ideo-motor Theory.*

The whole practice of Suggestion, in medicine, government and business as well as in teaching, is, indeed, a mixture of wise action, based on certain undoubted powers of ideas to produce effects in behavior and of more or less crass charlatanism. The same theory of ideo-motor action that is required for the former apparently can be used to justify the latter.

It is, of course, my contention that the theory itself is wrong—that an idea does not evoke the act which is like it, but the act which has followed it without annoyance—that successful suggestion toward an act consists in arousing, not the state of mind which is like that act, but the one which that act follows by instinct or habit, and in preventing from being aroused the state of mind or body which some contrary act so follows. If, whenever John Smith thought of running away howling, he did in fact stay and confront the foe, a most potent suggestion to courage would be to get him to think of himself as running away and howling.

Everyone admits that in a vague sense suggestion may be potent. What is needed is some principle that will distinguish between its successes and its failures, between its scientific use and imposture. The ideo-motor principle in its stock statements does not, the result being that efficiency in the use of suggestion either is falsely expected to result in cases where it can be proved not to do so, or is left dependent on an unpredictable combination of prestige, personal magnetism, rare skill and intuition born of experience.

If the doctrine of this book is true, suggestion will succeed in so far as it is a process of manipulating a person's ideas and attitudes so as to get him into a situation to which the desired response rather than another is connected by the laws of instinct, exercise and effect. It will fail in so far as it pretends to do anything more than this. An examination of the successes and failures of suggestion to see whether they do, in fact, follow this rule would be instructive, but I have found so great difficulty in getting the necessary data that I shall not attempt it.

CHAPTER TWELVE

Social Psychology (1924)

Floyd Henry Allport

New York: Houghton Mifflin, pp. 4–5, 242–52 [with elisions].

EDITOR'S INTRODUCTION

Nothing could have been further from the theorizing of Trotter or Le Bon than the work of Floyd Allport (1890–1979). Where they privileged the collective—the crowd and the herd—Allport saw only the individual. He rejected fundamentally the proposal that there existed a "crowd mind" or "crowd spirit" somehow independent of and metaphysically beyond the individual. Only individuals were real or concrete and as such must constitute the starting unit of any social analysis. The behavior of assemblages of people in crowds, or even institutions, had to be studied from the ground up, so to speak.

He also rejected McDougall's instinct theory, and, like Thorndike, adopted an early form of behaviorism as his theoretical tool of choice. At the same time, and in keeping with both men, he accepted the psychological essence of suggestion theory and integrated it into his larger theoretical framework.

It may be a cliché, but it would be a fitting one, to call Allport a giant in the history of social psychology. His 1924 book, *Social Psychology*, stands with the 1908 texts by McDougall and Ross as foundational in the field. Allport was of midwestern stock, one of four brothers, including another eminent social psychologist, Gordon Allport. Floyd Allport received his AB (1913) in psychology and PhD (1919) from Harvard University. After World War

I, he returned to Harvard as an assistant instructor then spent two years (1922–24) at the University of North Carolina at Chapel Hill before moving to Syracuse University, where he spent the remainder of his career. Appointed chair of the new Maxwell School of Citizenship and Public Affairs, Allport became a respected and well-liked researcher, teacher, and mentor, creating the university's doctoral program in social psychology.

Allport held that research in social psychology must be empirical and experimental. He pioneered experimental design in the field with a heavy emphasis on the careful measurement of attitude formation and change. But although the individual had to be the locus of measurement, the ultimate objective was to understand the influence of the group on a person's attitudes and behavior. One piece of the puzzle engaged the concept of suggestion, which Allport saw as integral in the larger cognitive mechanism of influence. Adopting and advancing a stimulus-response model, Allport accepted the idea of innate human predispositions, which he termed "prepotent tendencies" or "reflexes," but argued they were largely the consequence of social conditioning. A suggestion, then, denoted "a certain relation of stimulus and response operative between individuals." Functionally, a suggestion, in this view, could either help create a new conditioned attitudinal association or trigger an existing one.

"When we accept an opinion uncritically," he stated, "using it as a basis for our belief or action, we may be said to respond to a suggestion." The process, more specifically, was one in which "[the individual] who gives the stimulus controls the behavior and the consciousness of the recipient in an immediate manner, relatively uninfluenced by thought, and through the method of building up motor attitudes, releasing them, or augmenting the released response as it is being carried out."

In the following excerpt, Allport begins by dismantling the analytical claims ("illusions") of the crowd theorists, then moves to suggestion, considering extant definitions and detailing his physiological view of the spoken word and its suggestive effect "in the automatic and unconscious nature of language controls." He describes suggestion in the process attitude formation and in the activation of existing attitudes, and he reviews "the conditions of suggestibility." Here he cites by then long-standing variables, including age, gender, and the prestige of the speaker (wherein he alludes to McDougall's ideas on submission). He also describes the increased suggestibility of the individual in a group context: "We bow before the will of the majority." And he offers the applied example of advertising, which "play(s) freely upon suggestibility toward both prestige and large numbers." In conclusion, he offers a half dozen recommendations for strengthening the effectiveness of suggestion, including the use of indirect suggestion, positive rather than negative suggestions, and repetition as in the monotony and rhythm of chanting.

Allport's work pointed the direction for subsequent researchers for many years, and that included, at least until the 1940s, an important place for suggestion theory.—*P.P.*

Social Psychology (1924)

Social Psychology as a Science of the Individual. The Group Fallacy. Impressed by the closely knit and reciprocal nature of social behavior, some writers have been led to postulate a kind of 'collective mind' or 'group consciousness' as separate from the minds of the individuals of whom the group is composed. No fallacy is more subtle and misleading than this. It has appeared in the literature under numerous guises; but has everywhere left the reader in a state of mystical confusion. Several forms of this theory will be examined presently. The standpoint of this book may be concisely stated as follows. There is no psychology of groups which is not essentially and entirely a psychology of individuals. Social psychology must not be placed in contradistinction to the psychology of the individual; it is a part of the psychology of the individual, whose behavior it studies in relation to that sector of his environment comprised by his fellows. His biological needs are the ends toward which his social behavior is a developed means. Within his organism are provided all the mechanisms by which social behavior is explained. There is likewise no consciousness except that belonging to individuals. Psychology in all its branches is a science of the individual. To extend its principles to larger units is to destroy their meaning.

Psychological Forms of the Group Fallacy. 1. The 'Crowd Mind.' The most flagrant form of the group fallacy is the notion of crowd consciousness.[1] It has long been observed that persons in an excited mob seem to lose control of themselves, and to be swept along by tempestuous emotions and impelling ideas. It is therefore alleged that there is a lapse of personal consciousness and a rise of a common or 'crowd' consciousness. The objections to this view are

---

[1] An interesting point of difference, however, exists in the social as distinguished from other environmental relations. In the social sphere the environment not only stimulates the individual but is stimulated by him. Other persons not only cause us to react; they also react in turn to stimulations produced by us. A circular character is thus present in social behavior which is wanting in the simpler non-social adjustments.

fairly obvious. Psychologists agree in regarding consciousness as dependent upon the functioning of neural structure. Nervous systems are possessed by individuals; but there is no nervous system of the crowd. Secondly, the passing emotion or impulse common to the members of a crowd is not to be isolated introspectively from the sensations and feelings peculiar to the individual himself.

Another argument for crowd mind proceeds as follows. The turbulent and riotous deeds of a mob point to the existence of a 'mob consciousness,' for such behavior would be quite unthinkable for men in their right minds taken separately and in isolation. There is an element of absurdity in this argument: we are asked to explain the nature of crowd action by considering the individuals in isolation; that is, when there is no crowd at all. The mere adding up of the reactions of isolated individuals has no meaning whatsoever beyond mere enumeration. But given the situation of the word—that is, of a number of persons within stimulating distance of one another we shall find that the actions of all are nothing more than the sum of the actions of each taken separately. When we say that the crowd is excited, impulsive, and irrational, we mean that the individuals in it are excited, impulsive, and irrational. It is true that they would probably not be in this state if they were in isolation from one another; but that means that only in the close group each is so stimulated by the emotional behavior of others that he becomes excited to an unusual degree. The failure to take note of these interstimulations and reactions between individuals has given rise to the illusion that a 'crowd mind' suddenly descends upon the individuals and takes possession of them. The crowd as a whole has been attended to rather than the individual members. Spectacular mob action has thus combined with loose terminology to draw attention away from the true source of crowd explanation, namely, the individual. [...]

Suggestion

Various Definitions of Suggestion. The term 'suggestion,' like sympathy and imitation, denotes a certain relation of stimulus and response operative between individuals. Like sympathy it will be seen to involve no unique type of process, and like imitation it is a collective term embracing a number of distinct elementary mechanisms. When we accept an opinion uncritically, using it as a basis for our belief or action, we may be said to respond to a suggestion. Thus Professor McDougall considers suggestion as a process resulting in the acceptance of a proposition in the absence of logically adequate grounds. Professor Stern defines it as "the imitative assumption of a mental attitude under the illusion of assuming it spontaneously." Both these statements indicate the relatively unconscious nature of the process; but the latter broadens the notion from a matter of mere belief to a mental 'attitude,' thus implying some action or readiness to act. Professor Baldwin introduces an explanatory element in his definition, and includes, like Stern, a motor factor. He regards the process as a mechanism of attention which narrows the consciousness and motor impulses to restricted lines, and inhibits attitudes of discrimination and selection. It is here justly recognized that suggestion has a negative aspect, namely, the inhibiting of consciousness and action of a nature antagonistic to the suggested proposition. Finally, Münsterberg conceived the process entirely in the behavioristic terms of action and inhibition. A suggestion, according to him, is "a proposition to action which overcomes antagonistic impulses" in the subject. The only criticism one can apply to these definitions is that, while each suggests an important aspect of response to suggestion, each is too limited to do justice to all the types and phases of the process.

The Potency of Spoken Language in Bodily Control. Before attempting a complete analysis of suggestion, it will be profitable to consider the capabilities of the mechanism through which the suggestion is generally brought to bear, namely, the response of bodily effectors to language stimuli. The spoken word has a more profound effect upon the human organism than is commonly recognized. This effect is shown in two ways: (1) in the automatic and unconscious nature of language controls, and (2) in the far-reaching and complete character of the bodily changes produced.

The first aspect is illustrated by the circular speech reflexes, in which the sound of a word directly stimulates the response of pronouncing it. As adults we unconsciously employ these mechanisms in the reiteration of phrases spoken by others with whose opinions we are in perfect agreement. Echolalia is an abnormal extreme of the same phenomenon. Aphasia presents similar features in that spoken words, which the patient through his disorder has lost all means of understanding, may be written mechanically by him from dictation. "Psychopathic obedience" is a condition in which the patient immediately executes every action proposed to him. Perfectly normal individuals also show at times an immediate and undeliberated response to commands. These effects are based upon deeply fixed habits of association between word sounds and the bodily movements which they signify. It is convenient to regard them as sub-cortical or 'short-circuited' modes of response, having their centers at a lower level of the nervous system than the portions concerned with thought and meaning. While this explanation is still a hypothesis, it fits well with the description of the suggestion consciousness as an unreasoned and immediate acceptance of a proposal.

The influence of language not only approaches an immediate reflex; it is also remarkably thorough and far reaching. Hypnosis, which is essentially a state of heightened suggestibility, presents the clearest examples. By repeated suggestion the operator gains absolute control of all the mechanisms of the body. The resistance being broken down, the statement "You cannot open your eyes" takes immediate effect, and the subject actually cannot move his lids. The auditory impulse enters the central nervous system and goes immediately out to the effectors. It is as though one were talking directly to the muscles of the subject. [...]

Suggestion Defined as a Control of Attitude. This then is the type of physiological effect produced by verbal suggestion. An example of post-hypnotic suggestion will lead us to a still closer view of the normal mechanism. It is suggested under hypnosis that at six o'clock the subject will go to the telephone and call up a certain friend. A motor setting is thus prepared to perform this act at a certain signal, the approach of the hour of six; and when the time comes the subject, though now no longer under hypnosis, automatically performs the act. The motor set thus built up by suggestion we may call an attitude. In everyday life attitudes are built up in similar fashion. We talk over with our friend the feasibility of some civic project, or the merits of the new minister; and quite without knowing it we become set to react in accordance with this discussion when suitable occasion arises. We accept the words of an expert on any subject and repeat them to our friends as spontaneously as if they were our own. A suggestion from a friend regarding our appearance, manners, or habits may determine in us a fixed attitude to react in the direction suggested. A refractory child may with tact be talked into an attitude of yielding graciously to suggestions regarding his conduct. An enemy may often be handled in the same manner. All examples of this sort involve a preparatory setting of the synapses at the motor centers and possibly increases in tonicity of the muscles to be employed in carrying out the line of behavior suggested.

Suggestion is concerned with the control of bodily attitudes in three possible ways. First, it serves to build up or prepare the setting for a definite response when the releasing signal is given. The examples just mentioned belong to this category. Secondly, it may serve as the signal (social stimulus) which releases the attitude already established. And thirdly, suggestion may augment the released response as it is being carried out. These three effects of suggestion will be illustrated in the following sections.

1. Suggestion in the Formation of Attitudes. There is a great power in the spoken word; but it is not a magic power. Every normal suggestion builds up its attitude upon some deep-lying reaction tendency already present. Interests, emotions, sentiments, derived drives, and innate prepotent reactions (see Chapter III) serve as bases. A classic example is the jealousy and suspicion of Othello wrought upon by the persistent artifices of Iago until an attitude of infuriated vengeance toward Desdemona was developed. Advertisers notoriously exploit human drives in building up an attitude to purchase their products. Here also repeated suggestion is used in the attitude-forming process. Quality, good value, and the satisfaction of every form of human need are associated persistently with the particular trade name. [...]

2. Suggestion in the Release of Attitudes. There are situations in which previous events *have already* given rise to a motor setting, and in which the suggestion serves merely to release the act for which the body is prepared. Persons deprived of loved ones by the late war have developed an attitude of yearning expectancy concerning some future contact with the souls of the dead. Spiritualistic mediums and *ouija* boards have provided suggestions for the release of these tendencies; and an international craze for things 'psychic' has been the result. Yawning when others yawn is not sheer imitation. It occurs principally when we are tired and on the point of yawning ourselves. With this preparation the sight of the act serves as a release of the act in question. We have long standing attitudes of respect and obedience to age, prestige, and expert opinion. Hence any language suggestion from sources of this character liberates the response suggested.

The release of motor settings often involves the principle of allied and antagonistic responses. Suppose one is starting from home on a cloudy morning. The appearance of the sky is a stimulus which tends to evoke the response of getting an umbrella. Thoughts of inconvenience and of the chance that it may not rain represent a neural setting of an antagonistic sort, that is, leaving the umbrella behind. A friend suggests that the sky indicates rain, and immediately an allied stimulus is added to the attitude for taking the umbrella, and the antagonistic setting for leaving it is inhibited. The allied stimulus of the suggestion in this case is the deciding factor.

Both the formation and the release of attitudes are illustrated by familiar instances of suggestion. The art of the salesman is to build up a setting to purchase his product in the neuromuscular system of the prospect. When such a setting is developed and strengthened through argument and demonstration, the 'psychological moment' must be grasped and the contract blank produced or the direct suggestion to purchase delivered. The attitude is therewith released. [...]

3. Suggestion in the Increase of Responses already Released. The third effect of suggestion is related to the second. We have just seen that social influences help to discharge motor settings already prepared, as in going up to shake hands with the forgiven darky and in feeling an emotion of tenderness toward him. After these responses have been set off they may be *intensified* by a continuance of the same social stimuli that brought them about. Thus one would go forward *more quickly*, and his emotion would reach a *higher pitch*, because he continued to see others doing the same act. The social stimulus thus serves as a suggestion not only for releasing the reaction but for augmenting it as it is being carried out. In both cases it serves as an allied stimulus and is contributory to a motor setting already existing. The term *social facilitation* may be used to include both these effects (releasing and intensifying).

In the old-fashioned religious revival we find all three effects of suggestion upon attitude and response. First, through the preaching of 'hell fire' and 'conviction of sin,' the attitude of penitence is built up. Secondly, this setting is released by the invitation-hymn and the call to come forward. And thirdly, the acts bespeaking self-surrender and the cries of religious ecstasy from others increase the ardor of the emotional reaction of each convert. Situations of this sort will be more closely analyzed in the two following chapters. It is sufficient here to recognize them as forms of response to suggestion.

Conditioned Response in Suggestion. [...] Many suggestions not involving language are based on [...] the use of acts and objects usually accompanying a response as conditioning stimuli for bringing about the response at the will of the suggester. Boys, for example, enjoy the prank of sucking a lemon in front of the trombone player in a band in order to harass his performance by the conditioned puckerings of his mouth. The eccentric who goes hatless and gloveless in zero weather probably derives satisfaction in the knowledge that his habits are causing others to shiver. Hurrying to complete his lecture at the close of the hour, the professor is often distracted by the youth who leans forward and sits on the edge of his seat in order to produce a conditioning suggestion for bringing the remarks to a close.

The Conditions of Suggestibility. The main conditions favoring suggestion, like those for sympathy, represent the 'openness' of the organism to the stimulating suggestion, and are based, in particular, upon an attitude of submissiveness toward the suggester. High self-expression in personality traits, physical strength, superior social position, and prestige through power or knowledge place their possessors in an ascendant relation to those with whom they come in contact, thus giving their behavior a suggestive influence. Sex is sometimes a determinant of a suggestible attitude, females usually standing in the submissive rôle toward males, and hence susceptible to suggestions from them. Difference of age is also a strong factor in responsiveness to suggestion. Since most of the child's knowledge comes from his elders, and also because he feels his physical weakness before them, he has formed the attitude of accepting all their suggestions without question. Where, as in childish ignorance, conviction is based entirely upon the authority of the speaker, suggestion shades imperceptibly into simple belief. Poverty of ideas and extreme submissiveness are thus the causes of the notorious suggestibility of childhood.[2]

A situation which speedily places one in an attitude of submissive suggestibility is the presence of a group, or indeed the mere allusion to large numbers. We bow before the will of the majority. We rise irresistibly when the congregation rises, clap when the audience claps, and express disapproval in unison with the throng. Adherence to style and custom is based in part upon the attitude of submission to suggestion from great numbers. The mere fact of being in a crowd places one in this setting, and so prepares for the release of specific actions suggested by the behavior of the others.

Advertisers play freely upon suggestibility toward both prestige and large numbers. Placards announce that a certain remedy is endorsed by eminent physicians (a picture representing one of them often accompanies), or that thousands have been cured by it and are ready to extol its virtues. Professor H. T. Moore has measured the susceptibility of individuals to these forms of suggestion by having them pass judgment upon the seriousness of grammatical errors and moral faults, and upon the æsthetic value of musical cadences. A set of judgments was first obtained without any suggestive influence; and another set was taken later after telling the subjects (1) the opinion of the majority and (2) the opinion of 'experts' in regard to each of the items to be evaluated. The tendency to change their previous judgments to accord

---

[2]The same considerations apply to the unusual suggestibility of ignorant adults, and to the widespread belief in the Middle Ages in miraculous events backed by the authority of the clergy.

with the majority opinion on speech and morals was found to be almost five times as great as the change which might be expected by mere chance. The effect of suggestion in the case of expert opinion was slightly less, but still substantially large, the subjects altering almost half of their former judgments which were at variance with the stated opinion of experts.[3] [...]

To complete our account we may mention a number of devices and special conditions for rendering suggestions effective. 1. It is useful closely to concentrate the subject's attention by instruction or artifice so that the suggested proposal alone is received. 2. Monotony and rhythm, as in the chants of the medicine man or the passes of the hypnotist, relax and soothe the subject, and place him in a drowsy state of non-resistance. 3. Indirect suggestion takes the recipient off guard by avoiding the direct issue at first until a suitable attitude can be prepared for its acceptance. This method was employed in the story of the negro penitent. 4. A similar distraction of attention is produced by the interesting motions made by the conjurer with his right hand while his left un-obtrusively performs the trick. 5. Fatigue and intoxicants sometimes increase suggestibility. 6. It is important, finally, to word a suggestion in a positive rather than a negative manner. We have no response attitude for "thou shalt not"; therefore we often translate the phrase for purposes of action into "thou shalt." The skilled publicity agent never prints the slogan that "the cause cannot fail." He assures the public instead that "the cause is *certain to succeed!*"

Final Definition of Suggestion. Throughout the preceding discussion we have spoken of 'response to suggestion' rather than of suggestion as a form of response in itself. There are two senses in which the word may be used: namely, as stimulus, and as the behavior process of the response. The former use is rather more distinctive than the latter. 'A suggestion' is always a very definite thing; whereas the process of suggestion contains little that is unique. The attitude, for instance, of the runner crouching on the mark, and the release as he springs forward at the pistol shot, differ in no essential way from the physiological processes operative in cases that we would more appropriately term 'suggestion.' It might be stated that the suggestion process is characteristically, though not invariably, a response to a social form of stimulation, and that it implies a relation of ascendance and

---

[3]The effect of both classes of suggestion upon judgments of musical preference was much lower. Evidently we are most susceptible to social influences in regard to matters which are likely to affect our social standing, as in this case, our speech and conduct. In regard to standards of language the majority opinion was found to have somewhat more weight than that of experts. See reference at the end of this chapter.

submission, that is, the control of one person by another (cf. Münsterberg's definition). If we add that the neural pathways used are more immediate and less accompanied by thought consciousness than in other responses to language, the picture is fairly complete. The following somewhat cumbersome definition will serve to summarize the nature of suggestion, both as process and as stimulus.

Suggestion is a process involving elementary behavior mechanisms in response to a social stimulus; the nature of the process being that the one who gives the stimulus controls the behavior and consciousness of the recipient in an immediate manner, relatively uninfluenced by thought, and through the method of building up motor attitudes, releasing them, or augmenting the released response as it is being carried out.

'A suggestion' is a social stimulus producing the effect just described.

CHAPTER THIRTEEN

"Suggestion and Suggestibility" (1919)

Robert H. Gault

American Journal of Psychology *25: pp. 185–94 [with elisions]*.

EDITOR'S INTRODUCTION

While the forgoing illustrate the incursion of suggestion into instinct theory and behaviorism, the passages also speak to the sensitivity of the social psychological community to the variable conditions of suggestibility. As noted, this was a chord struck in the foundational work on the doctrine, but one that became ever more pronounced as researchers continued their studies of the phenomenon through the 1910s and 1920s.

The following two identically titled articles, one from the *American Journal of Psychology* and one from the *British Journal of Psychology*, offer illustrations. Given the nature of the publishing venues, they also underscore the prominence of suggestion theory in the literature at the time.

The first is by Robert Gault (1874–1971), who was a pupil of Ross. With his BA from Cornell University (1902) and PhD from the University of Pennsylvania (1905), Gault specialized in criminal psychology and criminology. He taught at Northwestern University for thirty years and authored three well-regarded texts in the field: *Social Psychology* (1923), *Criminology* (1932), and *Outline of General Psychology* (1925).

Suggestion and suggestibility, as the title indicates, are his foci in the following article. Like most of the authors of this period, he has abandoned crowd theory and positions suggestion in a stimulus-response paradigm that requires on the part of the subject "a readiness to respond to suggestion." It must operate "as an indirect appeal which awakens a determining tendency in such a way that the subject has more the sense of acting on his own initiative than of responding to external influence."

Beyond definitions, the article deals with the ways in which—and reasons why—differing demographic groups respond differently to suggestion. Here he diverges from prior authors, such as Ross, who see susceptibility to suggestion as innate in gender and ethnicity. Softening somewhat the misogyny and racism, Gault argues that resistance is a consequence of a psychological disposition to more thoughtfully assess a suggestion, and this is gained through life experience. Therefore, he writes, "the race and sex factors as determinants of the degree of suggestibility may very easily be overdone." The claimed suggestibility of the American Indians, he says, can essentially be accounted for by their culture, and "as women mingle more and more freely in the life outside of the home they will gradually build up those complexes which in time will undoubtedly place them on the same level with men in point of suggestibility." He concludes with the Progressive's optimism for improved thoughtfulness through improved education.—*P.P.*

References

Gault, Robert, and Delton Howard. 1925. *Outline of General Psychology*. New York: Longmans, Green.

Gault, Robert. 1923. *Social Psychology*. New York: Henry Holt.

Gault, Robert. 1932. *Criminology*. Boston: DC Heath.

"Suggestion and Suggestibility" (1919)

The words "suggestion" and "suggestibility" are the playthings of the tyro. He flourishes them as the key to most of the situations presented by human behavior as exhibited in crowds, mobs, and audiences. The reactions of one to another, as those of salesman and purchaser also, are often "explained" by the application of one or the other of these words.

In this article we (1) discuss two definitions of suggestion and suggestibility, and (2) describe the conditions that affect both. This should enable us (3) to understand the limitations of suggestion and suggestibility as means of arriving at large social unities.

Titchener defines suggestion as "any stimulus, external or internal, accompanied or unaccompanied by consciousness, which touches off a determining tendency."[1] For example, in the simple reaction experiment the instruction to react on a given signal sets off a determining tendency which releases the reaction movement. What made the reactor ready to accept instruction? What brought him into the laboratory? What brought him to the university? What brought him to seek an education in any university? In each case a previous suggestion. The reaction to this train of previous suggestion, each in its turn, has developed a complex disposition because of which the reaction is made as a matter of course, once the stimulus is presented.

This definition makes suggestion no different from a command or a sensory stimulus. To understand the response to a command or a sensory stimulus we must assume that a tendency or a disposition has already been prepared which is of such a nature that it may be touched off by the appropriate word, gesture, or other stimulus. We would not command an ox to attend to the demonstration of a geometrical proposition because we assume that the animal has no disposition favorable to such a reaction. Nor is suggestion in this case different from any stimulus in the technical sense. A certain visual impression awakens the train of processes which ends in the emotion of fear. But the visual stimulus occasioned by the presence of a serpent, e.g., could have no relation to fear were there not already a determining tendency to be touched off by it. It is difficult to conceive of any reaction that is not a response to a suggestion according to this definition.

Again we have suggestion defined by Bunnermann, not as an external condition or stimulus, but as a mental state of expectancy or emotional disturbance: as an unusual working of the function of interpretation due to expectancy or emotional disturbance.[2]

If we accept the view that expectancy is a state both of mental and physiological readiness or preparedness for response—more or less definite response according as attention is more or less sharply focused in a particular direction—then this definition confuses suggestion in Titchener's sense with the "determining tendency." But Titchener's "tendency" is as substantial

[1] *A Text-Book of Psychology* (New York, 1910), p. 450.

[2] G. Bunnermann, "Ueber psychogene Schmerzen," *Monatschr. fur Psychiat. W. Neur.*, XXXIV (1913), 142–71.

as human nature. Bunnermann's, on the other hand, is temporary. It is as fleeting as any emotion or state of expectancy. Titchener emphasizes the usualness of suggestion and response; Bunnermann describes it as "unusual."

Nearly all definitions of suggestion now in vogue closely approximate one or the other of the foregoing. There is, moreover, the intolerable popular definition of suggestion as the transmission of a conviction or an idea from one person to another.

An adequate treatment of suggestion and suggestibility must recognize the functioning of the stimulus and the more or less stable dispositions or tendencies of human nature. Nothing is gained by overlapping the command and other methods of obtaining response in the behavior of others. It should recognize suggestibility as a condition of readiness to respond to suggestion: as usual and normal, not as unusual and abnormal; as sharpened temporarily by fleeting expectation and by emotional disturbances. But suggestibility is not a wholly temporary emotional condition. On the other hand, a stable background of dispositions or complexes in our organization accounts for a certain degree of constancy in our readiness to accept suggestion. The sensitiveness of this background and its freedom from inhibitions determines our degree of suggestibility.

We will think of suggestion, then, not as a direct appeal such as a command issued by one person to another, nor as a sensory stimulus other than a command which immediately awakens a reflex motor response or a mental reaction, but as an indirect appeal which awakens a determining tendency in such a way that the subject has more the sense of acting on his own initiative than of responding to external influence. He appears to be acting on his own initiative because, as in the hypnotic state, there is a degree of dissociation between the tendency or disposition that is then active and others that would ordinarily hold its activity in check. It is not meant to be implied that in response to suggestion one is altogether passive. Indeed, in one aspect, active expectancy and desire is a determining tendency such as we have in mind.

Suggestibility is understood, therefore, as that condition of the organism in which one or another determining tendency or disposition may express itself with relative freedom. In extreme suggestibility this freedom of expression is most marked. It is untrammeled by the inhibitions that normally control. The active disposition or tendency has been, partially, at least, dissociated from others, to use a phrase that is current among students of the abnormal mind. In other words, it functions at least in a considerable degree of independence of the whole system of dispositions that make up the personality. This is the point of view that is represented by Sidis.[3] "Abnormal suggestibility is a disaggregation of consciousness, a slit, a scar, produced in the mind, a crack that may extend wider and deeper, ending at last in the total disjunction of the waking, guiding, controlling consciousness from the reflex consciousness; from the rest of the stream of life." In normal suggestibility the lesion effected in the body of consciousness is superficial, transitory, fleeting. In abnormal suggestibility, on the contrary, the slit is deep and lasting—it is a severe gash. In both cases, however, we have a removal, a dissociation of the waking from the subwaking, reflex consciousness, and suggestion is effected only through the latter. It is the subwaking, the reflex, not the waking, the controlling consciousness that is suggestible. Suggestibility is the attribute, the very essence of the subwaking, reflex consciousness. [...] Suggestibility varies as the degree of disaggregation, and inversely as the unification of consciousness.

If this is the correct view of the case we are prepared to understand that there are two large types of background for suggestibility. One is in our natural, the other in our acquired, dispositions. There is our superstitious nature which is never quite held in leash by our scientific and professional habits. Signs and portents, shadows in the moonlight, etc., affect our attitudes and our behavior more than we are often willing to acknowledge, and bring into the foreground of consciousness images and fears with their appropriate reactions which appear to the observer, in view of the occasioning shadow or what not, to be very far-fetched.

They produce their effects by reason of the existence in the organism of a disposition fostered in us by years of wondering at phenomena which we are unable to understand. This disposition is never fully integrated with our acquisitions; it is always more or less dissociated from those dispositions that would control it, and it is, therefore, so to speak, upon a hair trigger and ready to be touched off upon slight provocation. [...]

Again, it is the native disposition to follow after the strong, or those who show evidence of strength, that makes us peculiarly susceptible to the men and women of prestige, whether their prestige is due to social or economic, or professional position; to physical or mental qualities for leadership, or what not. The reports concerning testimony offered by children show how fatally the replies of the young are determined by the character of the questions that are put to them in court. Note, for example, a very striking case in

---

[3] *The Psychology of Suggestion*, pp. 88, 89.

Belgium in 1910: three little girls, aged nine and ten, had been playing by the roadside. In the evening they separated; two who were sisters went together to their home and the third set off in a different direction to her home. The next morning this girl was found by the roadside, murdered. The two sisters were awakened and asked of the whereabouts of their companion of the day before. They replied, "We do not know." Nevertheless the detectives in the case succeeded in putting into their mouths the statement that they had seen a stranger on the previous day, a man who stopped to speak with them. He wore a black mustache, a slouch hat, and black clothing. Such a man was then arrested and brought to trial. There was additional incriminating testimony by the two sisters: questions and answers aggregated hundreds of pages in typewritten form. The defense sought and obtained permission to try an experiment in testimony. He brought a group of school children into the courtroom and plied them with questions concerning the man who, on that morning, had crossed their school yard and engaged their teacher in conversation at the door of the school. The children's answers built up a detailed account of the appearance of the man, even to his necktie, and they spoke of their teacher's agitation when the stranger had gone. As a matter of fact no stranger had been seen on the school premises on that day. The questioner had been able to play upon their sensitive complexes and to stimulate spontaneous expression. The whole performance illustrates the play of suggestion upon a suggestible make-up. [4]

Children have not the advantage of acquired disposition, the results of experience, to hold in check their tendency to ally themselves with the apparently strong, and consequently they give assent whereas they would otherwise withhold it. The effect would be the same if these experiences had in fact been acquired but had been dissociated from more primitive tendencies.

The race and sex factors as determinants of the degree of suggestibility may very easily be overdone. It is true, as Ross says, [5] that the American Indian, far from being a thoroughly impassive creature, is extremely susceptible to suggestive influences. He cites the instance of the ghost-dance religion that spread among the Indians from 1889 to 1892, and took possession of probably sixty thousand souls. The central features of this phenomenon were a sacred dance and hypnotizing operations upon the dancers who had begun

---

[4] See Varendonc, "Les temoinages d'enfants clans un proces retentissant," *Arch. de Psychol.*, XI (1911), 129, 171.

[5] *Social Psychology*, p. 14. See also the *Fourteenth Annual Report of the Bureau of Ethnology*, p. 917.

to show signs of ecstasy. "They kept up dancing until fully one hundred persons were lying unconscious. They then stopped and seated themselves in a circle, and as each one recovered from his trance, he was brought to the center of the ring to relate his experience."

This is a case in which a superstitious disposition, or a crude religious nature, unhindered by the checks that prevail among most cultured people, has been able to express itself freely. It is probable that a member of any other race, brought up from infancy in an American-Indian environment, would behave in like fashion. The often-quoted data from Starbuck[6] to the effect that women are much more susceptible than men to religious influence; that in religious revivals "men display more friction against surroundings, more difficulty with points of belief, more doubt arising from educational influences, more readiness to question traditional beliefs and customs, more pronounced tendency to resist conviction, to pray, to call on God, to lose sleep and appetite" lend further support to the principle stated above—that suggestibility is to be explained on the ground of the degree of dissociation of a complex disposition, or system-complex from controlling dispositions. Practically such a dissociation is illustrated in the suggestibility of woman. Compared with man she has been in relative isolation from the affairs of practical life outside the home. Outside that sphere she has not acquired the disposition, therefore, to examine narrowly before judging or acting. She does not possess those complexes, normal among active men in contact with the world, which express themselves in the control that characterizes the conservative. [...]

As women mingle more and more freely in the life outside of the home they will gradually build up those complexes which in time will undoubt-edly place them on the same level with men in point of suggestibility. [...]

It is by no means wholly the native disposition which determines the degree and direction of suggestibility when it is partially or entirely dissoci-ated from controlling complexes. The acquired disposition or the product of education is potent also. You seat yourself before a bank of electric lamps and place your fingers upon a coiled wire which is apparently in circuit with the lamps, and when these are lighted the coil will seem to the unsuspecting observer to grow warm, even though a secret switch beneath the table may be so thrown as to allow the current to pass only through the lamps and not through the coil. Here is a suggestion that indirectly produces a thermal sen-sation. But the subject could not have been suggestible in this respect had he

---

[6] *American Journal of Psychology*, VIII, 271.

not acquired a certain disposition (an electricity-complex, we may say) in the course of his experience up to that time with electric currents and hot wires. Likewise, the professional disposition or complex of the physician renders him suggestible in the face of situations that leave the carpenter untouched. The physician, for example, responds with enthusiasm to a movement for paving the streets because it "suggests" to him what never occurred to the proposers—the improvement of sanitary conditions. [...]

Evidently if we have correctly analyzed the concepts of suggestion and suggestibility, the possibility of successfully employing these means alone to build up large social unities is limited by three factors: (1) racial and other native differences, (2) prejudices due to social and economic position, (3) inequalities in education and want of uniform experience among sections of the population.

Wherever there is a group of people with so much in common that they constitute a crowd, a mob, an audience, the readers of a particular periodical or the disciples of a particular *ism*, there is opportunity for a fairly wide-sweeping interplay of suggestion and suggestibility. As the means and frequency of communication among men increases, and as localism becomes swallowed up in nationalism and more, we should expect an increase in the waves of suggestive phenomena were there no counterbalancing factor. Such a factor is provided, however, more and more generously as the years come and go, in our institutions for higher learning, in industry and commerce, in as far as they cultivate a disposition to seek first-hand data and weigh the evidence.

CHAPTER FOURTEEN

"Suggestion and Suggestibility" (1920)

Edmund Prideaux

British Journal of Psychology 10, no. 2–3: pp. 228–41.

EDITOR'S INTRODUCTION

A somewhat different take on the plasticity of suggestion is provided by the British psychologist Edmund Prideaux (see note).He starts with McDougall, recommending that suggestion be explained in terms other than instinct theory and proffering—without much detail—a psycho-analytical approach that recognizes a strong affective element and draws on work from both psychotherapy (especially hypnotism) and social psychology.

He categorizes four "distinct states of suggestibility" which go well beyond the basic demographic categories reviewed by Gault and others. They include suggestibility that varies: (1) across individuals, (2) within any given individual under varying conditions, (3) to the extent a given suggestion comports with an individual's existing "system of ideas," and (4) according to the affective personal relationship between a suggestor and a subject.

The third state, "specific suggestibility," is interesting in that it foreshadows basic concepts of cognitive selectivity and confirmation bias. The fourth state, "personal suggestibility" also encompasses the concepts of suggestor prestige and authority and includes for Prideaux relationships involving love and/or sexual attraction. Prideaux further parses the process into types of positive, negative, and neutral responses to suggestion.

Note

No additional biographical information is available.

"Suggestion and Suggestibility" (1920)

§1.—Definitions of Suggestion.

THE controversies between psychologists and neurologists as to the nature and treatment of the psycho-neuroses are largely due to the employment by both parties of the same words in different senses, and, as a striking instance of this, the word "suggestion" has been responsible for considerable confusion. For many neurologists suggestion is the beginning and the end of all diseases of psychogenetic origin, both as an ætiological factor and as a method of treatment. Even amongst psychologists there seems to be no real agreement as to the meaning of the word, and it is often used as if it were an explanation for a mechanism which is not understood.

The various definitions which have been given of the term "suggestion" make it obvious that different degrees of the same process are being referred to. These definitions can be divided roughly into two classes according as they refer to: *(a) Normal suggestion,* which takes place in everyday life in all of us; or *(b) Abnormal suggestion,* which takes place in psychoneurotic patients, and in normal persons under abnormal conditions. It is difficult to draw any hard-and-fast line between the two, for the difference is one of degree only, and appears to depend on the individual tendencies of the subject, whereas the mechanism remains the same in both classes. The term "suggestion," as used by Janet, Dejerine, Grasset, and Babinski, refers to abnormal suggestion only. Janet defines it as "the complete and automatic development of an idea which takes place outside the will and personal perception of the subject,"[1] and Dejerine and Grasset hold a similar view. For Babinski the process is one of suggestion only when the idea conveyed is unreasonable.[2] The broadest definition is that of Bernheim, who defines it as "the process by which an

---

[1] Janet, P. "Mental State of Hystericals," p. 240.
[2] Bernheim, H. "Automatisme et Suggestion," 1917, p. 55.

idea is awakened in the mind of a subject, and accepted"[3]. This definition includes all varieties of suggestion; but does not clearly mark it off from other mental processes. The definition which is now often accepted by the English School of Psychologists is that of McDougall, given in his "Social Psychology," viz., "Suggestion is a process of communication resulting in the acceptance with conviction of the communicated proposition in the absence of logically adequate grounds for its acceptance."[4] This definition includes both normal and abnormal suggestion, but does not make it clear whether the action is limited to processes in which there is a relationship between two persons only—a limitation which seems to be unnecessary, as it excludes autosuggestion. McDougall could improve his definition and make it include every variety by making it read: "Suggestion is a mental process resulting in the acceptance with conviction of a proposition in the absence of logically adequate grounds for its acceptance"; and this is the definition which I put forward for the purpose of this discussion. McDougall classifies suggestion amongst his general innate tendencies as a pseudo-instinct,[5] and I think it would be profitable to discuss whether it is necessary to maintain this view or whether the process of suggestion cannot be explained in some other way.

We have then to explain why it is that we accept with conviction and act upon propositions made or occurring to us without any adequately logical grounds for so doing.

If there are logical grounds for accepting the proposition, the idea is generally called *persuasion,* but it is difficult to separate this from suggestion, and it seems better to include it—at any rate when used in psychotherapy as a form of normal suggestion, for there are often no logical grounds for accepting the proposition, but only logical grounds on the part of the physician for persuading the patient to accept it; moreover, to obtain conviction, affective processes must come into play, for the way of saying a thing is more important than what is said, which is expressed in the statement: "Manner is more important than matter."

There can be no doubt that *suggestibility* is the chief factor in the process of suggestion, and that the process is a subjective one; we have learnt as the result of psycho-analytical investigation that this state is not a passive state of receptivity, and that the mind cannot be compared to a vacant seat waiting for someone to fill it, as was originally held, but that it is the result of

---

[3] *Idem.* "Hypnotisme, Suggestion, Psychotberapie," 1903, p. 24.

[4] McDougall, W. "An Introduction to Social Psychology," Twelfth Edition, 1917, p. 97.

[5] *Idem. Ibid.,* p. 90.

active mental processes going on in the mind of the subject, and particularly of affective processes.

Ernest Jones has called attention to the distinction between verbal suggestion on the one hand, and affective suggestion on the other,[6] and maintains that the latter is the more fundamental, and is the necessary basis for the former, which view accords with Bleuler's statement, quoted by Jones, "Suggestion is an affective process."[7] This view seems to be by no means generally accepted, but a consideration of the facts with which we are familiar concerning suggestibility compels us to admit its truth, and an examination of those facts shows more clearly the general nature of the whole process of suggestion.

§2.—*Varieties of Suggestibility.*

The chief facts are that: (*a*) suggestibility varies in different persons irrespective of the nature of the suggestion, and of the suggestor; (*b*) suggestibility varies in the same person at different times and under different conditions; (*c*) suggestibility may have reference to a particular system of ideas only; (*d*) a person may be suggestible towards one person and not towards another. I call these four distinct states of suggestibility: (*a*) individual; (*b*) conditional; (*c*) specific; (*d*) personal.

Individual suggestibility.—The fact that suggestibility varies in different persons irrespective of the nature of the suggestion makes it important in psycho-therapy to be able to recognize what other characteristics are associated with exaggerated suggestibility. It is exaggerated in the child and diminished in old age: it is exaggerated in those whose egoistic instinctive tendencies are excessively developed and who make little attempt at self-control and so act on impulse, the class of persons originally described as having a sanguine temperament. This class corresponds to the "extrovert" of Jung, the "motor" type of Baldwin, the "objective" type of Bain, and the "tough-minded" of James. Suggestibility is also exaggerated in crowds, whose other characteristics are impulsiveness and incapacity to reason, with absence of judgment and of the critical spirit. Le Bon points out that "the decisions affecting matters of general interest come to by an assembly of men of distinction, but specialists in different walks of life, are not sensibly superior to the decisions that would be adopted by a gathering of imbeciles."[8]

---

[6] Jones, E. "Papers on Psycho-analysis," Second Edition, 1918, p. 319.

[7] *Idem. Ibid.,* p. 320.

[8] Le Bon, G. "The Crowd," Eleventh Impression, 1917, p. 32.

I think also that suggestibility is more marked in those who live in the south and warm climates than in those who live in the north and cold climates, and that those whose associations of ideas take place by contiguity are more suggestible than those who associate by similarity.

It is less marked in those who hold strong principles and ideals, in methodical thinkers, whose critical powers have been well developed, and in those with the so-called "bilious" temperament, who correspond to the "introvert," the "sensory" type, the "subjective" type, and the "tender-minded."

Suggestibility is very much exaggerated in the patient with "conversion hysteria," and this has led Babinski to enunciate his conception that hysteria is due to suggestion. This conception has been accepted by many neurologists in this country, who have little knowledge of the mental processes at work in the process of suggestion and use the term in a very limited sense. When we recognize suggestion as an affective process, then we can agree with Babinski that hysterical symptoms are produced by suggestion, but we shall not be able to accept his view that hysteria be limited to the symptoms of "conversion hysteria." I therefore think it is unfortunate that Rivers should have proposed the use of the term "suggestion neurosis" as a substitute for "conversion hysteria" in his paper, "War Neurosis and Military Training."[9] Moreover, so long as the present confusion exists in the meaning of the term suggestion the less we use it the better.

Investigations which I have been carrying out during the past year on the "psycho-galvanic reflex" point to the fact that exaggerated suggestibility is always associated with a low "emotive response," and Dr. Snowden informs me that similar results have been obtained by Dr. Golla and himself at the Maudsley Hospital. If it could be shown that the converse is true, that a low emotive response is always associated with exaggerated suggestibility, then we should have a means of measuring suggestibility. More work needs to be done on this subject, for apart from the fact that we are not yet decided as to the physiological nature of the reflex, it seems certain from the psychological standpoint that two factors must be taken into account, the liberation of emotion on the one hand, and the stimulation of "contrary" forces on the other. I use the term "contrary" forces in order to avoid the words "repressing," "inhibiting," and "controlling." I mean the forces which are brought into action by stimulation of mental processes on a higher level: they are "contrary" as applied to suggestion, and act in opposition to the instinctive processes on the perceptual level. Physiologically they are the forces set free

---

[9] Rivers, W. H. R. "Mental Hygiene," 1918, vol. ii, No. 4, p. 519.

by stimulation of the cerebral cortex; following Rivers in the symposium on "Instinct and the Unconscious," I might perhaps use Head's term and call them "epicritic." It is possible that the psychogalvanic reflex may be an indication of the strength of the "contrary" or "epicritic" forces stimulated by the liberated emotion, and that it is not merely an emotive response.

From a consideration of these facts we can explain individual suggestibility as being due to the varying degree in which the egoistic instinctive tendencies are developed and the manner in which the sentiments have become organized to form ideals and act as contrary forces.

(b) *Conditional suggestibility.*—The variation of suggestibility in the same person at different times and under different conditions seems to depend upon the affective state in which the person happens to be, and the relation of the suggested idea to that state. I have found that even patients who generally go into a deep state of hypnosis are resistant to hypnosis on one day and will go off into their usual state on the next. Suggestibility is increased during hypnosis, fatigue, illness, and prolonged emotional states, and by the effect of alcohol and certain drugs, conditions in which the "contrary" forces are weakened. A wife, for example, recognizes that a husband is more suggestible after a good dinner and chooses this time to get her propositions accepted.

(c) *Specific suggestibility.*—That suggestibility may refer to a particular system of ideas only is also an important fact pointing to the affective nature of the process. A person is specially suggestible to ideas that are pleasing to him and which satisfy his egoistic instinctive tendencies; according as those specific tendencies are developed so does his suggestibility vary towards ideas which evoke them, and we recognize that in the same family these tendencies are developed in each of the children in varying degree.

With the growth of sentiments and the appearance of complexes and interests, both actual and dispositional, as the result of experience, so does the suggestibility vary according as the suggestions harmonize with the affective states induced by them. Thus each person has his own particular sphere of suggestibility, and even under hypnosis the suggestibility is not the same for all suggestions. This is more clearly explained by a quotation from a paper by Ernest Jones on "Psychoanalysis and Education": "A desire that arises in a person's mind for the first time is not likely to be very effective or significant unless it becomes attached to others that are already present; in other words, a motive appeals more readily to him if it is linked, by resemblance, to earlier ones already operative in him."[10]

---

[10] *Idem. Ibid.,* p. 583.

(d) *Personal suggestibility.*—Suggestibility towards one person and not towards another depends on the affective processes operating between the two persons. Sympathy, respect and confidence between the subject and the suggester favour suggestibility. I have found it more difficult to hypnotize the patient of a colleague than one of my own.

Anything which tends to increase the authority and prestige, either personal or acquired, of the suggestor, increases suggestibility in the subject; thus a parent can produce suggestibility in a child, a teacher in a pupil, and a physician in a patient.

McDougall has pointed out that the personality comes into play in virtue of the relative strengths of the two instincts of "self-assertion" and "subjection." "Personal contact with any of our fellows seems regularly to bring one or other, or both, of these instincts into play,"[11] so that suggestibility is only evoked in us by persons who make upon us an impression of superiority of any kind in the particular situation of the moment. McDougall relies on the strength of these two instincts to explain individual suggestibility: but although they are important—especially the instinct of self-assertion in virtue of the part it plays in the organization of the sentiments on a higher level—other instincts play an equally important part. It is probable that prestige owes its power to the complex emotions of admiration and awe, and often of gratitude and reverence, which are evoked by the instincts of curiosity, subjection, self-preservation, and the parental instinct. Whether we accept Freud's view, that the above tendencies are but sublimations of the sexual instinct, or not, we have got to admit the influence of the sexual instinct, for we know that a sentiment of love or affection favours the sympathetic induction of emotion between two persons. According to Ferenczi: "Everything points to the conclusion that an unconscious sexual element is at the basis of every sympathetic emotion, and that when two people meet, whether of the same or the opposite sex, the unconscious always makes an effort towards transference"[12] and that this transference has its deepest roots in the repressed parental complexes. It is also significant that in the two classes of homo-sexuals, described by Ferenczi,[13] the "subject" and "object homo-erotics," the "subject-homo-erotic" has an increased suggestibility, and although my experience of these cases is small, it is that the "object homo-erotic" is not at all amenable to suggestion.

---

[11] *Idem. Ibid.*, p. 99.

[12] Ferenczi, S. "Contributions to Psycho-analysis," 1916, p. 55.

[13] *Idem. Ibid.*, p. 253.

It is outside the scope of this discussion to go further into the psycho-analytical standpoint, and Ernest Jones has already set forth the Freudian point of view in his paper on the "Action of Suggestion in Psychotherapy"[14] to the effect that "suggestion" is a special variety of transference, namely, that concerned with the transference of positive affects to the physician, and that suggestibility takes its root in the masochistic component of the sexual instinct. It is impossible for anyone to discover the truth of Freud's theories without psycho-analytical investigation; my own position is that I accept the greater part of Freud's theories in so far as the fate of the "pleasure-principle" is concerned, and his theory of sexual development and sublimation has been confirmed by my experience in psycho-analysis, but I think that the development and sensitivity of the "reality principle" is of much more importance than Freud seems to allow, and that Janet is right in so far as he emphasizes its significance.

A consideration then of facts shows that all four forms of suggestibility, which I have described as individual, conditional, specific, and personal, come into play in the process of suggestion, and that these are affective states evoked by the stimulation of different instinctive tendencies, sentiments, interests, and complexes.

§3.—*Classification of the Responses to Suggestion.*

Any explanation of suggestion must explain not only why suggestions are accepted, but also the circumstances under which they are refused, and even strongly opposed. If we take the results of attempts at suggestion in everyday life we can classify them into three groups:—

1. Positive response when the suggestion is accepted.

2. Negative response when the suggestion is opposed.

3. Neutral response when the suggestion is refused.

These results depend on the relationship of the suggested idea to the different states of suggestibility already described.

(a) *Positive response* may be immediate or delayed; the immediate response gives us the most typical example of the process of suggestion, for in the delayed response there are also at work other factors which I shall describe under "neutral response."

---

[14] *Idem. Ibid.*, p. 99.

Most writers are inclined to the view that if a suggestion is accepted it is due to the inhibition of other ideas opposing its acceptance, and that realization of the idea takes place simply by ideo-motor action. This view involves the difficulty that it depends on the meaning of inhibition, and that we do not understand the nature of ideo-motor action.

Hart in his paper, "Methods of Psychotherapy," [15] attaches great importance to inhibition, but recognizes that it is brought about by affective processes; for him "suggestion" is "complex thinking," by which he means thinking due to the action of a complex, using the term complex in a very wide sense. He speaks of the capacity of suggestion "for inhibiting conflicting ideas and tendencies." This seems to be an inadmissible use of the word "inhibition"; the verb "to inhibit" is an active and transitive verb, and the word "inhibition" thus conveys the idea of an active process. If I go downstairs, it might be true to say that by so doing I was inhibited from going upstairs, but it would hardly be a correct usage of the word; the idea of going up would never arise and would not require inhibition. Suggestion has no capacity for inhibiting ideas, but, if we speak in terms of inhibition, is rather the consequence of the inhibition of inhibiting forces normally involved in volition.

Moreover, the term "complex thinking" lays too much stress on the cognitive aspect of the process of suggestion, and though this is the first stage in the process, more than this seems to be involved; for example, if, during a railway strike, I merely thought of an engine as the means of transport for getting me to town, nothing further would result, but if forces were aroused in me sufficiently strong to make me "tip" the engine-driver, then I should be acting under the influence of suggestion. No other ideas would arise if the response was immediate, and no ideas would be inhibited.

The term "ideo-motor action" is a relic of the old psychology of ideas; for example, for Hegel, "an idea is a force, and is only inactive in so far as it is held in check by other ideas." [16] If the process of ideo-motor action be analysed, it is found that the action depends entirely on the affective forces aroused by the idea, and that no idea will realize itself unless it is reinforced by some affective force. Ideo-motor action is thus equivalent to the expression of emotion. We know that emotion is expressed normally through the autonomic nervous system, and, when excessive, through the central nervous system. It is evident that persons, whose instinctive tendencies are highly developed, and whose sentiments have not been well organized to act as

---

[15] Hart. B. *Proc. Roy. Soc. of Med.*, March, 1919.
[16] Wallace, W. "Hegel's Philosophy of Mind," 1894, p. 167.

"contrary forces," will realize their ideas in action through the central nervous system without opposition, and I have shown elsewhere that this may be an explanation why a patient with conversion hysteria develops symptoms attributable to the central nervous system, and a patient with anxiety hysteria develops symptoms attributable to the autonomic nervous system.

It follows from what I have already said that I here maintain the view that an idea is accepted because it harmonizes with some pre-formed interest, sentiment, or complex, that the affective forces involved give it the necessary reinforcing power to realize itself in opposition to all "contrary forces," and that it is these affective forces which produce conviction. Any condition which tends to weaken the "contrary forces" on the one hand, or strengthen the compatible affective forces on the other, favours the process of suggestion, and we have noted that the conditions which cause "conditional suggestibility" are those which weaken the volitional forces, and that individual suggestibility is exaggerated in those who are endowed with strong emotional tendencies and have a poor development of self-control.

McDougall has shown that it is the organization and strength of the self-regarding sentiment in relation to the other sentiments which determines our line of action and constitutes our self-control; as this higher control, though it relies for its strength on the self-regarding sentiment, involves the formation of ideals, and is, perhaps, influenced by the herd instinct, I have called it elsewhere the "social ideal self" as a contrast to the "individual self."[17] Individual suggestibility then depends very largely on the strength of the social ideal self; and the weaker the social ideal self, the greater the number of complexes that remain unsublimated, and the greater are the states of specific and personal suggestibility.

Wilfred Trotter has pointed out how one form of suggestion, "herd suggestion," is due to the action of herd instinct, and that "anything which dissociates a suggestion from the herd will tend to ensure such a suggestion being rejected."[18] It is owing to the influence of the herd instinct that we may accept propositions in regard to religion, politics, and education. Such beliefs are non-rational, and are accepted by us as the result of accumulated suggestions.

The exaggerated suggestibility of children, occurring when they have reached the age of paying attention, which is in its turn dependent on the interest aroused, is due to the evocation of the instinct of submission, the

---

[17] Prideaux, E. "Functional Nervous Diseases," 1920, chap. iv.

[18] Trotter, W. "Instinct of the Herd in Peace and War," Third Impression, 1917, p. 33

weakness of the social ideal self, and the absence of resistance complexes. For opposite reasons old people are less suggestible.

(a) *Negative response* is the response obtained when not only is the suggested idea incompatible with pre-formed sentiments and interests, but it arouses contrary emotions and sentiments. This is the process which is called "contra-suggestion." The mechanism is the same as for the positive response, but an opposing set of forces are set in action with the production of a state of "negativism"—a state which is the direct counterpart to suggestibility. This state, like suggestibility, may have individual, conditional, specific, or personal tendencies. It seems to be a form of over-determination due to the presence of antagonistic complexes, which more than counterbalance the forces of a weak social ideal self.

Like suggestibility, negativism may be exaggerated, and become pathological; it is most marked in dementia praecox.

Some people appear to adopt "negativism" as a habit; such are the people we call "cranks." I look upon the action of these people as being that of over-determination, owing to the formation of complexes associated with painful experiences in the past.

In psychotherapy, when we have established an atmosphere of cure, negativism signifies an unconscious resistance to recovery, and when exaggerated it must make us suspect dementia praecox, or malingering if it seems likely that the resistance is a conscious one.

(c) *Neutral response.*—It is hard to draw the line between the lower forms of volition and suggestion. If the idea is incompatible with the social ideal self and the social ideal self is strong, then the process is one of volition and we get a neutral response; this is what happens in those who hold strong principles and ideals. If the social ideal is too weak, and the affective forces aroused are strong, the idea is accepted and the process is one of suggestion.

If the idea has not made sufficient impression, we get a neutral response, and this is due to the fact that there are no pre-formed interests or complexes to which it can attach itself: in this case the suggestion is ignored. This is seen most markedly in certain imbeciles. The suggestion may need repetition to give it the necessary amount of prestige for acceptance, a fact which is taken into consideration as a basis for all advertisements. The suggestion may be incompatible with such interests and complexes as exist, and the forces involved simply neutralize each other, which is one of the reasons for the fact that the suggestions of the younger generation are not easily accepted by the elder.

A neutral response may also be the result of a conflict of motives due to the incompatibility of the interests aroused, with the production of a state of doubt, which is seen in an exaggerated form in cases of anxiety hysteria: in such cases the suggestion may be accepted after deliberation either to relieve tension, or when a decision is brought about by the reinforcement of one side of the conflict by further affective forces: or the conflict may be forgotten and only at some later period will one side of the conflict materialize by the stimulation of affective forces which harmonize with it. A neutral response will also occur in cases of "dementia."

CHAPTER FIFTEEN

"The Comparative Influence of Majority and Expert Opinion" (1921)

Henry T. Moore

American Journal of Psychology *32: pp. 16–20 [with elisions]*.

EDITOR'S INTRODUCTION

Among the more heavily studied sub-topics in suggestion theory was the power of the authoritative speaker (prestige) and the reference group itself. An experiment by psychologist Henry T. Moore (1903–1967) in 1921 is illustrative.

Moore had degrees from the University of Missouri (AB, 1903), Yale (AM, 1907) and Harvard (PhD, 1914). He was on the psychology faculty at the University of Minnesota and then Dartmouth until 1925, when he accepted a position as the second president of Skidmore College in New York, where he served for 32 years.

Although Allport was a—maybe *the*—leading exponent of laboratory experimentation in social psychology, he held no early monopoly on the method. Moore's work represents one of many examples of laboratory research applied to suggestibility in the 1910s and 1920s. Instead of sweeping sociological claims of the kind characterized by writers such as Trotter or

Ross, Moore focused on one narrow question, using a rigorous and elaborate design to gather quantifiable information. The question at hand was "the influence of the group upon the opinions of the individual," referencing, although not altogether favorably, Trotter's *Instincts of the Herd*. Moore also sought to compare the influence of the group with the influence of an outside expert.

His design marshaled ninety-five subjects, testing responses to treatments across three topics: linguistic judgments, ethical judgments, and musical preferences. He concluded, using terms of statistical probability, that there was evidence of suggestive influence in all conditions, although it was greater in matters of speech and morals than in music. The influence of group opinion was somewhat more powerful than that of the expert in matters of speech. The expert could exert some influence on musical taste, however, so "classical music has at least an even chance in its struggle with the popularity of the jazz band."

Referencing what we now label "generalizability," he noted in conclusion that similar tests of suggestibility in areas of fashion or orthodoxy "would give material which would be valid for general purposes."—*P.P.*

"The Comparative Influence of Majority and Expert Opinion" (1921)

The literature on Social Psychology contains numerous references to the influence of the group on the opinions of the individual. This one point has been made the subject of practically an entire volume by Trotter,[1] who refers to group opinion somewhat picturesquely as the voice of the herd. He represents this voice as coming with such a weight of authority that even the most eccentric individual feels compelled to seek some form of herd support for his opinions, and is completely at a loss when no such support is anywhere to be had.

The general fact is beyond dispute, but those who would like to see Social Psychology multiply its experimental findings are tempted to ask more specifically just how great this influence may be expected to be in any given situation. Can we hope to measure it? And if so, how does it compare with

---

[1] Trotter W. *The Instincts of the Herd in Peace and War,* 1916.

other influences that are likely to operate in determining an individual's social attitudes?

The group experiment here reported attempts a beginning at answering these questions for three types of situation, namely, speech, morals, and music. The method is somewhat similar to one used by Bridges[2] in a study of decision types reported in 1914. In general it consists of measuring a suggestive influence in terms of the number of reversals of judgment occasioned by it, as compared with the number that might have been expected by chance. The first problem was therefore to find out what was the chance of reversal of judgment in regard to each of the three kinds of material used. Ninety-five subjects were given eighteen paired comparisons for each of the three types of situation. The instructions for the linguistic judgments were that the subjects check the more offensive one of each pair of expressions. Examples of the expressions compared are: "Everybody loves their mother." "She sort of avoided him." "The party that wrote that was a scholar." "He never studies nights." The ethical judgments involved the checking of the more offensive of two traits of character in each of the eighteen pairs. Examples of the traits compared are: disloyalty to friends; willingness to get rich by questionable financial methods; cheating on an examination; willingness to overlook a business error favorable to oneself. The musical judgments involved an expression of preference for one of two resolutions of the dominant seventh chord, played on a reed organ. Eighteen paired resolutions were played, and the preferences recorded after each.

Two days later the same three series were repeated exactly as given before, and without the introduction of any special suggestive influence to alter the original judgments. Each subject was now scored on the basis of his percentage of reversals, and the mean of the ninety-five individual scores was taken as the chance of reversal for judgments concerned with that particular type of material. The average score thus recorded as representing the chance of reversal for linguistic judgments was 13.5 per cent with .55 P. E. of the mean; for moral judgments 10.3 per cent with P. E. of .50; for musical judgments 25.1 per cent, with P. E. of .84.

As a partial check on the above figures each of the three series of judgments was tried on a different group. The subjects in the check experiment were on an average about a year older than those in the original experiment, which probably accounts for their slightly lower per cent of reversals. Forty-

[2] Bridges, J. W., An Experimental Study of Decision Types and their Mental Correlates, *Psych. Rev. Mon. Sup.*, 1914, Vol. XVII, No. 1.

three subjects gave 11.4 per cent chance of reversal in linguistic judgments; 62 subjects gave 9.4 per cent reversals in ethical judgments; and 49 subjects gave 22.6 per cent reversals in musical judgments.

An interval of two and a half months was allowed between the experiment without suggestion and that in which suggestion was used. This seemed ample time to render negligible any memory effects from the preceding judgments. The experiment was now repeated as before, except for the addition of the suggestive influences. A new set of original judgments was taken, and after a two day interval the subjects were given the same series again, this time with the statement of what had been the majority preference for each pair. Great care was taken to convince them that these statements were being truthfully made, and the influence of suspicion was certainly not great. Each subject was now scored on the basis of the per cent of opportunities he had accepted to reverse his judgment so as to agree with majority opinion. The results are indicated in the three left columns of the upper chart. The average of such reversals in linguistic judgments was 62.2 per cent, with P. E. of 1.63; in ethical judgments 50.1 per cent, with P. E. of 1.69; in musical judgments 48.2 per cent, with P. E. of 1.52.

Two days later still the same comparisons were repeated, and at this time each judgment was preceded by a statement of the opinion of an expert in each field. These statements in some cases coincided with what had been given as majority opinion previously, but as often as not they were at variance with it. From these last records each individual was scored on the basis of the per cent of opportunities he had accepted for reversing his original judgment favorably to the statement of the expert. The results [...] show an average of 48 per cent reversals of language judgments, with P. E. of 1.4; 47.8 per cent reversals of ethical judgments, with P. E. of 1.6; and 46.2 per cent reversals in musical judgments, with P. E. of .9.

If now we take as our unit of measurement the per cent recorded as the chance of reversal, we find [...] that the probability of reversing favorably to the majority in matters of speech and morals is approximately five times chance; whereas in matters of musical feeling the probability is only about twice chance. By majority is meant here of course only the special type of majority provided in the experiment, but if generalization is permissible on the basis of the evidence available, we may venture the statement that a man is two and a half times as individualistic in his musical likes and dislikes as in his moral and linguistic preferences. Similarly we may conclude that expert and majority opinion hold about equal sway over the individual in morals and music, but that the chances are about ten to seven in favor of majority prestige in matters pertaining to speech. To take a concrete case, the struggle between the expert pronunciation which accents the word 'cantonment' on the first syllable, and the army pronunciation, which accents it on the second syllable, is likely to end with the doom of the expert, whereas classical music has at least an even chance in its struggle with the popularity of the jazz band.

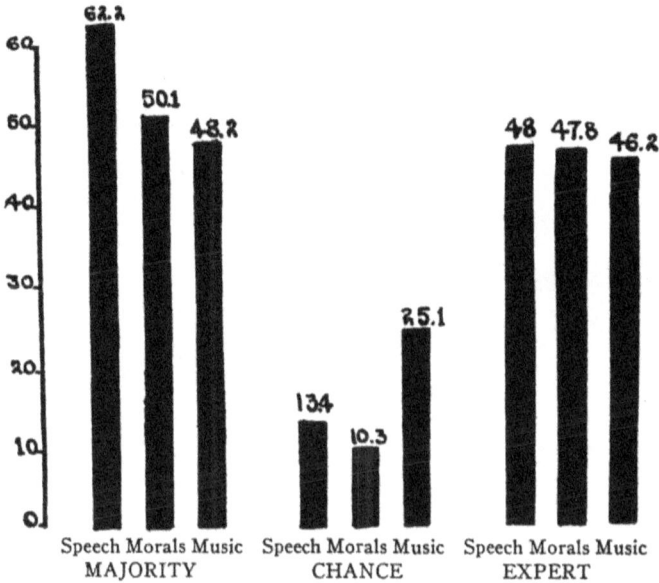

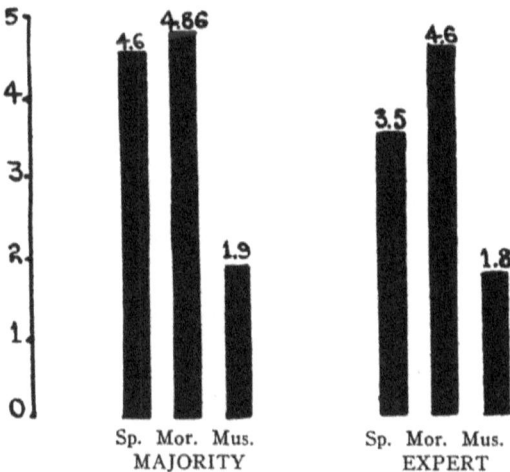

The type of experiment here described can, on account of the great range of individual variations involved, be valid only if applied to a large number of cases; and inasmuch as each particular experiment measures only a very particular type of suggestibility, any generalization from a single experiment will always be questionable. But it is believed that an extension of the method to cover a large number of typical cases in which such social influences as personal prestige, fashion, orthodoxy, etc., play a part, would give material which would be valid for general purposes. Whether the shrunken prestige of a defeated political candidate or of an abdicated emperor follows any accurately describable laws, one could scarcely venture to say; but it is sufficiently obvious that until so-called social laws rest on more than the personal observations of individual writers, we shall have a great excess of laws, and only a minimum of confidence in applying them. [3]

[3] Read at the Annual Meeting of the American Psychological Association, Cambridge, Mass., Dec. 31, 1919.

CHAPTER SIXTEEN

"The Psychology of Belief: A Study of Its Emotional, and Volitional Determinants" (1925)

Frederick Lund

Journal of Abnormal and Social Psychology *20, no. 2: pp. 174–96.*

EDITOR'S INTRODUCTION

In the 1950s, Hovland and his colleagues (1953) conducted what were later characterized as groundbreaking experiments in persuasion. They included the examination of variables such as source credibility, order effects, and channel effects. Order effects dealt with the organization of persuasive arguments. Channel effects involved assessing the relative efficacy of differing modes of presentation (for example, print versus a live speaker). Lowery and De Fleur (1983) later called this work the search for "the magic keys," noting it as one of the "milestones" in mass communication research. A closer read of Hovland, however, would have revealed his extensive citation of work done twenty-five years prior, including that of Frederick Lund (1894–1965), excerpted here.

Born in New Zealand, Lund emigrated with his family to the US, where he became a naturalized citizen in 1918. He took his bachelor's degree at the University of Nebraska (1918) and his master's (1923) and PhD in psychology (1925) at Columbia. He taught for two years at Columbia, spending most of the rest of his career at Bucknell and then Temple University. He also served as director of the Psychological Clinic in Camden, NJ.

As we've seen, researchers in the 1920s and 1930s studied assorted variables in the suggestion process, such as prestige and group suggestion, channel and order effects, and direct versus indirect message design; they even looked at message volume (loudness) and the time of day a suggestion was presented (Parsons 2021).

Lund's 1925 article from the *Journal of Abnormal Psychology and Social Psychology* is just one illustration of this kind of work. It combines a rigorous laboratory study with an eye for real-world application of findings. Cast in terms of belief and persuasion—Lund does not refer to suggestion in the study—it begins with a discussion of the nature of attitude creation in advertising. It then considers various "factors in persuasion," experimentally testing order effects and finding strong support for what he labels "the law of primacy."

Lund also references what later researchers would recognize as Leon Festinger's theory of cognitive consistency: "To have our ideas confirmed appeals to our ego, and our desire for consistency, while to have them attacked is likely to arouse a defiant and militant attitude, since our ideas and beliefs are in many instances so essential a part of our ego that they have become our most cherished possession." He concludes with recommendations on how the findings would be of use in applied settings, from advertising to argumentation in jury trials.—*P.P.*

References

Hovland, Carl, Irving Janis, and Harold Kelley. 1953. *Communication and Persuasion.* New Haven: Yale University Press.

Lowery, Sharon, and Melvin De Fleur. 1983. *Milestones in Mass Communication Research.* New York: Longman.

Parsons, Patrick. 2021. "The Lost Doctrine: Suggestion Theory in Early Media Effects Research." *Journalism & Communication Monographs* 23, no. 2.

"The Psychology of Belief: A Study of Its Emotional, and Volitional Determinants" (1925)

III. The Determinants of Belief and the Ideal of Rationality

The significant correlation between belief and desire, and the comparatively low correlations between belief and objective measures, leave little doubt as to the moulding influence of emotional factors. But the determination of this important relation does not preclude the absence of other factors instrumental in moulding our belief-attitudes. Nor does it tell us anything about the antecedents of our desires, granting their priority to belief, for our desires as our beliefs do not exist in any *a priori* fashion, but are in most cases the result of conditioning forces continually at work in social and economic relations.

CONSTRUCTION OF A LIST OF BELIEF-DETERMINANTS

In the earlier writings on the subject of belief much interest is shown in its determinants, but in the survey made of these writings no work was found outside of Balfour's "Foundations of Belief"[1] which is definitely devoted to the problem. Even in Balfour's classic work no attempt is made to present anything like a list of determinants. It is acknowledged that any attempt to construct such a list, the present one included, must of necessity be wanting and incomplete, since the forces at work giving form to belief are innumerable. Consequently, such a list will at best amount to a classification of these forces. [...]

BELIEF-DETERMINANTS IN ADVERTISING

"The fact that the American people," to quote Poffenberger, "are each year induced to squander millions of dollars in worthless securities through the medium of advertising in some form, and that warnings seem quite ineffective in protecting them, makes one curious about the basis of belief in advertising. It is not enough to say that the American people like to be fooled and that there is no scheme too wild to arouse the confidence of a large proportion of them."[2]

---

[1] Balfour, A.J. "Foundations of Belief." Longmans, Green & Co., London, 1895.
[2] Poffenberger, A.T., "The Conditions of the Belief in Advertising," *J. of Applied Psychol,* 1923, 7(1), 1.

Poffenberger agrees that belief is rarely the result of reasoning, and that logic when used comes in only to justify beliefs already established. In testing the relative weight of rational considerations in determining belief he gave fifty-seven students, graduate and undergraduate men, an advertisement of the New Gillette razor with the information and illustrations which the advertisement contained. They were asked to answer seven questions which were made out to test their belief in the new razor and their understanding of it. The answers showed that they were all agreed that the new razor was better than the old, and would in fact rather pay $5 for it than $1 to $2 for the old one. In supporting their belief they cited a statement from the advertisement about the "micrometric control of the blade position," but not one of them could explain how such control was gained, or how it was an advantage. Likewise, they believed the "channel guard" was an improvement, although they could not tell wherein the improvement consisted.

Poffenberger made another experiment which showed that the truth of the statements in an advertisement does not insure the public's belief in them. This is the case when the truth is too startling or surprising to be believed. A trunk advertisement showing a huge elephant standing on a trunk was presented to one hundred people with questions as in the former experiment. The picture was accompanied by signed statements as to the genuineness of the photograph, and as to the trunk being taken from regular stock. Thirty-eight per cent doubted the truth of the advertisement; 24 per cent questioned the genuineness of the photograph; and 21 per cent believed it impossible to construct a trunk which could withstand such weight. Experiments in which other advertisements of the same type were used confirmed the results of the trunk experiment.

"To create belief," Poffenberger concludes, "ideas aroused by an advertisement must not conflict too sharply with the reader's experience," and "must come from an authoritative source." He also contends that "we tend to believe what arouses our desires, our fears, and our emotions generally."[3]

IV. The Law of Primacy in Persuasion

FACTORS IN PERSUASION

In textbooks dealing with composition, oratory, debate, and argumentation, ample attention is given to intellectualistic factors, such as clearness, logic, and understanding, all of which play a part in conviction and persuasion.

---

[3] Op. cit., pp. 4—9.

Much less attention is given to the importance which attaches to habits of mind, habits of thinking, and common belief. Yet that these are significant factors in persuasion, and imperative in their demands upon the successful speaker, is apparent from data furnished on the subject, and should appear even from a superficial analysis of human motivation. To prove to an audience that the ideas advocated are in accordance with what they already believe is by no means unimportant in the art of persuasion. To have our ideas confirmed appeals to our ego, and our desire for consistency, while to have them attacked is likely to arouse a defiant and militant attitude, since our ideas and beliefs are in many instances so essential a part of our ego that they have become our most cherished possession.

That emotional factors, interests, prejudices, and desires, are elements in persuasion is also recognized by texts on the subject, but not proportionately to their value. The place assigned them should be determined by the results of empirical studies and by such correlations as have been obtained between belief and desire. To take special account of the self-interests of the individual, what is pleasing or displeasing or even what appeals to the vanity, ambitions, jealousies, and hatred of one's auditors or readers, may not seem commendable because of our social ideals and the atmosphere in which we are raised. However, their commendability is an ethical question, and in so far as such emotions and self-interests exist as important factors in persuasion, scientific interests must duly reckon with and account for them. An analysis of the most famous orations will reveal how very largely they depend for their persuasive appeal upon the primary emotions and "lower" impulses. These are usually camouflaged, however, or connected with "higher" motives which are more commendable. The rest is left to the rationalizing power of the individual. Frequently, skillful advertising will take account of the same principle.

Still another important factor in persuasion is the influence of order and arrangement in presentation. Should this follow the traditionally accepted notion of climax order, that is, from weaker to stronger? or should the order be reversed? Is there any significance to be attached to the order in which affirmative and negative arguments are presented? Who has the advantage the one who presents his side of the question first, or the one who presents his last? The experiment described in the next section was made with a view to answer these questions, and as a further means to determine the influence of emotional factors upon belief.

ORDER AS A FACTOR IN PERSUASION

The question of order arose in the first place out of a consideration of the possible influence which discussions pro and con might have upon a group's rating of a given proposition. The study of the effects of such discussions, depending upon their length and the nature of their persuasive appeals, might be a valid approach to securing definite estimations of the conditioning and determining factors in belief and persuasion. What, for example, would be the relative weight of discussions of the purely discursive type, as over against discussions relying mainly on their emotional appeals and question begging epithets? Important group differences depending on age, intelligence, and education, would doubtless become evident in such a study. [...]

The subjects in the test were six groups (A, B, C, D, E, F) of Nebraska undergraduate students. There were twenty or more subjects in each group. For all groups a rating of the thirty propositions on the belief scale was first secured by the usual procedure. [...]

The significant thing about the results is not so much the extent to which belief may be conditioned by such influences as the discussions present, but the importance attaching to the *order* in which these influences are present. The consistency with which the first discussion was most effective in determining the final position of the subject, confirms the presuppositions of a *law of primacy in persuasion*. The difference in the extent to which the principle operated, and the difference in the extent to which the subjects could be swayed from their original position, is only added confirmation of the principle. For if primacy is the factor then propositions upon which one has already had ample opportunity to form an opinion should be much less subject to persuasive influences. This must indeed be the case with the proposition on monogamous marriage, much more so at least than with the one on political rights, where the effects of the law of primacy are particularly in evidence.

An examination of the individual ratings of group A and group B reveal the following facts: 48 per cent of the subjects rated the proposition the same after reading the opposed discussion as they had after reading the first discussion; 30 per cent were swayed not more than two points (of a possible 20 points) after reading the second discussion; while 22 per cent changed their ratings on the average thirteen points, ranging from 5 to 20 with an A.D. of 3.4. Thus there was a tendency for 4/5 of the subjects to adhere doggedly to their original position (the position taken after reading the first discussion), while the remaining ones practically all changed their position from positive to negative or vice versa as the case might be. That the final position taken by four out of five seemed entirely determined by the first discussion may be considered as giving still further emphasis to the suggestion that there is a law of primacy operating in persuasion.

But if such a law is present, how are we to account for it? For an answer to this question we must leave the experimental field and rely on what seems probable in the case. We have noticed that a possible origin of belief and its desirability to the individual is to be found in the contentment and the feeling of stability and adjustment which it yields. Such satisfyingness is nature's device in encouraging belief and a certain amount of unquestioning acceptance necessary to social uniformity and organization. Man is continually therefore seeking points of attachment, and once they are gained he is loath to relinquish his hold. They have become intimate and necessary parts of his ego, and to have them assailed is equivalent to an attack upon his person.

Thus the first time a subject is presented to us we tend to form an opinion, and we do so in accordance with the influences present to shape it. Later such an opinion may gain a certain amount of emotional content if it is contradicted. This follows, not only because of its personal reference, but because we would not have our ideas appear fragile or inconsequential.

Another factor which may be responsible in a measure for the importance of primacy in persuasion is the *ideal of consistency,* an ideal closely related to the ideal of rationality because of its logical implications. We observe the ideal of consistency in the same way as we observe other ideals which have gained general commendation. We feel called upon to be consistent in the same way as we feel called upon to be rational. Once we have committed ourselves we frequently dare not change our positions lest we should be challenged with our former statements.

In accordance with this analysis, the students, having committed themselves after the reading of the first discussion, will remember this rating and will tend to be influenced by their desire to be consistent when asked to make another rating after reading the opposed discussion. But the consistency principle as determined by open commitment is not the only or perhaps even the primary factor as we have seen. A belief may gain a personal connotation though it has never been expressed. To have formed an opinion and inwardly to have yielded to its persuasive influence is sufficient to make it seem *ours* and something to which we owe our allegiance.

The significance which these facts give to primacy as an important constituent in belief and persuasion has certain practical bearings, some of which may be enumerated.

A. The speaker or writer engaged in a debate or dealing with a controversial subject, in observing the importance of primacy, should not follow the climax order in presenting his argument, but should weaken sympathy with his opponent *promptly* by attacking his strongest argument first, thus lessening the force of his adversary's case as quickly as possible.

B. In a debate, other things being equal, the affirmative, or whatever side of the question is first presented, should have the advantage according to the influence of primacy. However, in staged debates the principle is likely to be much less influential because of the more objective attitude taken by the audience toward the issue itself.

C. The advertiser interested in presenting a series of advertisements, which differ in magnitude or attention value, should get the best results by observing the anticlimax order. This point is, in fact, confirmed by the work of H. F. Adams who made an investigation as to the effect of climax, and anticlimax order, in advertising.[4]

D. Whether we are democrats or republicans, Protestants or Catholics, is frequently observed to be a consequence of paternal or ancestral affiliation. However, it is doubtful whether family ties or family considerations are nearly as important determinants as the fact that we *first* become familiar with the beliefs and the defenses of the beliefs of our family.

E. Our form of jury trial, just as our procedure in debates, assumes that both sides are given an equal opportunity. But the existence of such equality is based on logical considerations, and assumes that logical factors will control the decision of the judges or jurymen as the case might be. But our beliefs are rarely if ever fashioned through such dispassionate weighing of pros and cons. While the lawyer of the plaintiff is reviewing his case and making his appeal, the belief of the jurors is already in the process of formation, and they are not to be dissuaded from their position by an equal amount of evidence or persuasive appeal on the part of the defendant's lawyer, according to the law of primacy, which appears as an indubitable factor in persuasion.

---

[4] Adams, H. F., "The Effects of Climax and Anti-Climax Order," *J. of Applied Pyschol.*, Dec., 1920.

CHAPTER SEVENTEEN

Social Psychology (1925) & "The Concept of Imitation" (1926)

Knight Dunlap & Ellsworth Faris

Baltimore, MD: Williams & Wilkins, pp. 204–6 & American Journal of Sociology 3*2: pp. 367–78 [with elisions]*.

EDITOR'S INTRODUCTION

In the earliest writings, imitation and suggestion, as previously noted, were used almost interchangeably and frequently joined in the compound term *imitation-suggestion*. American social scientists quickly began efforts to untangle the concepts. Scholars such as Baldwin sometimes distinguished them by designating the suggestion as the stimulus and the imitation as the response. In this manner they remained paired as like phenomenon over the next several decades but, at the same time, developed their individual and unique psychological identities. So, suggestion became the term associated with general communicative influence, and imitation the replication of an observed behavior. As such, imitation, especially in children, would separate in research from studies on suggestibility and develop a life-history of its own, one that, by the 1960s, would lead to Albert Bandura's (1961) famous work on observational learning and the effects of media violence.

The intellectual history of imitation is beyond the scope of the present work, but the following two readings represent efforts through the 1920s to separate the concepts and more clearly articulate the characteristics of each, with special attention to imitation.

The first is by Knight Dunlap (1875–1949), an early leader in the field of experimental psychology. Educated at the University of California at Berkeley and Harvard, he taught for several years at Berkeley before joining the faculty at Johns Hopkins University in 1906. In addition to authoring multiple texts in the field, he founded the *Journal of Psychology*, was first editor of the *Journal of Comparative Psychology*, and served as president of the American Psychological Association in 1922.

In this short passage taken from his 1925 textbook on social psychology, Dunlap declares that suggestion and imitation deal "with the same process," yet he distinguishes them, as do others, by whether the stimulus that leads to an act is a spoken command (suggestion) or an observed action (imitation). In "normal life," he states, both contribute to "the springs of social action," but he associates imitation with the tendency to conform in social customs, manners, etc., stating that "the social effects of imitation are enormous."

While Dunlap's observations constitute a relatively small part of his much larger survey text, Ellsworth Faris's 1926 journal article deals exclusively with "The Concept of Imitation" and differs markedly from Dunlap by arguing for the impotency and even irrelevance of the idea.

Ellsworth Faris (1874–1953) obtained his PhD from the University of Chicago in 1913. He taught variously at schools in Texas and Iowa and returned to Chicago in 1919 to join the faculty, taking over as chair of the Department of Sociology and Anthropology in 1925. He served as editor of the *American Journal of Sociology* and president in 1937 of the American Sociological Society.

Heavily influenced by George Herbert Mead, he envisioned behavioral causality in a complex web of interpersonal and social relationships and disdained unidimensional and biological explanations of the kind proposed by McDougall. It was from this perspective that he critiqued the concept of imitation. In the following article, he positions imitation as a type of behavior with a multitude of possible, often unidentifiable, interacting sources, contrasting it with the simpler "functional treatment" of Ross and the French theorists, and concluding, by this view, that it cannot be considered "a justifiable psychological category."

He distinguishes imitation from suggestion, along the same lines as Dunlap, and identifies three types of imitative activity: immediate and un-planned (e.g., crowd behavior), long-term and unplanned (e.g., the acquisition of a dialect), and conscious and intentional (e.g., buying a new car like the neighbor's) and formulates each into a "law."

Ultimately, however, he concludes that imitation lacks a specific and clear causal mechanism, and is, therefore, "a result, but an irrelevant result." Contrary opinions, he declares, stem from "defective analysis." Neither social psychology nor sociology would agree with Faris in the end, but the article offers a reminder of the diverse views in scholarly discussion at the time.—*P.P.*

References

Bandura, Albert, Dorothea Ross, and Sheila Ross. 1961. "Transmission of Aggression through the Imitation of Aggressive Models." *Journal of Abnormal and Social Psychology* 63, no. 3: 575–82.

Social Psychology (1925)

Knight Dunlap

In *imitation*, the stimulus pattern afforded by the act of another person pro-duces, not the reaction of doing the act, but a perceptual reaction of some other type; and this first reaction, (the perception), produces an idea, (an ideational reaction), which includes the act. This ideational reaction may be produced immediately by the perception; or it may be produced mediately, by an intervening ideational reaction, or by a series of such. The distinguish-ing characteristic of the imitation reaction, in short, is the intervention of an *idea*, or a series of ideas, between the stimulus pattern of perception and the act which resembles that stimulus pattern.

The social effects of imitation are enormous, and are most conspicuous in the carrying out of the tendency to *conform*. Social customs, manners of speech, and details of dress are adopted from others mainly through deliberate imitation. No woman copies the type of costume of another woman except in so far as she has ideas that the costume represents a type which is to be worn by the group to whom she wishes to conform. Selective adoption of action is not impossible in the level of similitude reactions, but selection is vastly extended and facilitated by deliberation.

Ideas are simulated and imitated, along with other activities. Simply, or deliberatively, we adopt the religious, political, scientific, and other notions of others by repeating them. The expression of the idea by another person is the stimulus pattern; the thinking of the same idea is our imitative reaction. Although this is only one of the types of promulgation of ideas, and has been overemphasized in the theories of the past, it is important. All forms of the promulgation of ideas, including imitation, involve language, which is the most important of mental instruments, both socially and individually.

Neither similitude reaction nor imitation, therefore, is a means or method of learning, so far as specific acts are concerned. The reactor must have learned to perform the acts, or he cannot reproduce them. He cannot imitate the methods of speech of another person unless he has already learned to make the inflections and sounds involved, any more than he can imitate the starting of a motor car unless he has learned how to start it.

In another way, however, imitation may be an important method of learning; that is, in the synthesis of acts already learned as individual acts. One might learn to start an automobile by imitating the successive acts of a driver, provided one is already able to perform these successive acts. These acts being called forth in a certain order by successive imitation, may then become fixed in that order, in accordance with the laws of association, and the total reaction, comprising the series of previously learned acts, becomes learned.

In the simulation and imitation responses, the final act resembles the act of the other person which serves as the stimulus pattern; or else, the situation resulting from the act resembles the situation which constitutes the stimulus pattern. When one person's clapping his hands together causes another person to clap his hands, or when an American imitates a Britisher's drawl, we have illustrations of the first type. When the shop girl clothes herself, as nearly as skill and finances will allow, like my lady of the limousine, we have an illustration of the second type.

There is, however, another type of communication which is like imitation in that the ultimate act is the expression of an idea, not of a perception, but differs in that the idea does not result from a perception of an act or situation similar to the act or situation ultimately produced. This type of communication is properly called *suggestion,* and should be distinguished from imitation.[1]

---

[1] The confusion of the two types of action which has led to a fallacious explanation of all social behavior as "imitation" is due in part to the fact that we have the verb to *imitate* for the reproduction of a model; but we have no verb expressing the influence of the model

Suggestion is exhibited in a startling way in many of the phenomena of hypnosis; but it is no less present in normal life. On the other hand, neither hypnosis nor the social activities of normal life can be fully accounted for in terms of suggestion. If the hypnotist makes a bow to a properly prepared subject, the subject will bow in return; that is obviously imitation or else mere similitude reaction. If the hypnotist says "You will now greet politely Miss Blank, who is speaking to you," the subject again will bow. This is not imitation, but suggestion.

In both suggestion and imitation we are dealing with the same process, absent in similitude reaction, namely, "the tendency for an idea to express itself in action;" or more strictly, the tendency for the idea reactions to become strong and definite enough to produce outward effects of importance.

In normal life, suggestion and imitation contribute only part of the springs of social action. Many other factors contribute to the determination of the actions of man upon the stimulation furnished by other men, so that suggestion and imitation may be inhibited, accentuated, or reversed. Among these other factors, the influence of desires, and the process of associative recall of ideas are the most important. In hypnosis, both of these factors are reduced, so that the "suggestion" of a course of action fails to bring up associatively conflicting ideas, and the desires have less effect in impelling to or against the suggested acts. The effect of suggestion in normal life however, is very large.

"The Concept of Imitation" (1926)

Ellsworth Faris

The problem connected with those similarities of behavior called imitation has occupied the attention of most men who have written in the field of social psychology. Emphasized and slightly enlarged, the concept has given its name to whole schools of psychological and philosophical speculation. Formerly imitation was widely held to be a primary instinct, taking its place alongside the old standbys, pugnacity and fear. Recent writing on this subject has tended to introduce certain modifications. McDougall, for example, is unwilling to write it down as an instinct, but has worked out a

---

on the imitator; while, on the other hand, we have the verb to suggest for the influence which one man may have on another in this second way, but no convenient verb for the act of the person on whom the suggestion is made effective.

sort of imaginary switching arrangement by means of which the witnessing of the "expression" of an instinct may cause the same instinct to function in the beholder of the expression. Thus, while fear has its adequate and normal stimulus, the sight of a frightened person has a tendency on its own behalf to arouse the instinct of flight, which is the motor side of fear.

It is the purpose of this article to give an exposition of a point of view differing somewhat from those preceding. Imitation is a fact, or better, a name given to many types of fact. It is observed in many varieties of social experience, and must be dealt with in any thoroughgoing statement of human nature. But the thesis here presented is that imitation is not only a result of other causal or predisposing conditions, but that so-called imitation arises as a result from several widely different types of mechanism. Moreover, *the same causes or mechanisms or processes, which result in imitative behavior, can be shown to result also in behavior that is in no sense imitative.*

Imitation must clearly involve similarity in behavior to some copy or stimulus. To imitate is to behave like another, though all such likeness may not be imitation. There may be imitation of the movements of another, as when we copy another's dress, reproduce his movements, think thoughts like his, or have feelings and emotions which resemble those of another. Such, at least, is the usual and uncritical assumption.

The functional treatment of imitation, most fully presented in the writing of the French sociologists and engagingly stated by Professor Ross, assigns all these types of imitation to a single cause or mechanism. It is assumed that there is a tendency to imitate that is normal to human nature. Professor Ross goes further and assumes that suggestion is indissolubly linked up with the phenomenon. Man is a suggestible animal, and ideas, feelings, and movements are all thought of as suggestions, and produce in turn imitation. The behavior of crowds and mobs, the spread of fashions and conventions, the social heritage of customs, the conscious copying of new forms, and the unconscious imitation of gestures, dialects, and language elements, all these are assigned to the single and simple impulse of imitation, which comes to us through the avenue of suggestion.

Upon critical examination of the facts it seems necessary to make certain distinctions between different types of imitative behavior. There are at least three distinct and divergent sorts of reaction, which may be illustrated by three different types of phenomena.

I.

First, the behavior of crowds and mobs. A panic in a theater is picturesquely described as a sort of mental or emotional contagion. At first only a few are frightened, but their screams and frantic efforts to escape may be quickly taken over by others until the whole company is seized with uncontrollable fear. The anger of an excited mob is another instance of the same mechanism. Men find themselves in a mob by accident or join it from curiosity, but later describe their experience as being "carried away" by the emotion of anger. The voluminous literature on the behavior of crowds includes many descriptions of religious revivals, where those who come to scoff remain to pray, sucked into the vortex of religious emotion owing to the tendency to imitate the behavior of those who are observed. Into this class will also fall the panics and collective examples of enthusiasm which do not depend on the actual physical presence of the members of a group. Later in this discussion it will appear why this class should also include cases of hypnotism, in which one person responds to the suggestion of another when the inhibitions are removed by previously established *rapport*. These examples, which could be multiplied, are clearly cases of imitation, and the interpretation of them seems to be in general quite identical, but as will presently appear, the central explanation lies in the previously acquired habitual attitudes which receive a characteristic release.

Another quite distinct type of imitative behavior is the imitation of dialects and tricks of speech, which is a widespread if not universal phenomenon, and in the same category belong even more important imitative changes, which account for the acquisition of opinions, ideals, and social and political views, when one lives among other people, and is in communication with them. Evil communications corrupt good manners, and this is true imitation. Tarde's theory of criminality included this type of experience as well as the next or third category.

There remains a type of behavior differing from both the others. It is typified in fashion, and exhibited in all forms of conscious functional activity. Women who follow the new styles are hardly swept off their feet in an unconscious way, as the members of a mob are, nor do they gradually realize that they have bobbed their hair or shortened their skirts without knowing it. Much of our imitative life is of this character. It is a conscious copying. The model presented appeals to us first or last, and we go and do likewise. The interpretation of this type of behavior seems to be quite different from that of either of the other two.

If now we compare and contrast these three sorts of activity, it appears that the first type typified by panics and mob behavior is characterized by two adjectives, that is, it is *immediate* and *unwitting*. Sometimes it is spoken of as unconscious, but it is straining the word unconscious to say that an angry mob is not conscious. In typical mob behavior, however, it is not a deliberate purpose, but rather a partially realized activity which is most characteristic. Moreover, it is immediate or quick. Under excitement of a panic, there is not time to think and deliberate, and if one does think and deliberate, he finds himself acting differently from the others.

The second kind, typified by the acquisition of a dialect when it is not planned, differs fundamentally from the first. It is unintentional. It is often spoken of as unconscious, it is certainly unwitting. But unlike the first type, it is slow. It takes weeks or months sometimes, and certainly does not occur in the picturesque suddenness of the mob-activity type of imitation, though in cases of religious conversion, which are marginal to this, the climax may occur with a certain dramatic suddenness. In such cases we assume precedent processes.

The third type differs from both the others in that it is conscious, planned, intended, purposed. To buy a motor car because a neighbor has one, or to acquire a more expensive car like that of our social model, is to be under the influence of a distinct process, quite easily marked off from immediate, unwitting imitation, and also from the slow, unwitting type.

We have then the problem of interpretation which will reveal how these three distinct sorts of behavior come into existence. They appear not to be the result of the same motives or the same processes. Moreover, they are all complex, and ought to yield to an attempt to analyze them.

II.

When we examine carefully the first type it appears that mob activity involves a certain release of existing, that is of pre-existing, attitudes, habits, tendencies. The members of a theater party who are seized with fright are assumed to have already existing a fear of death and fire. Sudden alarm calls out, making kinetic and over-powering the tendency to save one's self from this danger. In the angry mob the situation does not differ. The fury of the members of the mob likewise rests upon already existing hostility, however latent or inactive this feeling may have been previously to the excitement. It is both picturesque and accurate to speak of the contagion of fury, but this contagion is the arousal of hostility and not the inculcation of it. The hostile attitudes are evoked, made active and kinetic. White men have been aroused to extremes of emotion quite surprising to themselves, when in a mob attacking Negroes, and in the Chicago riots the Negroes found themselves in a mob on more than one occasion, but it was a mob of Negroes. I can find no record of a Negro being swept into the contagion of a mob of white people attacking a member of his own race.

Consider the case of hypnotism. Under the abnormally suggestive condition of complete hypnotic control the subject responds immediately to what he is told to do. The subject will masticate a piece of paper and call it good, if he is told that it is candy or beef steak, but if a person without musical training be sent to the piano, when hypnotized, and told to play a sonata, he will not, for he can not. The abnormal condition makes it easy to release existing attitudes, but does not create new ones. A Trilby, when hypnotized, will sing and sing better than ever, for suggestion may intensify a potential activity.

We have then this formulation of the "law" of immediate, unwitting imitation exemplified in the crowd behavior: *Imitation in crowd behavior is limited to the release of attitudes or tendencies already existing and which are not new.*

The immediate responses to suggestion, which are most striking in hypnotized subjects, depend upon extreme dissociation, and are, therefore, the same type of behavior as crowd activity. Immediate response to a stimulus without inhibiting tendencies is almost a definition of suggestibility. The important point here is that the behavior of an excited member of a mob is precisely like the behavior of a hypnotized person. It is, therefore, not limited to crowd behavior, but crowd behavior is a special case in the whole general class of suggestion responses, and it is important to observe that the hypnotized person rarely imitates; he usually obeys. It looks like imitation when the stimulus and response are identical or similar, but if the operator says, "Jump," and the subject jumps, no one whose mind is really alert would call it imitation.

There is another type of behavior which requires mention. Cases of the sudden imitation of social models by little children are frequent in the literature, and, while by no means wholly authenticated, probably do occur. Whether they be entirely new, or the result of the process set forth in our second type, is at present an open question.

If the above "law" be true, there is no justification for the older formulation that the activity or feeling comes into the mind from without. If we inquire into the explanation of crowd behavior, it is apparent that we will need to know the past history or previous experience of the members of a mob, so that we may understand what attitudes are present that can be released. The one point here is that crowd behavior produces nothing new, but is limited to the intensification and activation of the habitual. There is a further point of the highest importance, namely, the failure of one emotional expression to produce its like in another, but this will be discussed later in the paper.

The first or mob type of imitation, being limited to previously existing habits, differs fundamentally from the second type, which consists essentially in new acquisitions. As stated above, this is typified by the widely observed and familiar phenomenon of acquiring a dialect, speech habits, tricks of manner, and gestures, as well as opinions, ideals, and beliefs. We have called this the slow, unwitting type. [...]

It is clear that we must seek for some other process than the evoking of an existing attitude, if we are to understand such behavior. The key seems to lie in the normal human tendency to converse with one's self, that is, to stimulate one's self, and to answer one's own stimulation, in which process one takes the role of the other, and new attitudes from the other enter the repertory of the person.

This analysis of the process of conversing with one's self has been most elaborately set forth by George H. Mead. Social experience consists in gestures and sentences directed to others, and in answering gestures and sentences addressed to us from others. We are stimulated and respond. Others are stimulated by us and respond to us, the social action consisting in the peculiarity that the response to a stimulus is also *ipso facto* a stimulus to a response.

Each gesture, therefore, is both answer and query, both stimulus and response. When, however, the person is alone this same type of activity tends to go on, following the pattern of associated behavior. The individual then comes to stimulate himself and to answer his own stimulation, and to proceed to respond to that answer, after which he goes on to answer that response. As far back as Plato is found the recognition of the fact that thinking is a conversation with one's self. [...]

Here we have an approach to the solution of the slow, unwitting imitation. To live over again the conversation or conflict is to say the words of the other in something resembling the same tone, and with the same attitude. It is literally to take the role of the other, to play the other's part, to assume the other's character. This would make it clear how the infidel might come to think like his clerical antagonist. It is utterly unlike mob activity, having little in it of the release of stored-up latent attitudes, but is the gradual taking over of new ones, which, indeed, may be organizations of old elements. It is the normal human tendency of playing the role of the other when we reflect on past social experiences and re-live the past.

A "law" of this slow, unwitting type of so-called imitation we may then attempt to formulate as follows: *When in rehearsing the past, emotional situations are re-enacted, taking the role of another sometimes gives rise to a new attitude, which is so like the attitude of the other person that it is often called imitation.*

It is evident that we still require further analysis and observation to reveal just how this process can operate. In extreme cases, such as pointing with the lips, and learning to shrug the shoulders, there is involved a form of attention to minimal stimulations which should be the object of research.

This process has been fully treated by Mead and others under the head of redintegration. The incomplete present act tends to be filled out when tension exists, and this filling out is an integrating anew, that is, a redintegration. It is often called imagination, and includes everything within that category and perhaps a great deal more.

The third type of imitation differs from both the others in that it is conscious, volitional, and planned. Many young people go to college because their friends go. Some go to the opera for the same reason. Others buy listerine. The explanatory principle here must involve an underlying purpose or ambition, which is furthered or achieved by the imitated activity. To go to college gives one a standing, a promise of success, or four years of pleasant loafing, and this ambition or desire takes its particular form because of the models that are presented. It is not the imitated act that is the center of interest, but rather the act is the instrumental activity which forwards or realizes the already existing purpose.

The attempt to write out a "law" for the third type of imitation would result in a statement somewhat as follows: *When a purpose or ambition appears to be achieved or furthered by acting like another, the result is the phenomenon known as conscious imitation.*

The three types of imitation then rest upon three different preconditions. To understand the first we must know what are the habitual attitudes that are ready to be suddenly released. To explain the second we must take account of the gestures and opinions or convictions of others, which by rehearsing we come to approximate, while to interpret the third, we must know the ambitions or unfulfilled desires which the mental and muscular activities are assumed to consummate. [...]

IV.

It is then the conclusion of this discussion that imitation is hardly a justifiable psychological category. We have seen that habitual attitudes produce crowd imitation, that talking to one's self produces another type, and conscious choice a third. On the other hand, the releasing of old attitudes, talking to one's self, and conscious choice, all three result in behavior that no one would call imitation. Imitation is then a mere accident of these three quite distinct types of mechanism. There is no instinct to imitate. There is no tendency to take over immediately a like thought or feeling, and all the uniformities which have received loosely the name of imitation are to be interpreted in quite the same way as the non uniformities growing out of the same processes.

Imitation then is a result, but an irrelevant result. It is an apparent, but not a real result in a causal sequence. It cannot be brought inside of any general statement or psychological law. The contrary opinion seems to result from that type of error which has given us so many wrong conclusions in the past, namely, defective analysis.

CHAPTER EIGHTEEN

An Introduction to Social Psychology (1922)

Charles A. Ellwood

New York: D. Appleton, pp. 155–57, 224–44 [with elisions].

EDITOR'S INTRODUCTION

As social psychology began to mature through the 1920s and 1930s, the foundational texts of McDougall and Ross were joined—as is often the case as a field expands—by new introductory and survey books, each providing their summary of the latest developments in the field. In nearly all cases, the authors discussed the question of social influence, attitude formation, and attitude change, and did so using the language and precepts of suggestion theory, sometimes nested in behaviorism, sometimes as a process of general psychological application. The following chapters offer three examples which illustrate not just the then state-of-the-art research on suggestion but speak to its standing as a widely accepted concept in the field.

The sociologist Charles Ellwood (1873–1946) graduated from Cornell University in 1896 but also studied at the University of Chicago under no less a cadre of stars than Albion Small, John Dewey, and George Herbert Mead. In Germany, he also took instruction from Georg Simmel. With his Chicago background, he became a leading exponent of the symbolic inter-actionist perspective and advocated the application of sociological theory in the solving of social problems. He taught at the University of Missouri-

Columbia and at Duke University and was president of the American Sociological Society in 1924. He wrote texts in several areas of sociology and social psychology, books so popular that he reportedly had sold a million copies by the end of his career.

Ellwood's 1922 *An Introduction to Social Psychology* gives special attention to the issue of public opinion, arguing that it is, by nature, the product of rational discussion among individuals. Following, without naming, Tarde, he states that public opinion arises in deliberative discussion; it is "the rational judgement of the group." The process must rely on a social system that protects free expression but, at the same time, can be channeled by those in leadership positions. He identifies the press as one important source of public opinion leadership, but worries that sensationalism, bias, and commercialism hamper its role as a positive social force.

Suggestion and imitation are treated later in the text. Despite his interactionist views, he appears to draw on instinct theory and habit to explain both processes, distinguishing between them and adding that both are normal and inherent in everyday life. He critiques the "suggestion-imitation theory of social life" as drawn by Tarde and Baldwin, in that they go too far in the assignment of social power to those processes. For Ellwood they are a component, not the central driver, of collective behavior. He dwells on imitation especially, using fashion trends as a practical example, and analyzes its role in "social order" and "social progress." A breakdown of types of and contexts for suggestion and imitation are implicit, but not detailed, in the text.—*P.P.*

An Introduction to Social Psychology (1922)

The Formation and Function of Public Opinion [1]

The highly dynamic societies of modem civilization control their social changes by what we call public opinion. To some extent, savage and barbarous societies did the same; only in these latter the opinion of the group was so bound by traditions and custom that public opinion, in the modem sense, could get no great development By public opinion, we mean a more or less rational collective judgment formed by the action and reaction of many individual judgments. Such a collective conscious opinion is obviously formed to mediate and control some change in the policies or institutions of the group. It implies, not so much that uniformity of opinion has been

---

[1] For collateral reading on public opinion, see Cooley: "Social Organization," Chap. XII.

reached by all members of the group, or even by a majority, as that a certain organization and coordination of the opinions and judgments of the individuals of the group has been reached. This is probably true even in those primitive groups which act only upon the principle of unanimity, and it is even more true in modem societies under the principle of majority rule. Of course, there is a certain core of agreement among the individuals of a group, or at least among a majority, but there is no absolute uniformity of judgment. As Professor Cooley says, public opinion is "an organization of separate individual judgments, a cooperative product of communication and reciprocal influence."[2] It does not represent, therefore, necessarily, as some social psychologists have claimed, the judgment of the lowest member of the group making the opinion, or even the mediocrity of its average individuals. It may well represent the matured judgment of leaders and specialists, after these have reacted with their public.

Whether control by public opinion will be control by the worst or the best minds in the group, however, will depend upon the circumstances of its formation, and the opportunities given for leadership to men of the highest intelligence. It will depend upon the appreciation which the group has of the judgment of the expert or of the superior mind, and that in turn will depend much upon the traditions of the group. It will also depend upon whether the conditions under which the opinion of the group is formed are such as to favor the wisest and most rational judgments circulating freely among the members of the group. Freedom of intercommunication and the encouragement of freedom of thought are necessary conditions for the formation of a public opinion of the highest degree of rationality. Without free speech, a free press and free discussion the highest development of public opinion is impossible, since it is formed by the action and reactions of many separate private judgments. Professor Giddings has rightly insisted that the highest type of public opinion depends for its development upon such conditions. He perhaps goes too far, however in saying that in those countries where free discussion and freedom of assemblage are interdicted, there can be no true public opinion.[3] In such countries, however, public opinion, while it develops, is usually of a very low order of rationality; and hence is either powerless to effect social changes, or, if it succeeds in effecting them, they are apt to be unwise. The proper functioning of public opinion in a social group demands, therefore, the fullest development of the mechanism of free

---

[2] "Social Organization." p. 121.

[3] "The Principles of Sociology," p. 138.

intercommunication. Such free functioning of public opinion is, on the whole, one of the best safeguards which societies have against social catastrophes, since it represents the free collective judgment of the group as a whole, and the most rational attempt it is capable of making to control collective action.

If the importance of a high development of public opinion in social life is such as we have just indicated, then it is equally important that the whole machinery of its formation be kept not only free, but also uncorrupted and alive, so to speak, to its social responsibility. Now, in the large, complex social groups of modern civilization, the formation and guidance of public opinion is becoming increasingly a function of the press. To the modern newspaper and magazine belongs especially the preponderant part in the guidance and formation of public opinion. If the press is commercial, if it is managed even to serve individual or class interests rather than to meet social needs, it will as surely fail to create the highest type of public opinion as if it were unfree. Means and methods yet remain to be devised by which the press can be kept free, and yet, at the same time, brought to realize in the highest degree its social responsibility as one of the most important parts of the machinery of our whole social life. Owing to sensationalism, to party and class bias, and to commercialism, it must be admitted that, even in the most advanced civilized societies of to-day, the press is still far from being the instrument of rational social readjustment which our social life demands.

The social function of public opinion, as we have already said, is to mediate in the transition from one type of social activity to another. It is a selective process, which has to do with the construction of new social habits and institutions. As our social life comes more and more under the sway of conscious and rational processes, custom, laws and institutions come more and more to rest upon public opinion. It is probably a mistake to trace the origin of these back to the public opinion of primitive groups, because, as we have already pointed out, customs and institutions very often have their origin in the lower stages of social evolution from instinctive reactions, or even in some cases from accidental adjustments on the part of primitive society. But in the later stages of social development, especially in free society, the rational judgment of the group, which we call public opinion, comes in to modify profoundly customs and institutions. In these stages public opinion is often the decisive element in establishing a law or institution; and in this sense the laws and institutions of democratic society may be said to rest upon public opinion.

In democratic societies, public opinion is, then, a force lying back of the power of all regulative institutions. It is to be regarded, perhaps, as the chief instrument of social control in highly dynamic societies, inasmuch as the other institutions of control, especially government, very largely rest upon it. Moreover, it seems to be playing an increasing part in controlling all social adjustments. If it can be developed to the highest degree of rationality as well as of power, the social life of the future may evidently expect much from it; for the most important problems before our civilization are capable of solution through the development of rational public opinion. [...]

Chapter X: Imitation and Suggestion in the Social Life

There remain three social mental processes of such great importance in the social life that they demand further and more specific consideration. These are, imitation, suggestion and sympathy. They are closely related processes, and are so intimately bound up with social life that whole social psychologies have been built upon the study of their action, without much regard to other elements in either the individual or the social mind. Following our usual method, we shall take up first the active, or motor, side of these processes, namely, imitation.

The Psychology of Imitation. The word "imitation" is often used for three very distinct kinds of psychic processes. First it is used as a name to cover the social method of developing the instincts. In such cases, imitation is a more or less unconscious copying of the instinctive behavior of one animal by another, usually of the same species. The perception of the instinctive activity excites a similar activity in the observing individual from a similar instinctive basis. We say, in such cases, that the instinctive response is excited sympathetically. This social method of developing the instincts is peculiar to the higher animals. In lower animal forms, instinctive reaction can be excited only through the appropriate stimuli in the environment; but in many of the higher animals, including man, the seeing of the activity going on in other individuals, usually of the same species, excites the impulse also. [...]

A second sort of imitation is seen in the tendency to conform, or to be like one's fellows. It is the passion to do as others do, and is usually more highly conscious than the type which we have just described, but is still largely without consciousness of the purpose of the imitative act. It also characterizes animals that live in groups and show a relatively high development of intelligence. It is certainly more than a mere neural tendency to do what we see others doing. Rather, it must probably be considered a specific manifestation, or differentiation, of the gregarious impulses. When we strive to conform our ways of action and even of thinking to those of our group, without specific reason for doing so, we are at once gregarious and imitative. The re-enforcement of the general neural tendency to imitate by the gregarious impulses would undoubtedly produce such a result. This copying of others for the sake of being at one with one's group is, in human society, then, mainly an instinctive matter, as is shown by the fact that very few people could give intelligent reasons for so doing.[4] It is also manifestly one of the most important features of the social life of mankind. It is, moreover, imitation in its purest form.

Still another sort of imitation is rational imitation, or the copying of the action of another, not merely for the sake of social conformity, nor yet because it satisfies some primitive impulse, but because it is in accord with some rational purpose to do so. Thus, the imitation we see in fashions is largely of the second sort, it expresses a mere instinctive desire to conform; on the other hand, when we adopt some improved tool to accomplish something, the imitation is of this third sort. Such rational imitation doubtless in part grows out of the preceding sorts of imitation, but it is quite different from them on account of its large rational and purposive element. It is no longer pure imitation, but a rational response which is imitative in form, just as the first sort of imitation was an instinctive response, merely imitative in its form. Rational imitation is, however, like the other two preceding sorts, closely connected with the social life of man. It has been a chief factor in his cultural evolution. [...]

The Connections of Imitation With Suggestion and Other Mental Processes. To be rightly understood, imitation must be correlated by the student with other mental processes. Imitation is but one of the types of interstimulation and response. It is an outcome of instinct and habit and is mediatory of both of those fundamental aspects of the mental and social life. Not only are instinctive reactions in man developed and modified by imitation, but the same statement is of course true of our acquired habits. Without imitation to mediate the expressions of instinct, habit and adaptation in human social groups, anything like harmonious social life would be impossible. For imitation in the broad sense in which we have just used the term, is nothing less than that type of mental interstimulation and response which results in uniformity of activity in the interacting individuals. It is closely connected, therefore, with other processes, which tend toward mental uniformity in a

---

[4]Compare the argument in Trotter: "Instincts of the Herd in Peace and War," pp. 18–32.

group. It is especially closely related to suggestion, which is a process tending toward *intellectual* uniformity in a group, and to sympathy, which in a broad sense is any process which tends toward *feeling* uniformity in a group. We might define these various terms very simply, indeed, respectively as socially induced activity, cognition and feeling. Imitation, suggestion and sympathy are therefore, all closely related processes. This does not mean that wherever we find one, we must necessarily find the others also; but it does mean that these three processes are continually associated in actual social life, and may perhaps be regarded as the motor, affective and cognitive aspects of one socio-psychic process which for the want of a better name, we may call "mental induction."[5] In discussing these factors in our social life, therefore, we should be careful not only to see that they are related, but to bring them together in our actual descriptions of social activity. This is usually done in the case of imitation and suggestion, imitation being regarded as the active side of the total suggestion-imitation process; but sympathy is not less the affective side of the same process. [...]

The Psychology of Suggestion. By suggestion, we mean the process of communicating an idea from one individual to another, which idea is accepted uncritically without rational ground for its acceptance. The state of mind which is necessary in order that a suggestion may work is called suggestibility. It is the tendency to believe without proof and to act without sufficient reason. It is a state in which an idea or image, particularly one that is associated with some original tendency of human nature, becomes more or less isolated in the mind from inhibiting or controlling processes and tends to work itself out automatically. Hypnotism is an extreme example of the working of suggestion and suggestibility. The normal individual in every day social life is, however, more or less suggestible. The critical faculties are rarely fully awake. Indeed, suggestibility is a normal and necessary accompaniment of gregarious, or group, life. The social animal must be ready at all times to respond to the ideas communicated to him by the fellow members of his group, and he usually does so more or less uncritically. We can scarcely agree with Boris Sidis that man is "social because he is suggestible"[6]; but we must admit that no high development of group life is possible without suggestibility. It represents the receptive, plastic side of consciousness with reference to the rest of the group. It is evidently the cognitive side of the same process which manifests itself actively as imitation.

---

[5] Compare the statements in Ellwood: "Sociology in Its Psychological Aspects," p. 293.

[6] "The Psychology of Suggestion," p. 310.

The psychology of suggestion is, therefore, essentially the same as that of imitation. Suggestibility manifests itself particularly in connection with all of the great subconscious tendencies of original or acquired human nature. It particularly manifests itself, therefore, in connection with the instinct-emotions and deeply established habits. It is a form of interstimulation between individuals which makes for the intellectual unity of the group. It thus tends toward uniformity in activity, and while, like imitation, it has its pathological manifestations, it must be regarded as a normal and necessary quality of the socialized individual. It is so uniformly present in all forms of imitation as the receptive, or cognitive, side of the process, that usually it will not be necessary for us to discuss it as a separate process.

The Suggestion-Imitation Theory of Society. Since Bagehot published his "Physics and Politics," in 1869, sociologists and social psychologists have put forth suggestion-imitation theories of the social life. Bagehot himself said: "The main force which molds and fashions men in society as we now see it is unconscious imitation. The more acknowledged causes, such as change of climate, alteration of political institutions, progress of science, act principally through this cause."[7]

In 1890, Gabriel Tarde, an eminent French sociologist, put forth, in his "Laws of Imitation," the theory that human social life must be interpreted fundamentally in terms of the suggestion-imitation process. Tarde believed that the influence of one mind upon another was entirely through the suggestion-imitation process. In as much as he accepted the psychological view of society, he proclaimed that imitation is "the elementary social phenomenon," "the fundamental social fact."[8] He even went so far as to say that imitation is the criterion of the social, and that "society is imitation."[9] Social unity, according to Tarde, is therefore wholly the result of the suggestion-imitation process. It is not due to organic heredity, but rather to "the effect of that suggestion-imitation process, which, starting from one primitive creature possessed of a single idea or act, passed this copy on to one of its neighbors, then to an other, and so on."[10] While Tarde left a place in his social psychology for conflict, or opposition, and invention, yet he found the essential elements of these in the suggestion-imitation process. He believed that the laws of imitation are to sociology "what the laws of habit

---

[7] "Physics and Politics," p. 97.

[8] "Social Laws," p. 56.

[9] "Laws of Imitation" (translation by Mrs. Parsons), p. 74.

[10] "Social Laws," pp. 38, 39.

and heredity are to biology, the laws of gravitation to astronomy, and the laws of vibration to physics."[11]

In 1895, Professor J. M. Baldwin, an eminent American psychologist, put forth independently a similar theory of the social life. Like Tarde, Baldwin found imitation to be fundamental in both the mental and social life, but he guarded himself against Tarde's extreme formulas and maintained only that imitation was the method of social organization and development. The individual develops intellectually and morally by imitating the mental attitudes and the actions of those about him, Baldwin said, while society changes through the imitation of the thought or activity of some individual who is accepted as a social leader.[12] In contrast to Tarde, Baldwin found that the content, or the matter, of the social life, in distinction from its method, is thoughts. Thus in Baldwin, the imitation theory is combined with an intellectualistic view of social life. His theory may be briefly summarized as follows: (1) the matter of social organization, or the content of the social life, is thoughts; (2) the method of their organization is imitation; (3) these thoughts originate with the individual; (4) certain of these thoughts are imitated and thus generalized by society.[13]

It is not necessary to criticize in detail this theory of society. As a theory it unduly simplifies the social life by overlooking, or slighting, the working of other factors than imitation and suggestion. There is no evidence to show, important as imitation and suggestion are in the social life, that they are more important than many other factors in the individual and in the environment. Habits are not wholly acquired by imitation, nor is it true that the learning process is fundamentally an imitative process.[14] Recent psychologists have tended to minimize the importance of imitation in the process of learning, or of acquiring new habits. The student also must not forget that psychology shows that the imitative tendency is constantly modified and controlled by a great number of other elements in human nature and in the environment. We cannot interpret society in terms of one of its very general aspects or processes, apart from all the rest of the processes of collective living. If we should do so, we would get a very abstract and one-sided view of the social life, one which is separated in particular from the great forces of organic and social evolution, which have made even imitation itself; for man is social,

---

[11] *Ibid.*, p. 61.

[12] "Social and Ethical Interpretations in Mental Development," Fourth Edition, Chaps. II, III, XII, XIII.

[13] *Ibid.*, pp. 504–524.

[14] Compare Thorndike: "Educational Psychology," Vol. ii, "The Psychology of Learning."

not because he is imitative, but because his whole nature has been evolved under conditions of group life. Hence he is imitative because he is social, rather than social because he is imitative.

Imitation is, then, not the foundation of the social life, but an instrument which the social life has developed to perfect its coordinations. It is, as we have already said, and as Baldwin has insisted, the chief means of propagating the *acquired* uniformities in human society. It is this because it is the type of interaction between individuals which results in uniformity of activity. It is, therefore, the great and indispensable means of bringing about unity in groups when uniform, concerted action above the purely instinctive level is necessary or desirable. Imitation makes for social uniformity, and so makes for social unity, except in those cases where unity rests upon difference rather than upon similarity of activity. [...]

Fashion in the Social Life. The work of imitation in the social life is perhaps best illustrated by fashion, for, as we have already said, fashion is imitation at its purest. Fashion is copying the members of one's group, not for the sake of utility, but for the sake of conformity. Fashion may be accompanied by utility, but its real motive is the advantage of conformity. It is perhaps best seen in clothing, but it affects all the methods, or "styles," of living and thinking. There are fashions, for example, in houses, in furniture, in behavior, in morality, in values and even in ideas. Because all of these things press upon the individual with the weight of mass-suggestion, it is very difficult to avoid conformity to them. And yet they may have very little inherent utility, value or truth in themselves.

It is a mistake to set fashion in opposition to tradition or custom. In small isolated communities the only fashions which obtain are usually the customs of generations. They are none the less fashions, however, because they are clearly imitations on the basis of social conformity. In larger communities, more or less in contact with the whole civilized world, fashion becomes chiefly an imitation of contemporaries, rather than of the past. In such communities, owing to emancipation from tradition and custom, to the accumulation of an economic surplus, and to competition in social self-exhibition, fashions change often with great rapidity. As soon as a fashion or style has become generalized in the mass of the group, those who maintain their social prestige by "conspicuous consumption" and other means of attracting attention to themselves, feel that they must change their style of dress, of behavior, or even of general living, in order that they may assert their superiority to the mass. Here evidently the instinct of self-assertion comes in to modify the tendency toward social conformity. The elite, to whom the masses have come to took for standards along some given line, change the fashion in order to assert their superiority, or perhaps to gain some economic advantage. The masses of the group, with their habitual tendencies to follow their leaders, imitate the elite. Again the elite change the style, and again modes of living in the group change. Under the conditions of modem civilization, while this results in great variety in the social life, it also results in much economic and vital waste, and not infrequently in social confusion. How to control fashion imitation along all lines by the reason has accordingly become one of the great problems of Western civilization. The mere fact that such a problem exists, however, shows the relative independence and the great power of the imitation process in human society.

It must be admitted that fashion imitation has good as well as bad sides. New ideas of great social value, superior social standards, and even superior modes of general living may be spread to a large extent by fashion imitation; that is, they may become accepted by the masses because they are imitated as fashions from social superiors, rather than because their utility, or value, is rationally perceived. As a matter of historic fact, superior religions, moral codes, artistic productions and even mechanical inventions, have often been thus diffused, largely through the power of fashion imitation. As a rule, such things have to become "fashions" before they can become embodied as a part of the social tradition. Fashion imitation here shades, of course, imperceptibly into the broader "conventionality imitation," that is, any imitation of contemporaries, of which fashion imitation is manifestly a part, and which we have already discussed as a factor in social change.

The Psychology of the Crowd. Another good illustration of the influence of suggestion-imitation in the social life is in the psychology of crowds, or mobs. In the socio-psychological sense, we have a crowd only when we have some unity in the activity of a large group of individuals gathered together in one place. This unity of activity usually comes through some stimulation, which excites the whole mass of individuals in the group. This stimulation at the same time serves to fix the attention of all the members of the group upon one object, or in a given direction. Under such conditions, a group of human beings usually becomes highly suggestible. The fixation of attention and the excitement which characterize the psychological crowd serve to inhibit the free working of those habits, ideas and standards, which normally guide the individual in ordinary social life. Moreover, the mere presence of a great number of individuals in close proximity increases nervous excitement, emotion, and so suggestibility. A group of individuals in such a condition are very manifestly apt to behave differently from what they would in ordinary social life. Acquired habits and the control of reflective thought drop away, and individuals are left with only their emotions and instincts to guide them. Moreover, one instinct-emotion excited under such circumstances exerts a strong inhibiting influence upon all of the rest. It is no wonder, therefore, that civilized men act like savages in crowds. The whole crowd becomes, as it were, a mere creature of impulse, liable to follow any extreme suggestion in the line of the emotion which has already been excited. Crowds become thus capable of performing the basest deeds, though at the same time they may often appear to act heroically. Social and moral conduct on a high scale, however, is impossible for the crowd, because its actions are simply the result of a suggestion-imitation process acting upon the level of instinct emotion. That civilized men are capable of such behavior is again a forceful illustration of the power of suggestion and imitation in human society under certain conditions. It is also a proof that the forms and conditions of association are of themselves powerful influences upon social conduct. [...]

Imitation as a Factor in Social Order. Both conventionality imitation and custom imitation are powerful factors in furthering social order. The imitation of one's contemporaries brings about a great deal of the unity and order which we find in human groups. This is especially true where the social intercourse of the members of the group is close and intimate. Social classes, professions, communities, groups of all sorts, under such circumstances, readily fall into similarities of activity and of habit, which they pick up from one another. This serves greatly to aid in keeping the life of the whole group harmonious at any given time.

But it is chiefly custom imitation which acts as a conservative factor favoring social order in human groups. The social importance of folkways, of custom, of usages and of traditions in preserving social continuity has already been pointed out, and the importance of these factors is, of course, the importance of imitation. The spiritual possessions of the race are thus handed down from one generation to another mainly through the imitative process. Children get the bulk of their habits, ideas and standards from association with their elders, and, as we have seen especially from their family circles. From a very early age the child absorbs imitatively the examples in the way of behavior and character furnished by his intimate group of associates. Language, moral standards, religion, esthetic tastes and political traditions are thus acquired by the child. In many cases these imitative absorptions from early environment remain the dominant elements in the mental and moral character of the individual throughout life. Thus are to be explained, without any doubt, in the main the peculiar local traits which we find in nearly all human groups. National peculiarities, for example, are very largely acquired by the participation of each individual in the customs and traditions of his country. The whole content of cultural development, indeed, because it is made up of acquired habits is passed along from generation to generation very largely by imitative methods. Even in the industrial and technological realm, where utility is supposed to reign supreme, custom, usage and tradition are found not less than in the other phases of social life, only more under the control of other factors.

Social order and organization, therefore, are very largely conserved through imitative processes. Nearly all forms of the social life are handed down from one generation to another through imitation. Only the simpler forms may be supposed to spring directly from human needs, or from mere habituation to physical environment. In all other cases, practically, imitation acts as a mediating process by which social and cultural forms are preserved. The harmony and order of human social groups are, therefore, very largely a product of conventionality and custom imitation.

Imitation as a Factor in Social Progress. Conventionality imitation is one of the main methods, as we have already seen, by which changes are brought about in human societies. This imitation may be of two sorts, either of its own leaders by a group, or of one group by another group. This latter sort of imitation, the imitation which results from the contact of groups, especially of dissimilar cultures, has been one of the most powerful influences in human history. Civilization has been spread very largely through the imitation of one group by another. No civilization, so far as we know, has been developed by a people without borrowings from other people. In the history of existing modern nations these borrowings have been so extensive that no nation can be said to have developed its own civilization. Even Western civilization, so-called, has borrowed extensively from the civilizations of the Orient; and we now know that every existing culture in the world has borrowed to a greater or less degree from every other culture.

An Introduction to Social Psychology (1926)

Luther Lee Bernard

New York: Henry Holt, pp. 282–321 [with elisions].

EDITOR'S INTRODUCTION

Luther Bernard (1881–1951) was a student of Ellwood (University of Missouri AB, 1907) and also a graduate student in the University of Chicago's famed sociology department (PhD, 1910). In his peripatetic career, he taught at more than a half-dozen colleges and universities from Cornell to the University of North Carolina to Penn State University. He was president of the American Sociological Society in 1932 and held numerous editorial board positions. His theoretical orientation was behavioristic, and he was said to be successful in helping move sociology away from biological determinism.

Four years after Ellwood's survey text, Bernard published a book with the identical title. It covered, as one might expect, the same ground, but with a stronger emphasis on the social implications of suggestion. In the following excerpt, Bernard sets suggestion inside Floyd Allport's behaviorism: "Suggestion exists when any relatively uncritical and immediate response occurs to a stimulus by means of behavior mechanisms which have already been prepared." Stimuli, further, are described in terms of conditioned symbols and stereotypes.

Capturing much of the extant thinking of the time, Bernard details the variously identified forms of suggestion, such as direct and indirect, and reviews the findings on the suggestibility of differing classes of people. In the end, he finds the suggestion process to be an irrational one and sees great danger in the public's potential susceptibility: "Suggestion operates in almost every sphere and aspect of life. It is a short cut method of controlling effectively conditioned behavior." Referencing specifically the power of the media, he warns, "Through the home, school, church, movie, theater, radio, and newspaper and press generally, we are told what to think or believe in almost all relationships in life." Concern about propaganda—political and commercial—was a growing theme following World War I, and as illustrated by Bernard, was intimately associated with the psychological power of suggestion.—*P.P.*

An Introduction to Social Psychology (1926)

CHAPTER XIX: SUGGESTION AND PERSONALITY DEVELOPMENT

DEFINITIONS—Suggestion exists when any relatively uncritical and immediate response occurs to a stimulus by means of behavior mechanisms which have already been prepared. A suggested response is conditioned ordinarily to a symbol or cue and not to the perception of a total situation, although the term suggestion is also sometimes used to indicate the skillful organization and presentation by another person of stimuli which will compel or induce logically or emotionally the response desired. Since it is a concept adopted for the description of phenomena of a social character, its use is ordinarily limited to behavior in social situations, and especially to behavior in response to symbolic or cue stimuli coming from another person. The cue itself may be either a concrete perceptual or an abstract stimulus. In any case the stimulus is in the nature of an object, act, or symbol which is ordinarily perceived concretely and immediately.

A suggested response may be either imitative or nonimitative, according as it does or does not reproduce the behavior which originally served as the stimulus and which the symbolic or foreshortened cue now represents. If the response has been conditioned to a total stimulus situation which it does not reproduce or resemble, or if it has been conditioned to a symbolic stimulus merely by association of stimuli it is not imitative. In such a case it is even possible for the response to resemble the behavior of another, some part of which behavior serves as the cue to the response, without its being an imitated response. Such resemblance between the behavior of the two persons is accidental, and is likely to be confused with true imitation.

Suggested and Rational Behavior Distinguished—The suggested response may occur consciously or unconsciously. As a matter of fact most suggested behavior, in the sense in which we are here considering it, is only partly conscious. The greater the degree of the interruption of the suggested behavior, the more conscious the response is, and the more critical or analytical we are of it. Hence the less immediate and more rational the response is, the less truly suggested is the behavior. Purely suggested behavior would be wholly unconscious, or at least unpremeditated and immediate. But there are all degrees of modification of the suggested response from that which is purely automatic and is conditioned to an abbreviated or symbolic cue to that which is in the nature of a rational response. The characteristic of suggested behavior is that it approaches the automatic, while rational behavior is ordinarily highly conscious and is controlled by abstract psychic mechanisms. In suggestion the stimulus situation is ordinarily reduced to a symbolic cue, while in rational behavior the stimulus situation may take on a succession of forms, sometimes even contradictory, and be highly differentiated and spread out over a considerable period of time. Also the suggested response, in its purest form, comes almost immediately after the stimulus is given. Delay in the response means either that thought is entering in to elaborate the response on a more or less critical or rational basis or that there is some hidden unconscious conflict which will not allow the impulses normally arising from the stimulus to go over into immediate action.

Suggestion occurs in the realm of ideas and attitudes or neuro-psychic behavior as well as in that of overt behavior, but the purest forms of suggestion go over immediately into overt responses. Psychic responses to suggestion are never rational in character, for by becoming rational they would cease to have the characteristic of suggested behavior, such as immediacy, automaticity, and unconsciousness. Suggested psychic responses are stereotyped responses, such as conventional beliefs, emotions, desires, opinions, and expressions of polite intercourse. The mechanism for the psychic response is already present, and all that is necessary to put the mechanism into effect is to present the appropriate cue or abbreviated stimulus. The essential characteristic of suggestion is that the stimulus, usually in the form of a cue or a symbol of the total stimulus, is conditioned definitely to the response, with the result that the conditioned response occurs immediately upon the occurrence of the stimulus or cue. [...]

Abbreviated or Symbolic Conditioning of the Response in Suggested Behavior—The response may or may not have some similarity to the stimulus. If it is similar to it, the chances are strong that the response was at one time consciously imitative, and that it has now been transformed into suggested behavior by becoming relatively automatic and perhaps by dispensing with the necessity for a perception or recognition of the total behavior stimulus. In such cases of substitution of suggestion imitation for conscious or rational imitation, some conspicuous portion of the total behavior stimulus will ordinarily be singled out to serve as a cue and will condition the response as a whole to itself. This specific portion of the original complete stimulus is now sufficient to produce the total response. Perhaps in the organism's attempt to economize attention no more than this particular selected portion of the stimulus is any longer perceived or recognized. Yet, in real life, such an isolated or selected portion of the original stimulus-giving behavior is not likely to operate alone, unless it be artificially isolated by the subject's attention. In most cases the original total behavior stimulus continues to function, and to the uncritical or unanalytical observer it appears to be necessary to set off the response. Therefore, even if the observer has made the delimitation of the stimulus which we have set forth above, he is likely to mistake such a response for a conscious act of imitation.

This is as true of psychic as of overt responses in suggestion imitation. For example, the mere sight of a certain book or picture or the oral or visual presentation of its title, may be sufficient to set up the habitual or stereotyped line of thinking which we have previously established through abstract imitation of it. It is not necessary actually to reread the book in order to recall the contents which have become conditioned to the title or to the image of the book through their constant association with these symbols. Much also that we do of a similar nature when in the presence of others, although it was originally consciously imitated behavior, is no longer such.

We have the mechanisms of response already fixed or stereotyped and it is merely necessary to receive the selected conditioning stimulus of the presence of the other person or of the perception of some article belonging to him or associated with him to put the behavior in operation. Thus the mere presence of people in a crowd looking toward the top of a building will cause us to look up, expecting to see a man climbing the wall or smoke issuing from the windows. A picture of people at a football game in the attitude of cheering or singing will call up in the inner or attitudinal behavior of the subject the words of a cheer or of a song, which may or may not be the one which these people are shouting or singing. Acting under the influence of the selected stimulus or cue he responds with the behavior pattern which is preconditioned in him. Such a response is still truly imitative, but it is suggestion imitation, and is not rational or even necessarily conscious imitation. However, non-imitative suggested behavior operates by the same partial or substitute mechanism.

Stereotyping the Symbols Conditioning Suggested Responses—Thus the stimulus which sets off a suggested response is nearly always a symbol which has come by substitution or by selective elimination to condition the original response. In the type of cases just described, where suggestion imitation behavior is substituted for conscious imitation behavior, selection of an outstanding portion of the original total behavior stimulus by means of elimination is the method ordinarily used. The effective stimulus is here a selected partial stimulus. But in many, perhaps in most, other cases the stimulus is a complete substitution, depending wholly upon similarity or association in time or spacial contiguity for its chance to condition the original response. In such cases there may be no recognizable similarity of the stimulus to the response which is conditioned to it. In fact the stimulus or cue may not even be a part of the behavior of another person. This substitute conditioning of the response occurs especially in connection with language symbols. Any word or phrase or gesture or facial or other expression may become associated with any response and thereafter call forth the response by suggestion, although it may have nothing to do with the situation in which the behavior was originally learned or imitated. Thus the word "eventually" has come to have the power of suggesting Gold Medal flour to millions of people. Likewise such conditioning symbols as commands, prohibitions, words or gestures denoting things, qualities, action, etc., must at some time in human history have come to be associated with behavior which they conditioned for the first time in this manner. Consequently in the life of each child they are made, as a part of his training, to condition his behavior through such arbitrary association. Words and gestures as language symbols are also associated with our ideas and attitudes in exactly the same manner and become capable of calling up any sentiment, belief, judgment or train of thought which has become stereotyped and has been conditioned to these stimuli. This is in fact the method of the origin of language and shows how meaning is conveyed through language from one generation or age to another. This fact will explain why certain stock phrases, shibboleths, proverbs, and the like are so effective in gaining the desired response through advertising, propaganda literature, newspapers, the oratorical efforts of revivalists, political spell-binders, and the like.

The Continuity of Meaning and Stereotyped Symbols—A very large portion of the symbols which serve as suggestion stimuli for the release of conditioned responses are of this long time stereotyped character. That is, they remain the same or almost the same from year to year and from generation to generation. Each child does not create them for himself, but acquires them or learns them from others. They are a part of his social heritage. This is true not only of words and phrases and sentences and systems of knowledge, such as sciences and philosophies, but it is also true of those symbolized personal and social values which condition our behavior with reference to men, groups, and things. It is as true of emotional as of intellectual symbols. The esthetic values in art are transmitted from one generation to another and from one individual or group to other units of the same character. Although we do not always fully realize it, pictures, statuary, music, ritual, poetry, have meanings which are dependent primarily upon this continuity in transmission, just as is the case with meaning which reposes in intellectual symbols. The meaning of art and of science is not a function of the symbols which represent or condition them to us, but it resides in the persons whose responses, overt and internal or attitudinal, are conditioned to the symbols. The symbols are merely the communicative media which carry the meaning from one person to another through the process of conditioning by association. Once the chain of conditioned responses is broken by omitting a generation of men thus conditioned to respond psychically and overtly to these symbols, their meaning is gone. Such has actually happened at times in history, where whole systems of symbols, like the languages and the writing and culture of the Hittites and the Philistines and the Minoans have been lost because the chain of conditioned responses which preserved the meaning of their writings was broken. As yet no one has been able to recondition his responses to these symbols in the same way in which these ancient peoples had conditioned theirs and thus to interpret their meaning. Consequently their cultures are to us sealed books and their symbols have lost completely their original power of suggestion. [...]

Direct and Indirect Suggestion differ primarily in the extent to which the ultimate stimulus is recognized as the source of our suggested behavior and the purpose of the manipulator of the suggestion is perceived. In direct suggestion the manipulator relies upon the strength of the conditioning of the response to the stimulus and does not hesitate to bring himself out clearly into the foreground and issue commands or statements which he expects the other person or persons to accept and act upon. This method of suggestion is most effective when used by people who have prestige with the subject. Thus parents, teachers, ministers and priests, officials, employers, and others with authority or who are our recognized superiors, can afford to employ direct suggestion and may secure effective results from its use. They save time and energy simply by giving directions or commands or making descriptive and positive statements. But even when used by persons in authority this method of suggestion must be employed with tact and consideration for others. If the directly suggested person gets the impression that he is being manipulated contrary to his advantage and for the selfish purposes of another person, or if he feels that the suggestions are given harshly and without sympathy, or that they are commandments merely and not "suggestions," or advice, as that term is sometimes understood by induction, they are likely to lose their moral effect, although they may continue to be obeyed as a matter of policy. Many a parent has lost his or her moral prestige with a child by employing direct suggestion too baldly and with too much show of authority. Employers and superintendents or foremen are more often hated because of the brutal directness and unsympathetic character of their suggestions or commands to laborers than for being hard taskmasters.

Superiority of Indirect Suggestion—Indirect suggestion is usually better in every way except for the lack of economy of time and energy involved in using it and sometimes in the lack of clearness of the instructions. Sometimes there is even a saving of time and energy in the long run as the result of the use of indirect suggestion. Ministers perhaps should always employ it and teachers usually, parents and employers at least frequently. The public lecturer and the newspaper and periodical almost invariably make use of indirect suggestion. Its method is merely that of selecting by chance or intention some type of stimulus which calls forth the desired response in the subject without revealing the motive, or perhaps even the source, or the identity of the suggester. Thus one may say to a child who objects to taking his medicine that the medicine looks like honey, or some other substance which appeals to the child. Perhaps even this method is too direct and is likely to lead to suspicion or detection of ulterior motives on the part of the suggester. It may be better to ask the child what he thinks it looks like before offering it or if he doesn't think it looks like honey. Or it may sometimes be advisable for some one else to sample the substance and declare it tastes very much like honey. The child's eating responses are sufficiently closely conditioned to the stimulus of honey that he will take the medicine unless he suspects the purpose or content of the indirect suggestion.

Methods and Examples of Indirect Suggestion—Indirect suggestions are best made by means of an incidental appeal to the appetites or interests and close associations of the subject. Indeed, no indirect suggestion can be very effective unless thus made. An indirect appeal to vanity is almost invariably successful. People will decide as if of their own initiative to do almost anything if the suggester has succeeded in conditioning the response to the stimulus of his approval of their personal appearance or conduct. The best way for lovers or married people to make up after quarrels is for the offender, or at least the one who must assume the rôle of the offender, to become enraptured with the attractiveness of the other or to speak appreciatively of her many virtues, skillfully conditioning the desired response to the imputed qualities, which will readily be accepted and approved by the subject. This method does not always work so well with marital parties as with lovers, because the element of suspicion of motives or the lack of novelty of the device may have entered into the equation. Tom Sawyer's method of getting his fence whitewashed is a classic example of the employment of the method of indirect suggestion. The political orator's flattery of the reputed wisdom of the people, which he has skillfully associated with the response of voting for his candidate, affords another excellent illustration. The successful insurance salesman or book agent is a master of indirect suggestion. He tells you of all the élite who are his patrons and of the large amount of insurance they carry through his company or of the fine bindings they have purchased.

Dangers of Indirect Suggestion—But indirect suggestion is not without its faults and dangers. It can be employed for socially bad as well as for socially good ends even more effectively than direct suggestion. Direct suggestion brings the moral issue more clearly into view and if a choice is permitted more opportunity is provided for a rational decision on the merits of the proposition. The act or belief desired by the suggester is called by its own name and it is not hidden behind a simile or a compliment. But in the case of indirect suggestion the chief art is to cover up or lessen the direct adjustment significance of the response and to condition it to a motive or an attitude which is really extrinsic to the situation. One is induced to take medicine because it tastes or looks like honey, not because it cures an ill. Another yields to a lover because he thinks she is beautiful. A third votes for a bad candidate because he has been told that he (the voter) is a patriotic American Citizen. A fourth purchases insurance of an agent because he is told that a railway president did likewise. There is always the danger that a decision may be a wrong one when made for extrinsic reasons. Certainly it is not good moral training to be coddled and teased into doing things only on the basis of a personal selfish appeal to vanity or to the sense of approbation of superiors or to personal pleasure. It is better for one's moral fiber and self-respect, especially for his social and ethical outlook, to face propositions on their own merits. Perhaps there has been too much indirect suggestion used to control the younger generation. It is possible that they have come to feel that they must be wheedled into meeting their obligations to themselves and society. It sometimes looks as if they felt they were doing others a favor in living up to the best social and personal ideals. It is a difficult question to decide in any particular case, whether to use direct or indirect suggestion. [...]

CHAPTER XX: THE CONDITIONS OF SUGGESTIBILITY

After what has been said in the previous chapter about the kinds of suggestion, the meaning of suggestibility will be sufficiently clear. One is suggestible in the degree to which (1) he has ready made stimulus-response mechanisms which are effectively conditioned to definite stimuli, (2) in the degree to which interrupting and inhibiting stimulus-response mechanisms or psychic behavior patterns are absent, and (3) the immediacy and unreflectiveness with which the response follows the stimulus. This is a general statement of the conditions of suggestibility or of the effectiveness of the conditioning of stimuli to suggested responses. These conditions may be stated in more detail under two general headings: the external and internal conditions of suggestibility. The external conditions will be discussed first. Conditions (1) and (3) have already been considered.

The *External Conditions of Suggestibility*—It is not enough to state the internal conditions favorable to the effectiveness of suggestion in the purely negative manner of freedom from the outside interference which tends to stimulate internal conflicts. There are also certain positive external conditions which increase suggestion. Duration and repetition of the stimulus are other important external conditions of suggestibility. [...]

Duration and repetition are made use of in all "educational" campaigns, such as political or religious propaganda, the advertising of commercial products, reform movements, and formal education or training itself.

Persistence wins the convert to any cause. "At first we endure, then we tolerate, and next we embrace," is another way of saying that we condition a favorable response through constant operation of some stimulus which formerly was ineffective.

Volume of stimuli is closely allied in method and results to duration and repetition. The latter attributes in fact, when taken consecutively, constitute volume. The propagandist and the advertiser and the proselytizer know well the uses of volume. What one hears or sees or tastes constantly, if it is at all tolerable, becomes essential to one's comfort. Thus men learn to use narcotics and intoxicants, develop habits of labor, or fall into the dissipations of vice. Volume of suggestion works negatively as well as positively. It cuts off former stimuli from operation and concentrates attention upon new ones which thereby are afforded a clear field for the conditioning of responses. There is no particular reason why we should eat K's cornflakes instead of A's, except that we see them advertised more persistently and with greater frequency. If we hear of nothing but the lost condition of our soul we will eventually save it according to the method prescribed by the particular religious propaganda which we have the good fortune to hear. We are Protestants or Catholics, Jews or Christians, Republicans or Democrats, not because each system of belief or interests is superior to all the rest—a contradiction in itself—but because the volume of suggestion in that direction has been overwhelming. We establish our conditioning of responses almost unconsciously (some people erroneously say, instinctively) and thereafter we respond readily to Protestant, Catholic, Jewish, Christian, Republican, or Democratic stimuli, according as we have been conditioned to respond. If the other side challenges us, we learn, that is, condition, arguments with which to confound them. Since they have done the same, and since the whole argument is a contest of suggestion instead of reason, neither side wins, unless one side is more suggestible, or there is greater vitality or volume or prestige on the one side than the other. Volume is perhaps not so exclusively limited to the conditioning of responses as are duration and repetition. The greater the volume the greater, within limits, is the opportunity for the suggesting or conditioning stimuli to be effective, that is, to cross the threshold of stimulation.

Prestige in the stimulating object, usually a personality, group of personalities, or a theory or a system of thought, or belief, conditions a strong readiness to respond to this object. This readiness is due to the fact that the responses of the subject are conditioned strongly through previous experience by certain attributes or powers possessed by the object. Thus prestige as an external factor means simply power to give suggestion and relates primarily to the power of the object to release a ready made response and secondarily to its power to condition such a response to itself as stimulus. Prestige is the prime external essential condition of suggestibility. If it exists, volume, duration and repetition are not necessary in order to make the suggestion effective. Prestige is effective conditioning plus a strong affective evaluation of the stimulus. [...]

The Internal Conditions of Suggestibility are both negative and positive. The positive condition is, as has already been stated, the existence of a strongly conditioned association between stimuli and response mechanisms. The negative internal condition is the absence of any conflicting or inhibiting psychic processes or competing stimulus-response mechanisms. This absence of inhibiting mechanisms may arise either from the fact that such competing tendencies or psychic behavior organizations have never been introduced into the psychic personality or from the fact that dissociation of conditioned overt response or inner behavior processes has been effected. These two negative conditions are very similar, except that the former is simpler and more negative than the latter. In such cases the mind or inner behavior organization has never been filled with inhibiting dispositions, with the result that there is little chance for inner conflicts or interruptions to occur. In the second case the development of conflicting conditioned responses may have occurred, but the conflict is prevented by isolating the inner behavior mechanisms either by means of concentrating the attention upon certain stimuli to the exclusion of others or by developing some internal control over psychic content which leads to dissociation of inner mechanisms, such as occurs typically in auto-suggestion. This inner control is probably effected by fixing the attention upon some external or, more frequently, psychic or mnemic symbol or cue which organizes the psychic and overt responses in the desired manner as preconditioned. Thus concentration of the attention upon external involuntary stimuli or voluntary fixation upon an external object, as in crystal gazing, or upon an internal symbol, as in automatic trance, is essential to that degree of dissociation of psychic processes which renders one readily suggestible in a unilateral direction.

Where one is suggestible to a large number of stimuli at the same time we say he is excited. He is as truly suggestible or suggested in this as in other cases of suggestion where the behavior is more direct and unified, but since we have associated the term suggestion with a fairly well integrated and isolated type of response which excludes other types we do not speak of response by general excitement as suggested behavior. Of course, excitement may also be due to conflicts in imitation or of some other form of stimulation. The more intense and concentrated or isolated the relatively automatic and uncritical conditioned responses are, the purer and more profound the type suggestion, according to conventional usage.

The Unfilled Mind as a Condition of Suggestibility—The unfilled mind operates as a favorable factor in suggestibility in a great many types of cases. But it can thus operate only if there are certain behavior mechanisms in the mind which are effectively conditioned to stimuli. This condition is likely always to exist, even in those of the lowest intelligence quotient or with the least training. Because all animals, human or otherwise, have certain natural drives or prepotent dispositions, such as the need for food, and the desire for sex satisfaction—to which they soon add other and acquired drives for at least shelter, protection from enemies, and possibly for association with their kind, as a minimum requirement for existence—certain habits of response grow up to supplement whatever instinctive behavior processes there may be for the effective realization of such drives. These responses, native and acquired, become conditioned to appropriate stimuli and render the subject suggestible to these stimuli which call for the satisfaction of his native and acquired interests by whatever means he has learned or inherited. What we really mean when we speak of a mind unfilled by inhibiting behavior mechanisms is that the higher and more socialized, esthetic and ethical, behavior patterns which we find in cultivated or civilized man have not yet been, or cannot be, added to our behavior complexes to serve as restraints upon the relatively irrational satisfaction of our wants and desires under the dominance of suggestion. Certain classes of animals and human beings are particularly suggestible because of this fact. [...]

Feeble-minded persons, like lower animals, are highly suggestible in line with their fundamental drives, but find it very difficult or impossible to condition their responses effectively to cultural or social stimuli of a high order, especially when a considerable degree of intelligence is involved. The higher grades of the feeble-minded can be successfully conditioned to stimuli to sympathetic response, acquiescence and loyalty and tenderness of a high degree of concentration in simple relationships, and are thus made highly suggestible to some of the finest simple emotional values in our culture. But, without constant reënforcement of the suggestion through the presence of the stimulus or even some supplementary stimulus, the cultural and more complex and abstract acquired conditionings give way before the more nearly instinctive and appetitive. [...]

The young, like the feeble-minded and lower animals, are highly suggestible in the direction of their relatively few preconditioned responses. But unlike the feeble-minded and animals, they can build up a rational psychic content or rival conditioned responses, which inhibit the more appetitive responses to suggestion. The conditioning of rival responses is in effect a process of rendering the subject responsive to new and more cultural or more highly socialized stimuli to broader range of stimuli which serve to condition responses away from the more appetitive stimuli and thus to sublimate and intellectualize and socialize behavior is, in the broadest sense, the process of education, whether it be in schools or elsewhere. [...]

The uneducated and those inexperienced in the problems of life adjustment are much like children both in their lack of the development of susceptibility to rival stimuli of a cultural character to condition or inhibit their prepotent or previously conditioned responses and in their capacity to develop a high degree of susceptibility under proper circumstances. The same is also true of backward races and peoples. In fact, there is a very close social analogy between the backward peoples of all races, whether they come from isolated districts in the midst of a highly cultivated civilization, as from mountainous regions, or from the slums of great cities, or from larger geographical units of isolation in the midst of a world civilization. [...]

Men and women of culture are also highly suggestible, by skilled manipulators, in those fields in which they lack experience or scientific data with which to check stimuli. Insurance agents, book agents, and other persistent salesmen, usually find women easier prey than men, and a pretty woman can sell some men almost anything in spite of their experience with agents. In the one case, the woman's responses are conditioned to the glowing words of idealism and day-dreamy promises, which her experience or knowledge is not able to contradict. Living a more or less repressed and inexperienced life, she consequently responds to the stimuli of hope or to the suggestion that all the other women of intelligence and fashion have purchased the article, instead of to the actual merits of the object which is before her. In the second case, the average man responds by previous conditioning to the artfully manipulated sex stimuli, while he thinks he is rationally considering the value of the books or other articles. Thus in reality women sell sex appeal while the men frequently buy this stimulus and pay for books they never open. It is not possible, however, under normal stimuli conditions, to suggest a social false step to a well-trained woman of fashion or the purchase of worthless oil stock or submerged real estate to a keen businessman. In their own fields men and women are "hard boiled," unless their responses are conditioned by analogy and unconsciously to stimuli that release other responses which are ordinarily censored and kept in the background. This is what happens in the case of the man buying books for which he has no use because the saleswoman appealed to his unconscious admiration for a pretty woman while his critical financial judgment was in temporary abeyance. On the whole, it may be said that women of good intelligence are more likely to be suggested contrary to reason where a matter of lack of experience is involved. Both men and women are likely to be suggested contrary to interest where the suggester can make a covert and unrecognized appeal by conditioning a substitute stimulus which operates strongly in the subconsciousness of the one being manipulated, but is carefully kept out of the argument. [...]

Somewhat more radical is the dissociation in the case of what we call prejudices. A prejudice arises from the strong conditioning of certain psychic behavior or attitudes to certain corresponding stimuli and the dissociation of inhibiting tendencies, with the result that the inhibiting processes are not adequate to break these conditionings. As a consequence the prejudiced person has a fixed idea or is radically suggestible in the direction of his belief or allegiance. Such prejudices are particularly liable to form in connection with religion, politics, sex matters, one's kin or property, art, or any other objects which call from us strong emotional responses. It is very difficult to be rational and objective, or unprejudiced about things which are close to us or for which we have made sacrifices or which we have molded to our own liking, that is, things to which our responses have become strongly conditioned. We are strongly suggestible in favor of our friends, family, party, creed, property, and the like, and just as strongly suggestible against our enemies and the friends, families, and property of our rivals. A "good" Republican or Democrat will believe almost anything he reads or hears in favor of his own party or in opposition to the rival parties. It is only recently that we have persuaded ourselves not to consign the adherents of rival religious creeds to the flames in the world to come or as surely to expect to meet all of those who profess our own faith, regardless of their morals, in the realms of bliss. Prejudices, from which no one is free, are the result of a mild form of dissociation. Nevertheless they cause a vast amount of distortion of functional adjustment in our world. [...]

The Ubiquitousness of Suggestion—Suggestion operates in almost every sphere and aspect of life. It is a short cut method of controlling effectively conditioned behavior. It is in itself quite devoid of moral character and may be used indifferently for ethical, non-ethical, or anti-ethical ends. It is frequently said that rationally directed conduct is of a higher type socially than suggested behavior. This is of course true, but it is not possible to be self or socially conscious about everything. Short cut controls in behavior are inevitable. The greater volume of suggestion occurs in the direction of everyday contacts, as was pointed out in the previous chapter, where it is ordinarily unmanipulated by some supervising agency. But there is also a vast amount of manipulated suggestion. This comes especially through the family, the school, the church, politics, the stage, the newspaper and periodical, and advertising. The newspaper, through its news articles, editorials, and advertisements, does much to control public opinion. Commercial advertisements to a large extent determine consumption, at least with reference to brands and styles, if not with regard to the contents and quality of the articles themselves.

Through the home, school, church, movie, theater, radio, and newspaper and press generally, we are told what to think or believe in almost all relationships in life. Sometimes this suggestion is direct and sometimes it is indirect, according to the degree of resistance which the person or public offers to the suggestion. The control of propaganda suggestion for proper social ends has become one of the serious problems of our day and must be attained by some method or other if society is not to be increasingly manipulated for selfish or partisan purposes. Controlled by suggestion we probably shall be, but this control should be for legitimate social purposes. It is not the function of this work on the principles of social psychology to go into details regarding either the methods of suggestion employed in concrete cases or types or the methods of controlling such propaganda. This belongs to the applications of social psychology, especially to the subjects of social organization, social control, and social ethics.

Principles of Sociology (1928)

Frederick Elmore Lumley

New York: McGraw-Hill, pp. 220–27 [with elisions].

EDITOR'S INTRODUCTION

Frederick Lumley (1880–1954) was among the first wave of scholars to study the social role of radio, publishing several journal articles on the nature of the radio audience and the use of the new medium in education. With a PhD from Yale (1912), he joined the faculty at The Ohio State University in 1920 and rose to chair of the Department of Sociology in 1932, retiring in 1945.

In addition to radio, Lumley had a strong and related interest in propaganda, expressed in his books *Means of Social Control* (1925) and *The Propaganda Menace* (1933). There he warned, "We have now come to recognize that wherever there is any sort of connection between individuals, there the propagandists flock to pour in their poison" (192). Propaganda is treated more fully in the next section of this anthology, but Lumley's work is a reminder here that throughout the 1920s and 1930s, writing on suggestion theory, in both the academic and popular press, was usually bound up to a greater or lesser extent in discussions of the media's capacity to create and alter the public consciousness.

In his 1928 survey text, excerpted below, Lumley reviews by then well-trod ground, laying out for the student the definitions, categories, and conditions of suggestion, as well as imitation, and citing many of the figures already sketched here: Baldwin, Bechterew, Judd, Ellwood, and Bernard.

He offers examples of suggestion-based manipulation along the way, stating that "an increasing amount comes from books and magazines and especially the newspapers and the movies. These tell us more and more what to think and what to do and how to feel." In many ways, his analysis is a glum one. He describes "the vast numbers" who for various reasons make up "the suggestible part of the population," adding, moreover, that "none of us is free; we always have some weak point or several weak points by which we may be taken captive." Lumley was not totally without hope, however. While not included in this excerpt, in other work he expresses the Progressive's faith in the prophylactic of education to provide adequate protection against "The Propaganda Menace."—*P.P.*

References

Lumley, Frederick. 1925. *Means of Social Control*. New York: Century.

Lumley, Frederick. 1933. *The Propaganda Menace*. New York: Century.

Principles of Sociology (1928)

CHAPTER XI: SUGGESTION-IMITATION

We are still considering major social processes, social interactions, characteristic "goings-on"; these are the plots of the social drama which interest us now. The next social process selected for treatment is a double affair, a social Siamese twins. We can hardly think of imitation without at the same time thinking of what is imitated—which leads directly to suggestion—and we can hardly think of suggestion without thinking of what comes out of it—which leads often to imitation. In this chapter, then, we have to deal with a more obviously circular form of interaction—the activities of people forming a continuous hail of suggestions, these being taken up by others who act imitatively and suggest to yet others, and so on without end. [...]

SUGGESTION

1. Definition

Suggestion has been defined in various ways. Bechterew describes it as "the direct infection of one person by another of certain mental states" or "the penetration or inoculation of a strange idea into the consciousness, without direct immediate participation by the 'ego' of the subject." This is passive suggestion. But there is also active suggestion wherein the subject necessarily takes part by attention, reflection, judgment, and will. These two phases of the process are obvious to all of us, for while we are actively attending in one direction, we are at the same time open to impressions from other directions, and thus active and passive at the same time; we may be intent upon the book we are reading—direct suggestion—but become vaguely aware that we have been called to do something about paying our overdue taxes—indirect suggestion. Our environment is continually furnishing us with hints, noted and unnoted, for our next or for future movements.[1]

"By suggestion" says Ellwood, "we mean the process of communicating an idea from one individual to another, when the idea is accepted more or less uncritically or without rational ground."[2] According to Allport, suggestion may be regarded from three points of view and thus defined in three ways. First it is a process of building up predispositions toward behavior in certain ways. We might think of these predispositions as being organized around the native drives or urges such as hunger, sex impulses, fear, and the like; and we can also think of them as being organized about and enlargements of certain acquired patterns, such as habits of action and belief—religious, political, aesthetic, and others. Looked at in this way, suggestion is the process of forming attitudes or prejudices; the emphasis here is upon what takes place within the subject; it is suggestibility.

In the second place, suggestion may be regarded as some external signal or stimulus which releases or sets off predispositions already built up. When we are already very fond of pie or detest it, attracted to foreigners or abominate them, emotionally aroused by the flag or untouched, deeply in love with some one or antipathetic;—these are predispositions which are easily touched off. This is what we mean when we say that a person is "quick on the trigger"; we mean that he is like gunpowder—ready to "go up in the air"

---

[1] Cf. Park and Burgess, op. cit., p. 410.
[2] "The Psychology of Human Society," p. 347.

or, like a turtle "sink into his shell" at the mere mention of a certain matter; we mean the cue that touches off our readiness to respond in certain ways.

In the third place, suggestion may be defined as that process by which these predispositions are augmented or intensified. Thus, if we are fond of pie, we may be made to be more fond of it by certain acts or words of others; or we may be made to detest it. If we dislike foreigners, we may be made to hate them by the suggestions of others. We find that advertisers and propagandists are all the while working to enlarge our predispositions in certain directions and dwarf them in others.

It will be evident that these three views are all important for a well-rounded view of the subject. It will also be apparent that the first and the third views are similar, the latter referring to an advanced stage of the process indicated by the former. It will also be obvious that the second view is the more common one. This view stresses the fundamental characteristics, namely, the strength of the predispositions, the immediacy and automaticity of the responses. [3]

2. Suggestibility

These points but confirm our own observation that, in certain ways and upon certain matters, we are all very impressionable; we are very suggestible; we are "quick on the trigger" when certain hints are given but are left cold by others; we "go up in the air" when some matters are mentioned but are quite indifferent to others; and we vary in suggestibility. Why is this? What are the reasons why some stimuli affect us always and others do not or why the same stimuli affect us differently at different times? In other words, we come now to inquire briefly into the nature and causes of suggestibility. We might consider first the internal conditions and second the external conditions.

1. Internal Conditions.—The first part of the answer to the question of our impressionability is found in our *predispositions*, native and acquired; it is found in the response mechanisms present at the moment. Illustrations are abundant and at hand. If we already fear Catholics, then we are very sensitive to hints from the Klan; fearing, we are already getting away from Catholics as quickly as possible, and hints from the Klan but help us in our flight; or, fearing them, we are ready to believe that they are planning to dominate the country, and cues from the Klan but nerve us to fight them the more viciously. Thus, the Klan works with a set-up which we already have, either to set it off or to strengthen it. If we need or believe we need a

---

[3] Cf. Bernard, "Introduction to Social Psychology," p. 284.

new suit of clothes or a new dress, then we are especially attentive to the announcements of the advertisers about bargain sales and the new fashions; our wants are a weakness into which these manipulators put their verbal and pictorial hooks; our needs are systemic conditions which are ready for inoculation. If we are Republicans, then we are especially susceptible to favorable remarks about Republicans and are ready to believe terrible things about Democrats. If we are laborers and members of unions, then we are impressionable to hints against capitalists. Thus, our suggestibility is partly a matter of our training, our moulding, up to date; it is partly a matter of our mental structure and how we have been in the habit of responding. Since we all have prejudices, we are all susceptible; since we are all brought up in groups with certain folkways and mores dominant, we all have prejudices.

Again, we are suggestible in proportion to the *absence of inhibiting* or competing set-ups. This is but the negative aspect of the situation described above which might be regarded as positive; it is equivalent to saying that while we are strongly conditioned in certain directions and upon certain matters, we are unprotected and weak at others. For instance, if we are drinkers, we are impressionable to stimuli from liquors, liquor bottles, the clink of glasses, the smell of a barroom, conversation about drinking, and the like—unless we have made a New Year's resolution or pledged ourselves to the temperance society to quit drinking; this acts as an inhibiting factor to these suggestions. If we are fond of football or the theater, then the preparations of others about us to go to the game or the show, their conversation, their enthusiasm are suggestions which we find it hard to resist unless we have determined to study or to do something else.

Says Bernard:

> The unfilled mind operates as a favorable factor in suggestibility in a great many types of cases. But it can thus operate only if there are certain behavior mechanisms in the mind which are effectively conditioned to stimuli. This condition is likely always to exist, even in those of the lowest intelligence quotient or with the least training. [4]

The animals below man are highly suggestible in the direction of their instinctive and simple acquired interests or needs. Feeble-minded persons, like the lower animals, are highly suggestible in the same way and thus find it impossible to meet the highly developed and complicated restraints of ordinary social life. The young, like the feeble-minded and the lower animals,

---

[4] "Introduction to Social Psychology," p. 305.

are highly suggestible in the direction of their relatively few preconditioned responses. They can build up, however, many conditioned responses whereas the feeble-minded and the animals cannot do so. The uneducated and the inexperienced are like children with respect to suggestibility. The same is true of the so-called backward races. Men and women of culture are also very impressionable to the suggestions of skilled manipulators in those fields in which they lack experience or other rational inhibitions; the most careful scientists are often sold "gold bricks" by high-powered salesmen.

Many *mental diseases*, such as hysteria, functional amnesia, absent-mindedness, dual personality, and the like are very favorable to suggestibility in some directions. During great emotional stress, one is usually more suggestible—at the time of a death in the family, for instance. Fatigue, fasting, and intoxication make us all more susceptible. These interfere with the nerve pulsations, cause the weaker, because acquired, reactions to cease functioning, and the individual is given over to the control of the older and stronger impulses. Thus, the tired person or the one who has fasted some time is usually more irritable and less reasonable than the one who has not poisoned the tissues in these ways. It is under such conditions as these that excellent and sensible people often do the most fiendish things.

We might also speak of the presence of *fixed ideas*, manias, and various fears as heightening suggestibility in line with these outgoings. There are all degrees of intensity here, from the mild peculiarities, foibles, hobbies, up to and including the wildest insanities. To sum up, we have, then, among us and everywhere vast numbers of biased people, empty minds, sick minds, children, absorbed folk, who constitute the suggestible part of the population; and, indeed, none of us is free; we always have some weak point or several weak points by which we may be taken captive.

2. External Conditions.—What takes us captive? The answer is, very naturally, the stimuli which impinge upon us from without. Suggestions reach us from many parts of our world; but we are interested in the suggestions which reach us from other people, from the members of our own species. Then, of course, wherever there are people in action, there are suggestions. This leads at once into the problem of imitation; but there are several points to be made before we take up that matter.

Monotony and rhythm in the stimuli reaching us are important factors in aiding these stimuli to do their work. If the teacher talks in a monotonous tone, we either become fixed upon it, as it were, or we utterly lose interest and go to sleep or do something else. The rhythm of the music and the dance take us in almost invariably—unless we are righteously opposed to dancing and dance music, which is inhibition. We seem to be very susceptible to stimuli in these forms in our work, in recreation, in worship, and elsewhere.

Very important, also, are the *duration and repetition* of the stimuli. The criminal who is stolid and unyielding finally breaks down and confesses when put through the "third degree," which is almost the severest ordeal any man has to go through. In the evangelistic meeting, the perpetual re-iteration of the same theme finally weakens the sin-ridden and gains the results sought; as the result of high pressure for a time, some begin to sur-render, then more, and, finally, droves respond. In a certain hymn, the idea "where He leads me I will follow" is repeated three times in the chorus, and the chorus is sung with each stanza, so the singers say this phrase a *dozen* times. Again:

— It's the old time religion,
It's the old time religion,
It's the old time religion,
And it's good enough for me.

This same thing is found in advertising, no one being able to go out any more without being assailed at every available point by glowing descriptions of numerous commodities.

A closely allied feature is the *volume* of stimuli. This is well illustrated again from advertising. Indeed, we might truly say that duration and repetition constitute volume. Volume of stimuli cuts off other pressures by outdoing them and thus leaves a clear field for the particular pressures applied. There is no particular reason why we should chew A's gum more than B's except that we see it advertised more frequently, more sumptuously. If we have been continually plied with the idea that our soul is lost, then we are apt to save it or have it saved according to the pattern prescribed by those who have been most persistent in helping us reach the fixed idea that it is lost.

That undefinable but real thing which we call *prestige* also has its weight. The factors composing it are numerous and various, but some of them are old age, special skill, high position, erudition, or superiority of some kind. The Bible has immense prestige with many because it is a very old book and is supposed to be inspired. When the makers of a certain cigarette recently plied us all with the idea that great singers and public speakers were tes-tifying that this particular brand of "coffin nails" did not hurt but actually improved their voices, they were using prestige. When some one clinches an argument with the assertion that some great author, banker, military leader, statesman, or scientist did this or said that, he is using prestige; and we find it very difficult to resist such an argument; we tend to respond promptly and automatically. We are "charmed," or "hypnotized," or "fascinated" by the big, the overpowering, the superior.[5]

3. The Ubiquitousness of Suggestion

According to Bernard:

> Suggestion operates in almost every sphere and aspect of life. It is a short cut method of controlling effectively conditioned behavior. It is in itself quite devoid of moral character and may be used indifferently for ethical, non-ethical, or anti-ethical ends. It is frequently said that rationally directed conduct is of a higher type socially than suggested behavior. This is of course true, but it is not possible to be self or socially conscious about everything. Short cut controls in behavior are inevitable.[6]

The greater volume of stimuli reaches us from our immediate surroundings—the home, the school, the playground, the local clubs, in short, the primary groups. But an increasing amount comes from books and magazines and especially the newspapers and the movies. These tell us more and more what to think and what to do and how to feel. These things "make up our minds" for us all along the line. We think we are acting of our own accord and in the light of our own judgment, when, as a matter of fact, this is almost impossible considering the amount of pressure, the strength of it, and the ubiquitousness of it.

Besides that inevitable pressure which we cannot escape simply because we live among people with these developed means of communication, there is a vast amount of special interest manipulation. Having nothing to meet but the pressures applied by the members of our families, our friends, and the like makes the problem of individual decision tremendously difficult; but when we have sharpshooters of skillfully directed stimuli all about us trying to impregnate us with their own special charges, and when we rarely can know who they are, where they are, or how they work, the problem is immeasurably complicated. The advertisers are bad enough, but the propagandists are worse. According to these, we must always be doing

---

[5] Cf. Bogardus, "Fundamentals of Social Psychology," p. 124.
[6] *Op. cit.*, p. 320.

something different from what we are doing. We do find some relief in the struggles which they have among themselves to outdo each other in getting our attention. But, in spite of this, the pressure they apply is terrific. We are everlastingly watched. The Evil Eye of primitive man was no more potent for direction than the pressures which modern experts use. But now we are ready to consider imitation.

IMITATION

1. Some Definitions

According to Judd, imitation is used to "designate any repetition of any act or thought which has been noted by an observer. Thus one imitates the facial expression of another or his mode of speech."[7] The conception is narrowed by Kirkpatrick:

> In general, we think of acts as imitative when they reproduce acts that have been observed by the performer. The psychological basis of imitation is the general tendency of the idea of an action to result in the action. In imitation the idea of the act comes more or less directly from the perception of the act as performed by another. It is imitative just in proportion as the idea and the impulse are derived from the perception of the act.

He points out that if a hungry child begins eating when he sees some one else eating, the act is not properly imitative, since the child knows how to eat and is hungry; it would eat at the sight of food. But when it tries to eat *like* someone else or eats when it is not hungry because it sees some one else eating—that is imitation.[8]

The term is broadened again by Baldwin who uses the notion to cover the kinds of actions already noted and, in addition, repetitions of actions of the imitator himself. Thus, one imitates oneself and sets up what is called *circular reaction*. Stout points out that we must carefully distinguish between the ability to imitate and the impulse to imitate. We might take again the case of the child eating. It knows how to get food to its mouth—that is its ability. But its impulse to eat may be set off by the sight of food or by somebody else trying to eat; this latter would be imitation if the child were not hungry. When the cough of one man sets another man coughing, it is evident that

---

[7] Park and Burgess, *op. cit.*, p. 390.
[8] "Fundamentals of Child Study," p. 129.

imitation here applies only to the impulse to cough; the second man does not learn how to cough from the first man; he is simply prompted to cough at this time by the coughing of the other man.[9]

Bernard says:

> Imitation is the doing what the other person does because perception of his behavior sets up in the imitator the same or similar responses to those which serve as stimuli. The imitated behavior may be either a total overt response or symbolic behavior. It is not possible to imitate or copy the behavior of another unless that behavior has been conditioned as a response organization in the imitator to the behavior of the one imitated, or of some one behaving as he does, as stimulus . . . Thus imitation is a social category within the field of the conditioned response.

2. Kinds of Imitation

Two types and four subtypes of imitation are distinguished by Bernard. These are suggestion imitation—automatic and accidental, and purposive—by trial and error and projection. We must understand what these things mean.

1. Suggestion Imitation.—*a.* There is first of all that sort of imitation which we might call *automatic*. We go to the tap and turn it, and the water runs out. Similarly, we act on people. We say to a person: "You are a liar." That speech is a turning of the tap or a pulling of the trigger—whichever simile seems the more appropriate. The point is that there is something ready to come forth—of itself, automatically—and we simply occasion the coming. We do not force it out; we simply make its coming possible.

Conditioned as we all are to react to certain stimuli, we are ready to be angry at such a speech, we are ready to lift our hats when we see others doing so, we are ready to run when we see others running, we are hungry when we see others eating, we are ready to get in step on the sidewalk when we are walking with others, we are ready to beat time with our foot, we are ready to yawn when we see others yawn. We do these things automatically, without taking thought, without our being aware what we are doing. And we have already pointed out that there are many copies about, many cues to follow, many hints to take, many stimuli plying us all the time.

---

[9] Park and Burgess, *op. cit.*, p. 390.

CHAPTER TWENTY-ONE

Social Psychology (1931)

Ernest Théodore Krueger & Walter C. Reckless

New York: Longmans, Green, pp. 117–31 [with elisions].

EDITOR'S INTRODUCTION

By the 1930s, the paradigmatic template of suggestion and imitation was well set, as evidenced in the 1931 survey text by Krueger and Reckless. Walter Reckless (1899–1988) was a University of Chicago PhD in sociology (1925) and a student of Robert Park and Ernest Burgess. He taught at Vanderbilt University and Ohio State and was particularly known for his work on criminology and juvenile delinquency. Ernest Théodore Krueger (1883–1945) was a classmate of Reckless's at Chicago (PhD, 1925) and for some years a colleague on the sociology faculty at Vanderbilt.

In the following excerpt, Krueger and Reckless appear to accept, unlike some in the field, the basics of French crowd theory, including the power of social contagion and characteristics of mob behavior. But they then extend the concepts to mass movements and social epidemics. In these passages they offer some frighteningly prescient observations relative to today's social media. They declare, "Not merely do fads, fashions, and fancies take on contagious proportions, but bugaboos, rumors, scares, dreads, unrest can like-wise spread and become epidemic."

Their treatment of crowds versus publics is more sophisticated than that of other scholars of the period. They note that there isn't just one all-pervading public but rather "many different kinds of publics." And here they delve, even more than Bernard, into the applications of theory to media practice. The public leadership previously provided by political and religious authorities now must compete, they write, "with the impersonal leadership of news, publicity, and propaganda." In fact, it is the particular media consumed by the heterogeneous groups that bind them together: "Whether a public in its organization is mixed or specialized depends on the material presented in the medium or journal which holds the group together. Hence it is that modern publics can be labeled sociologically by the papers or periodicals they read."

Broadly speaking, then, much of the work in social psychology, including the survey texts, treated suggestion first and foremost as a theoretical issue, with practical implications noted, sometimes anxiously, to provide illustrations of the psychological phenomenon. The following section turns that emphasis around and looks at work that was directed specifically at the social role of the media, using suggestion theory as an explanatory model.—*P.P.*

Social Psychology (1931)

CHAPTER V: SOCIAL BEHAVIOR ANALYZED

Social Behavior Defined.—While in the preceding chapters we have indicated the effect which interaction, contacts, and definitions have on human beings and the part which these factors play in molding human nature and personality, we have left still the problem of analyzing more definitely the ways in which a person's behavior is affected by the behavior of other human beings. An act performed under the direct or indirect influence of others or in the close or distant company of others has, to be sure, some claim to be called social since two or more persons are involved. But an act which is impelled, so to speak, by the behavior of company has another claim to be called social, because this act would not have emerged in the first place or would not have taken the form which it did take, had not company been present. Social behavior, therefore, is that activity determined by the activity of others.

For purposes of this chapter, we assume that the individual has all the necessary equipment, both native and acquired, to "take in" what others are doing and to respond to the activity of those about him. And furthermore, we shall not deal with the psychological individual (the organism) but the sociological individual, the person who is an organism plus all the accumulated effects of social experience. Consequently when we assume that the person has the necessary equipment to "take in" the behavior of company, we simply mean that he has a central nervous system, sensory apparatus, language, and ability to understand and interpret the activity of others. When we assume that the person has the equipment to respond to the behavior of surrounding persons, we have in mind that he can act reflexively, automatically, emotionally, temperamentally; that he can move and co-ordinate the limbs, hands, fingers, tongue, mouth, head, shoulders; that he can act habitually, tastefully, sentimentally, purposefully, and restrainedly. Moreover, the socially developed human animal (the person) usually has more than enough equipment to "take in" and "respond to" the demands of his social milieu.

The Characteristics of the Crowd.—The simplest and most elementary form of social behavior takes place in the crowd. The crowd consists, in the first place, of a collection of physically proximate individuals. The closer the physical distance, the greater the influence of organism on organism. The main effect of physical proximity is *barometric*. Individuals feel one another's presence. They feel the weight of collective pressure. The accompanying emotional disturbances are usually shortness of breath, discomfort, contraction, depression, until the crowd as a crowd gets into action, when the emotional reactions are registered in quickened heart beat, thrill, exhilaration, expansion.

The next characteristic of the crowd is focus of attention. A happening, an event, a crisis, a leader, may be the cause of individuals' being drawn within range of each other's influence. But whatever the circumstance, the minds of a collection of individuals must be oriented centripetally. Heads must be turned in the same direction; eyes and ears trained on a dominant object, in order for physically proximate persons to constitute a crowd. Focus of attention, after the attention is captured, brings about a control or a dominance at a center not necessarily an exact geometric center.

When attention is focused and dominance of the center established, rapport is set up. Rapport, as we shall use the term in connection with crowd behavior, means the state of mutual responsiveness or the condition where everybody is attune or responsive to everybody else, so that what happens at the center can be communicated to the circumference and what happens at the circumference or any other point within it can be diffused throughout as well as carried back to the center.

The Bases for Contagious Behavior.—In this condition, where everyone is held within range of influence of every one else inside the circumference, behavior becomes contagious. This simply means that the state of rapport facilitates the uninhibited release of responses, whatever they may be—spoken phrases, shouts, applause, laughter, waving of arms, stamping of feet. The usual inhibitions which ordinarily lend propriety, caution, deliberation to the behavior of persons break down. Reserve is cast to the winds; restraint disappears, and abandon ensues. The individual's defense is down; his self-control is relaxed. He, therefore, is not in a position to offer resistance to the suggestions of others—whether these suggestions be verbal or motor. Thus it is that members of a crowd, in which control at the center is established and rapport pervades to the circumference, can follow suit on any suggestion which merges out of the mass action and survives long enough to circulate throughout the entire mass.

The Crowd More than a Collectivity.—Without assigning the crowd any mystical properties, we should note that it is more than a mere collection of people. It is a collectivity plus the effects of interaction and mutual responsiveness. While it is composed of individuals, still all these individuals with their responses cannot be added together statistically and total a crowd. In other words, a crowd is not composed of a number of "like-minded" individuals who are acting in "like-minded" ways. Although all individuals who finally get swallowed up in crowd behavior bring to the situation a repertoire of responses, this repertoire is by no means the same in every case. Even the detectable differences in equipment are not so important for collective action.

Development of a Collective Representation.—The significant point is that individuals get something from the atmosphere of their own presence, something from the collective interplay—something they did not bring to the situation. For the want of better terms we shall say that this something is a collective representation—a derived impulse to act in a specific way, a point of orientation, some plan or some gesture satisfying to those concerned. And this is developed just as a slogan or a battle cry is developed—collectively. "Berlin or Bust," "Onward Christian Soldiers," "Down with the Bastille," "Fifty-four Forty or Fight," are examples of collective representations which crowds in the past have developed. No matter how restless, indignant, outraged, or mad people are before they are turned into a crowd, individuals of the mass did not possess the collective gesture before the crowd experience.

Circular Response and Collective Behavior.—Furthermore, by virtue of the interstimulation, the individual's responses are intensified as we have indicated before. This applies mainly to his motor and emotional reactions. The process by which the activities of a group of individuals gain momentum, become accelerated, are reënforced by the collective interplay, is known as *circular response*. If the milling and interaction in a crowd goes on long enough, without distraction or disturbance, the group will work itself up to a point of frenzy, which is attended by violent bodily movements and wild, ecstatic behavior. Thus crowd activity at the beginning is usually mild in comparison with what it becomes when the group gets under way or is warmed up. Hence it is that the old-fashioned camp meeting or revival starts lethargically and ends in riotous orgy. If the circular response of crowd action proceeds up to the point of frenzy and delirium, individuals will continue, hypnotized by their own rhythm and momentum, until they fall exhausted. When persons are in this state, it takes more than an intellectual or a verbal stimulus to bring them back to their separately conscious selves. They must be given a severe shock in order to be revived. The cowboys have learned that one way to break up the milling of animals is to shoot off a gun over their heads. This turns the animal crowd into a panic of individual animals going their separate ways. Most crowds, however, do not reach the limit to which the process of circular response could take them. At best the crowd is doomed to a temporary, fleeting existence. And this is why a particular crowd has no future as a group. The excitement instead of being reënforced may die down; individuals may be distracted and break the rapport. The crowd as a unit may meet its Waterloo, that is, an obstacle or counteractant from without, which disperses it. Mob demonstrations in continental cities are now being broken up by cold water from fire hoses. And finally, the crowd may achieve its goal, which has the effect of consummation. Then comes the realization that there is no more to be done and "it's time to go home."

The Mob an Acting Crowd.—We have used the term *crowd* in the discussion thus far in a technical sense, namely, as a collection of physically proximate individuals, bound together by a focus of attention and a condition of rapport. This type of crowd has carried the label of "psychological crowd" (a term originally coined by Le Bon), although in common sense, a crowd means anything from an assembly or collection of people to a mob. We have seen that a crowd is something more than a gathering of people, despite the fact that at a gathering individuals may be in close physical proximity. A mob has usually meant mass action, even in common usage. We may rightfully say, therefore, that a mob is an acting crowd. It is a crowd that finally does something, whether this something is the storming of the Bastille, the lynching of a criminal, the tearing down of a house. The final act, the climactic gesture, usually has legal and political consequences. Mobs have been associated with popular justice—mob rule—and mob action is curbed, so far as possible, in order to prevent violent demonstrations.

Orgiastic Crowds.—While we have crowds whose collective milling results in a final consummatory act of political consequence, there are crowds which are purely orgiastic—feeling and expressive crowds, so to speak. The bacchanalia is an example of an orgiastic crowd. Festal and ceremonial gatherings are prone to turn into orgiastic crowds, provided the occasion is not too formal. A revival service likewise is readily converted into an orgiastic crowd. It has been said that the religious sect is a chronic (orgiastic) crowd. By this is meant that many sects have developed a ritual by which their meetings become protracted.

The Sociological Significance of Crowds: Mass Movements.—The manifestations of collective behavior which we may observe at student mass meetings, at football games, and at conflagrations, should not minimize the sociological importance of the crowd in history. Periods of transition, in which political, economic, and religious changes are taking place, have had their dramatic mob and orgiastic episodes. Revolutions have had their mob scenes. The rise of new religious denominations, like Methodism for example, has been accompanied by throngs and demonstrations. The struggle of labor against capital furnishes us with many instances of mob action. The big strikes of the past thirty years almost inevitably have been colored by crowd behavior. The mass meetings at which the strike is called, the riots between strikers and police, the battles between the union men and scab laborers are cases in point. Reform movements, like suffrage and prohibition, have had their parades and demonstrations. Crowds gathered when war was declared and when the armistice was signed. The crowds of wartime tend to be mobs, which make political gestures. The crowds of armistice are orgiastic, with their "victory balls" and frenzied celebrations. And it may very well be, as some have contended, that crowd behavior functions as a safety-valve, as a device to release steam and pressure accumulated through periods of unrest.

How Suggestions Circulate.—The rapport established in a crowd means that behavior can become contagious. Hissing, applause, laughter, running, waving of hands, when once picked up, circulates rapidly from center to circumference. The assumption is that individuals bring to the situation equipment which enables them to join the circulating pattern and that, due to the effects of focus of attention and rapport, individuals offer no resistance to joining. Under such conditions an act or a gesture of one person is a suggestion to be acted on, none too consciously, by another person. And contagion simply means that a suggestion—not necessarily a verbal one at all—has been picked up and acted upon by several individuals. Contagion is the diffusion or spread of the suggestion. Now suggestions in a crowd do not light on unprepared soil. Under crowd stimulation persons are usually prepared to act; they are "all set" to act in some way. The suggestion, which is picked up and which circulates, therefore, is presented at the ripe moment, when individuals are prepared to act somehow but need a form to follow. When the hiss or the hooray reverberates throughout the throng, we have here something more than mere stimulus and response. For under ordinary conditions we might look askance upon an enthusiastic outburst of a companion and not follow his lead (suggestion) at all. But the interaction in a crowd experience prepares the body for action and makes the individual gullible. Consequently, the person is ready to follow suit, when the stimulus (suggestion) occurs.

Leadership in the Crowd.—The leader of the crowd is one who can deliver suggestions at a moment's notice. He is a "quick-trigger" man rather than a deliberate, phlegmatic person. He is more of an actor than a thinker. His leadership consists in being sensitive to the crowd and finally establishing himself at the center. It is possible for him to emerge out of the crowd itself and bring the circumference under his dominance. If such is the case, he becomes the focus of attention and substitutes himself for the crisis which brought the crowd together. He gains ascendancy by being able to deliver a suggestion at the very time the crowd needs a gesture to follow. And, what is more, he is able to produce a suggestion which is not only picked up but which trains all eyes, ears, and nerves on him. He remains leader as long as his suggestions are followed. His achieving and maintaining dominance depend not merely on his ability to act at the right moment, but also on his being sensitive to the mood of the throng. He is in the delicate position of having to offer a suggestion to the multitude, and make it palatable, when the multitude itself wants to do something and does not know what it wants to do. Suggestions thus rest on the lap of the gods. They may or may not be taken up and they may or may not fit into the mood of the crowd, since they are subject to the whim and caprice of the multitude. If, after gaining ascendancy, the leader presents the crowd with suggestions that are not taken up, he is dethroned, howled down, or forced to go off on a new tangent. However, those suggestions which fall flat, those which are not picked up or cause resistance, help to create a consensus of exactly what the individuals of the crowd want to do. While leaders may rise up out of the rank and file of the throng, it is also true that a person who has started in a position of dominance (like the orator) may convert his audience into a crowd. Orators are frequently capable of moving their audiences into action. They must be able to depict an impending crisis so as to bring the audience to the same point of rapport and inverted attention which would have been established by a natural crisis—the very point at which, if the throng is to act as a crowd, a leader must arise.

Social Epidemics.—Suggestions can traverse a much wider area than the small closed circle of the crowd. And they can be diffused from person to person, place to place, independent of the collective behavior within crowds. Contagious behavior, it should be remembered, is not limited to the crowd, although it finds in the crowd all the facilitating conditions. The circulation of fads and fashions, the waves of popular fancies are examples of the diffusion of suggestions which run beyond the narrow limits of a crowd and take on nation-wide proportions. Not merely do fads, fashions, and fancies take on contagious proportions, but bugaboos, rumors, scares, dreads, unrest can like-wise spread and become epidemic. Gold rushes, migrations, business panics, crusades, chauvinistic demonstrations, renaissance movements have assumed the character of epidemics—human landslides, so to speak.

Preparation for Following Suggestions.—Those individuals who join these mass movements are prepared ahead of time for the leap. That is, they are already restless, discontented, expectant, or yearning for something to happen. The behavior of others, whether through direct or indirect contact, presents a lead for the aroused person to follow. In many instances a definite concrete wish or an attitude is created by the suggestive activity of surrounding persons. In other instances, where the individual seems to leap into the current and to act immediately on a suggestion presented him, it is difficult to say whether a particular conscious motive is created first before overt action takes place, or whether the suggestion merely opens an outlet or channel for a pent-up charge in the body. Apparently in most social epidemics, some time (a few days or weeks) elapses before the idea or suggestion takes hold and then it takes hold because it has created in the individual a desire to go that way. [...]

Characteristics of Publics.—In contrast to the collective behavior which takes place in crowds and social epidemics, we have also the interplay of individuals within publics. While there is a considerable borderline between the crowd and the public, we might say that a public is a discussion group. A public does not require physical proximity in order to function characteristically, although the forum may bring individuals together in an audience. It is important to note that the press and the radio have enabled publics to exist over a wide area and have eliminated contiguity as a necessary condition for collective action in the public. Sociologically speaking, there is not one all-pervading public. Rather are there many different kinds of publics. They really represent groupings of persons who are held within range of one another's influence by sharing a common interest or issue and by having a medium through which to express and exchange ideas and opinions. We might say, therefore, that a public is a group sharing a given universe of discourse. The individuals within a public are not merely responsive to the events which claim their interest and attention, but they are sensitive to what others think. While wrangling and differences of opinion are expected to be present within a public, yet out of these social dialectics develops some sort of consensus. If consensus is impossible at any point, a public is then ready to split, as has happened over and over again in the field of religion and politics. New creeds or new doctrines usually have represented the consensus of the dissenters from an older public.

Leadership in the Public.—The leader of a public is a thinker rather than an actor. He leads by statement rather than by movement. His appeals are, for the most part, intellectual, rational, logical. His leadership consists in formulating ideas, programs, goals, policies which his constituents will accept. After he has once brought his followers under dominance, he may, by virtue of his reputation and prestige, be able to make his followers accept his ideas uncritically, even prelogically. This, of course, depends on the extent to which he has been able to bring about consensus. If the leader of a public has been able to inspire confidence, get his leadership recognized, to implant a firm foundation of belief and faith in certain principles, individuals who comprise the constituency will blindly follow, meek as lambs.

Impersonal Leadership of News.—New types of leadership have developed in modern times. The leader who gets to the people, shows them the way, interprets life for them through the medium of the pulpit, the forum, the editorial, even through personal touch (e.g., the ward boss) must now compete with the impersonal leadership of news, publicity, and propaganda. News places control in the hands of reporters and city editors, although it is a record or a recitation of events so written that the common man will understand. Instead of reacting to a leader's judgment as to what happened, individuals are now able to formulate their own opinions and make their own comments on the events of everyday life which attract notice. The newspaper has thus made the reader a witness to the significant events of a world-wide area, and enables him to know what is going on in the same sense that the villager sees about every happening in the small town. The responses made to news are determined largely by the direction of one's interests and the set of one's attitudes (such as intolerance, open-mindedness, shock, prudery, detachment, etc.). As a rule, the reading public is not satiated, and can be depended upon to react to news. The reaction may be in the nature of a changed notion (i.e., the acquisition of a new definition of conduct); it may take the form of mere comment (i.e., expression of opinion without registering any change in attitude); it may become translated into mass action, which represents an awakened or an aroused public's gesture. The "sob story" has created a sympathetic attitude towards the delinquent, who was formerly a scapegoat, while the exposures of crime and graft have led directly to definite crusades against the underworld and corrupt politics.

Publicity and Propaganda.—Publicity works on the principle that people must become familiar or acquainted with an object before they will react favorably towards it. Publicity agents assume that unfamiliar things, persons, or situations tend to breed caution, suspicion, fear, although they may arouse curiosity just because they are unfamiliar. It may be said that publicity defines objects for the public, calls attention to new values and in so doing creates attitudes and, in some instances (as in the case of commercial advertisements), even concrete desires. And, furthermore, it should be noted that publicity starts talk, provokes discussion which will win more adherents and strengthen the (favorable) consensus of opinion. Propaganda seeks to convert individuals to a cause—win them over to a side. It uses intellectual and sentimental materials for its appeals. Facts, figures, and logic are used as well as art, dramatics, and graphics. The former appeal to one's rational mind; the latter, to attitudes and sentiments. War posters depicting the enemy's violation of womanhood and childhood defined the situation in such a way as to produce righteous indignation. Propaganda, therefore, usually taps some previously existing sentiment or attitude which has been lying dormant. If the wets give out figures on the cost of prohibition enforcement, the increased taxes, the loss of revenue following the abolition of the liquor traffic, they are exploiting a stereotyped distaste for high taxes and expensive government. It appears that any given public may be mixed, that is, be interested in many different issues—politics, religion, science, and sport. Or a public may be very specialized—such as a musical public, the horse-racing public, etc. Whether a public in its organization is mixed or specialized depends on the material presented in the medium or journal which holds the group together. Hence it is that modern publics can be labeled sociologically by the papers or periodicals they read. The newspaper undoubtedly creates the most heterogeneous public, since it runs the widest assortment of material and makes the most varied appeals.

Social Control and the Public.—No matter how heterogeneous or homogeneous, scattered or local a public is, it usually acts as a censoring group. Divergent human behavior has always been the object of scrutiny, and if it entails violation of convention or moral code, it creates a sort of crisis. The public through expression of opinion deals out criticism or punishment. The reason a public can exert pressure on the individual's conduct is just that it holds the person's position or status in its hands. Public disapproval, scorn, rebuke, means loss of status and a fall in the estimation of the group. The censoring public is called into being when a violation or infraction is discovered. The board of censors then has something to talk about, to discuss, to take action on. Villages, neighborhoods, large communities, even nations are converted into a public when a startling or shocking personal episode comes to light. The effect of public censorship is usually suppression; the violation is given judgment and the would-be violators are reminded of what will happen to them if they are caught. However, public suppression does not act as a complete deterrent; since there are certain individuals who will run the risk of being exposed or who are indifferent to the consequences of disapproval and since infraction has now become a popular way to attract notice to oneself. It has been said that one of Chicago's beer-running gangsters gets more attention in the press than the President of the United States, and that gangsters realize this.

"The Influence of Newspaper Presentations Upon the Growth of Crime and Other Anti-Social Activity" (1910 & 1911)

Frances Fenton

American Journal of Sociology 16, no. 3: pp. 342–71 [with elisions]; and American Journal of Sociology 16, no. 4: pp. 538–64 [with elisions].

EDITOR'S INTRODUCTION

This section considers writing focused on the influence of media in social and political life and conducted within the suggestion paradigm in the first decades of the twentieth century. In 1921, Park and Burgess had observed, "At the present time there are many promising developments in the study of suggestion in special fields, such as advertising, leadership, politics, religion" (424). Such work, indeed, was well underway by then.

One of the first and most ambitious efforts involved a study of the impact of newspaper reading on crime and antisocial behavior. It appeared in sociology's leading journal, the *American Journal of Sociology*, which devoted the better part of two issues to the report. It was the published doctoral dissertation of Frances Fenton (1880–unknown). Fenton was one of the rare women in the field at the time. She earned her doctorate in the University of Chicago's sociology department in 1911. That same year, she married a fellow graduate student, Luther Bernard (whose work appears earlier in this anthology). While they divorced in 1922, she retained her married name and, as Frances Fenton Bernard, later joined the faculties at Wellesley College, Mount Holyoke College, and in 1924 was named dean of Smith College, where she served until 1928.

Her study was impressive for its time in its use of empirical data, as Fenton employed both a methodical content analysis along with data from courts records and a survey sent to two hundred members of the justice system. The conclusion drawn—that newspaper reading could trigger antisocial behavior—lacked the analytical rigor required by today's social science, but seen through the lens of suggestion theory, which was the lens used by Fenton, a causal relationship appeared to be a reasonable conclusion. "On the basis of the psychology of suggestion," she wrote, "a direct causal connection may be established between the newspaper and crime and other anti-social activities" (370).

The following excerpt includes Fenton's detailed discussion of the suggestion doctrine, with a thorough review of the extant literature on the topic (again demonstrating its ubiquity in the field). She describes the relevant forms of suggestion's impact—"conscious" and "unconscious"—and offers the qualifying note that the degree of influence can vary from person to person: "Whether a person exposed to (external stimuli) gets a suggestion or not depends, in general, on the kind of person he is" (368).

While the study is narrowly directed at "the suggestive power of the newspaper," Fenton adds, in conclusion, that similar pernicious effects could be expected from moving picture shows, the theater and even literature. She also offers recommendations for newspaper reform that include laws "to restrain newspapers from, or to punish them for, detailing certain types of anti-social facts."—*P.P.*

References

Park, Robert, and Edward Burgess, eds. 1921. *Introduction to the Science of Sociology.* Chicago: University of Chicago Press.

"The Influence of Newspaper Presentations Upon the Growth of Crime and Other Anti-Social Activity" (1910 & 1911)

CHAPTER I: INTRODUCTION

(1) STATEMENT OF PROBLEM; (2) EXPLANATION OF STANDPOINT; (3) PRELIMINARY DEFINITIONS

1. The present study is an attempt to investigate the question, How and to what extent do newspaper presentations of crime and other anti-social activities influence the growth of crime and other types of anti-social activity? That is, do people get the idea of, or the impulse to, committing criminal and other anti-social acts from the reading of such acts or similar acts in the newspapers? It is not necessary at this point to define criminal acts any further than to say that, although they vary somewhat in different states and at different times, penal codes adequately define them as "an act or omission to act forbidden by law and punishable upon conviction." The expression, "other anti-social acts" refers to activities not technically criminal, but perhaps immoral in character, and detrimental to group life, which have not yet, and may never, become incorporated in penal codes. [...]

The causal relationship implied in the question proposed above, "Do people get the idea of, or the impulse to, committing criminal and other anti-social acts from the reading of such acts or similar acts in the newspapers?" is intended to include in general all the influences of newspapers upon anti-social activity, both conscious and unconscious on the part of the person so influenced, and more specifically those influences coming from the general-news section, to a consideration of which this study is mainly limited. That is, it includes (1) cases of so-called pure suggestion in which the person affected is unaware, in part or wholly, of the part the newspaper account has had in influencing his activity; (2) cases in which the person consciously models his act upon a similar act related or described in the newspaper; and (3) cases in which newspaper accounts have had an influence in the gradual building up of standards, ideals, images, which are partial, even if only remote, causes of anti-social activity.

The aspect of the newspaper question here dealt with has been distinctly limited to the problem as above stated, and to the attempt to get actual evidence for or against the assumption made so generally today, that the newspaper has an influence, through suggestion, upon the growth of crime and other anti-social activity. Many other phases of newspaper influence as a social factor of immense importance need scientific investigation. But in this particular study no attempt is made to deal with them, nor is any attempt here made to discover what is the chief difficulty with the newspaper, nor the causes of the difficulty or difficulties. [...]

The suggestive power of the newspaper through its accounts of anti-social activities, through its comic supplements, through its possible influence on children, on the weak and unstable, on women, etc., has been emphasized by a number of writers.[1] The psychology of suggestion has been mentioned in this connection and explained in a popular way.[2] Also on this assumption, various practical steps have been taken to protect certain classes of people mentioned above from the effects of newspaper suggestion to anti-social activity. An example of this is to be found in the following statement from a letter written by Mr. F. G. Pettigrove, President Massachusetts Prison Commission, that "no daily papers are given to prisoners in the state prison or reformatories" of Massachusetts, and also "it is the general policy of penal institutions in America not to admit a daily newspaper." [...]

The present problem is a phase of the general problem of the control of stimuli to activity for the purpose of diminishing crime. It is scarcely necessary to point out the importance of this problem. However, a few general statements will indicate *how* important it is, as well as emphasize its connection with the present study.

We know very little as yet about the way in which habits grow up in the individual. Orthodox psychology, while it has given us many conclusions which are of value for social practice, has centered its attention almost exclusively on conscious processes in the individual and, with the exception of the studies of certain French and American writers[3] who have definitely treated suggestion and hypnotism, but who in only a few cases may be classed as orthodox psychologists, has dealt very slightly with the unconscious and only slightly conscious activities which form so large a part of our conduct.[4] Any valid control of conduct, individual, or social must be

---

[1] "Crime against American Children-Comic Supplement of Sunday Paper," *Ladies Home Journal*, January, 1909, XXVI, 5; "Are Newspapers Weakening Our National Fibre?" *Current Literature*, XLI, 517; "Newspaper Responsibility for Lawlessness," *Nation*, LXXVII, 151; "Newspapers' Sensations and Suggestions," *Independent*, LXVII, 449–51.

[2] S. W. Pennypacker, "Sensational Journalism and the Remedy," *North American Review*, CXC, 590.

[3] Notably Binet, Janet, Ribot, LeBon and Sidis, Ross, James, Morton Prince.

[4] Cf. William McDougall, *Introduction to Social Psychology* (Methuen & Co., 1908), 3,

based on a knowledge of this unconscious source of our stimuli to activity, as well as on a knowledge of conscious processes.

Little as we know in detail of the way in which habits are unconsciously acquired or grow up in the individual (because we know so little of what the individual starts out in life with), we do know the general fact that habits are unconsciously as well as consciously acquired, and that a part, at any rate, of the material out of which they grow are the social stimuli with which individuals come in contact—other people's activities, the drama, literature, art, newspapers, etc. We have enough evidence, certainly, to be sure that social control, the control of conduct, is in large part the control of unperceived stimuli to conduct, especially early in the lives of individuals. We are just beginning to evaluate our education, our drama, our novels, and our other forms of art and social stimuli on an objectively social basis and thus on a functional basis. The really preventive and constructive work of the juvenile court and of juvenile protective associations, as well as that of other ameliorative and preventive organizations, such as the New York Society for the Suppression of Vice, is really based on this principle, that of pushing preventive measures as far back in the environment as possible, and thus of controlling the conscious and unconscious formation of habits.

In this process of evaluation, the newspaper as a social factor of immense importance, must be included. For the reason, then, that the newspaper is far-reaching in its influence,[5] and that it repeats and includes stimuli from other sources as well, from the drama, the novel, etc., and because of the general conviction that newspapers do incite to anti-social activity, this study has been undertaken.

2. The general standpoint from which the investigation is made is that of a study of both conscious and unconscious suggestion and the effect of such suggestion from a constructively social point of view.[6] It is necessary

---

15; also *Physiological Psychology* (J. M. Dent & Co., 1905), 1, 2. For statements as to the province of psychology bearing out the above assertion, see James, *Psychology* (Henry Holt, 1889), 1; Wundt, *Outlines of Psych.* (tr. Judd 2d revis. Eng. ed.; Wilhelm Engleman, 1902), 3, 23; Titchener, *Outlines of Psych.* (Macmillan, 1905, 3d revis. ed.), 6; Stout, *Manual of Psych.* (Hinds & Noble, 1889), 4, 5; Thorndike, *Elements of Psych.* (A. G. Seiler, 1907, 2d ed.), 1; H. Hoffding, *Outlines of Psych.* (tr. Lowndes, Macmillan, 1893), 1; Angell, *Psychology* (Henry Holt & Co., 1908, 4th ed.), 1.

[5] The number of daily newspapers in the United States reported by Ayer and Sons' *Newspaper Annual and Directory*, 1910, is 2,467. On the basis of figures for 1905, the *Bulletin of the Bureau of the Census*, U.S. Depart. of Commerce and Labor, Table 76, gives the average circulation per issue as 21,079,130. This would allow an average of one paper for every four inhabitants or one paper for every family.

[6] Cf. p. 342. In chap. iii this general standpoint will be discussed in detail as a basis for the

here merely to state the fact which has been pointed out above, that much of our conduct is of an unconscious and but dimly conscious sort, as compared with fully conscious and reasoned activity; that it is stimulated by a great variety of suggestions, over which we have, as yet very little control. The process of stimulus and response between newspaper and human activity, which goes on sometimes consciously and sometimes unconsciously, is the subject of study here. [...]

CHAPTER III: THE PRINCIPLES OF SUGGESTION WITH SPECIAL REFERENCE TO THE NEWSPAPER

The problem of this study is that of the general connection between the newspaper and crime and other anti-social activity. The emphasis in this chapter is upon an analysis of the activity as it goes on, rather than upon the types of sources, that is, sections of the newspaper, from which stimuli to that activity come. The standpoint in the most general sense is that of suggestion, if the latter be taken in its broadest meaning to cover all stimulus and response relations, such as are included in the definition of suggestion given in the *Dictionary of Philosophy and Psychology:* "The coming into the mind from without of a presentation, idea, or any sort of intimation having meaning for consciousness which effects a lodgment and takes the place it would have if internally aroused by association."[7] Within this field there are all types and gradations of stimulus and response relations, from so-called pure suggestion, in which there is no perception by the actor of the relation between stimulus and response up to so-called reasoned activity, in which there is such consciousness of this connection. We are accustomed to think chiefly of this latter type in connection with the newspaper and similar stimuli because we are used to thinking of activity as consciously caused, and because we can get direct introspective evidence of the connection from the actor, that is, the person involved can tell of the stimulus

---

whole treatment.

[7] The word "consciousness" as here used, if the writer is consistent, must connote merely mental processes as such, and not necessarily consciousness of, or attention to, the particular relation of stimulus and image. In other words, "entrance into consciousness" here means simply the process of setting off an activity. The word "consciousness" is, of course, an ambiguous term to all but psychologists. As a matter of fact, we have no adequate definition of consciousness. Nervous terms, terms of stimulus and response, are the nearest ones in which we can express it, and we call conscious acts those in which more than one stimulus is present, and in which therefore there is necessity for inhibition or selection of stimuli. In this discussion "consciousness" is not used in any metaphysical sense, but merely to denote "attention" or "inhibition."

and connection in such cases. The other class of cases at the opposite pole from these, we are not accustomed to connect with the newspaper, cases of so-called pure suggestion or unconscious suggestion, in which there is no perception of the relation between stimulus and response and regarding which, therefore, we can get no direct introspective evidence from the person concerned. Nevertheless, for reasons which will be set forth, these latter cases form a very important share of all cases of newspaper suggestion. It is unconscious suggestion, or suggestion as it is commonly understood, that constitutes a large number of the cases of newspaper influence on crime and other anti-social activity. As yet these cases are an unexplored portion of the field of suggestion and cannot be analyzed introspectively because they elude introspection by their very nature; and, finally, they enter into the other less purely suggested acts and even into reasoned acts as part content of those acts. It is necessary, therefore, to make an objective study of cases of unconscious newspaper suggestion. In no other way can we gain a control of it, and of the stimuli to it.

The only kind of activity stimulated by the newspaper that admits of introspective evidence is that in which there is some degree of conscious planning, and in which, therefore, the person remembers where he got his model or idea. Activity in which unconscious suggestion plays a large part cannot be checked up, except indirectly by the employment of objective methods of analysis, that is, for example, where a resemblance is noted between a newspaper account and the act by some third person, or where, as in cases of suicide, robbery, etc., a marked account of a similar act is found in the person's room or on his person. But all acts are mixtures, complexes of many activities, and suggested parts enter also even into those acts in which conscious planning is the predominant element.

In a later chapter cases of reasoned activities, which constitute direct introspective evidence of suggestion, will be analyzed in detail and it will be shown just how the act goes on. Here, the preliminary theoretical basis for that analysis will be laid by dealing in some detail with the psychology of this more narrowly suggested type of activity for which there is no direct introspective evidence, and which enters into the reasoned type. Suggestion, in this narrower sense, will be defined here and its operation described and illustrated with especial reference to the newspaper.

The first question, then, is, what is unconscious suggestion? The orthodox textbooks on psychology, such as those of James, Angell, Judd, Titchener, Royce, and others, do not contain explicit definitions of suggestion. The facts of suggestion, when treated in them at all, are dealt with as part of the subject of hypnotism. Consequently these writers cannot be cited in this connection. Definitions of suggestion must be drawn from those who have actually treated this matter. Binet says of suggestion:

> Suggestion when successful, consists of an idea impressed upon a person and reigning dominant in the consciousness [8] of that person; reason, critical power and will are impotent to restrain it.... For suggestion to develop itself accordingly, it is necessary that the subject's field of consciousness do not contain too many antagonistic ideas. [9]

The first part of this definition is too ideational. Ideas are not the only things that can be "impressed" upon a person. Images and bare impulsive tendencies as well may be thus impressed. Otherwise, however, the definition does point out the unitary character of activity in suggestion. Moll says,

> The externally suggested idea of a movement, induces the movement; the idea of an object causes a corresponding sense-delusion.... Ideas aroused in us have an effect which sometimes shows itself as other concepts (ideas, sensations, etc.), and sometimes externally as movement; in many cases, perhaps in all, there is both an internal and an external effect. What effect appears, what idea, what feeling, what movement will be induced by the first concept, depends upon the individuality of the person, upon his imagery, upon his character, his habits, and upon the species of the concept. [10]

Moll is here considering suggestion chiefly in connection with hypnotism as a method of producing an effect. Nevertheless, this definition does point out the close relation between stimulus and response (idea and movement), and the external source of the stimulus.

In his *Psychotherapy*, [11] Munsterberg makes the following statement among others, regarding suggestion,

> A suggestion is, we might say at first, an idea which has a power in our mind to suppress the opposite idea. A suggestion is an idea which in itself is not different from other ideas, but the way in which it takes possession of the mind reduces the chances of any opposite ideas; it inhibits them. Every suggestion is thus

---

[8] "Consciousness" is apparently here used broadly as in the first definition cited.

[9] *On Double Consciousness*, Open Court Pub. Co. (1894), 70, 71.

[10] *Hypnotism*, 63; (tr. Hopkirk), 4th enlarged ed. Scribner, 1909

[11] Moffat, Yard & Co., 1909, p. 86.

> ultimately a suggestion of activity....[12] By small steps, suggestion shades over
> into ordinary exchange of ideas, propositions, and impressions, just as attention
> shades over into a neutral perception.[13]

This definition also limits suggestion to an ideational process, but it brings out its quick going-over into activity, its inhibitory character with relation to other ideas, and the fact that the line between suggestion and what we call ordinary stimulus and response relations is not exact.

"'Suggestion' is only another name for the power of ideas, *so far as they prove efficacious over belief and conduct,*" says James in his *Varieties of Religious Experience.*[14]

To take a more involved definition: The question of suggestion becomes, then, that of the mechanism of attention in working three results: (1) the narrowing of consciousness[15] upon the suggested idea, (2) the consequent narrowing of the motor impulses to simpler lines of discharge, and (3) the consequent inhibition of the discriminating and selective attitude which constitutes belief in reality.[16]

This definition also limits suggestion to an ideational process, and in so far it is too narrow, but it emphasizes the unitary character of the activity, as does the definition of Binet, and it makes explicit the part of inhibition in suggestion, that is, the absence of conflict of stimuli. Although the third point, as stated, simply means absence of inhibition, it serves to emphasize the uncritical attitude in suggestion.

Boris Sidis says, By suggestion is meant the intrusion into the mind of an idea; met with more or less opposition by the persons; accepted uncritically at last; and realized unreflectively, almost automatically.[17] This definition is bound up with Sidis' theory of double consciousness, or disaggregation of consciousness (for which he has been much criticized), which comes out in the phrase, "met with more or less opposition." Otherwise, barring its limitation to "idea" this definition covers the facts of suggestion.

Cooley says of suggestion: "The word is here used to denote an influence that works in a comparatively mechanical and reflex way, without calling

---

[12] *Ibid.,* 104.

[13] *Ibid.,* 106.

[14] Longmans, Green & Co. (1902), p. 112.

[15] Cf. note at beginning of the chapter.

[16] J. M. Baldwin, *Mental Development in the Child and the Race* (MacMillan, 1906), 3d ed., 104.

[17] *The Psychology of Suggestion* (D. Appleton & Co., 1898), 15.

out that higher selective activity of mind implied in choice or will." [18] This definition implies the main facts of suggestion; its unconscious character, the absence of conscious selection and choice, that is, of attention, and consequently its quick going-over into action.

In short, for the purposes of this study, suggestion is the process by which ideas, images, impulsive tendencies, or any sort of stimulus, enter from without into the composition of the neural make-up or disposition and, at times more or less in the focus of consciousness, at other times not in the focus at all, are transformed into activity by the agency of a stimulus which bears an effective though unrecognized relation or similarity to the image or neural set, and in which there is in large part, or wholly, failure to anticipate the results of the suggested act. For example, when one reads an account of a murder he images it visually, or auditorially, or in whatever terms are characteristic of his type of imagery. These images and motor tendencies stay in his mind, that is, in his neural disposition, and later, when they are called up by some new stimulus, they may become cues, causes, of immediate activity, as appears from the following account of an act. Professor Woodworth says,

> The complete determinant of a voluntary motor act—that which specifies exactly what it shall be—is nothing less than the total set of the nervous system at the moment. The set is determined partly by factors of long standing, instincts and habits, partly by the sensations of the moment, partly by recent perceptions of the situation and by other thoughts lately present in consciousness; at the moment, however, these factors, though they contribute essentially to the set of the system, are for the most part present in consciousness only as a background or "fringe," if at all, while the attention is occupied by the thought of some particular change to be effected in the situation. The thought may be clothed in sensorial images but these are after all only clothes, and a naked thought can perfectly well perform its function of starting the motor machinery in action and determining the point and object of its application. [19]

The fact that the reading of the murder case, as referred to above, was the source of the initial imagery, or that there is a connection between the present stimulus and the image, is not recognized in this type of suggestion, and the activity follows unreflectively upon the calling up of the image;

---

[18] *Human Nature and the Social Order* (Scribner, 1902), 14.

[19] "The Cause of Voluntary Movement," *Studies in Philosophy and Psychology* (Garman Memorial Volume; Houghton, Mifflin Co., 1906), 391, 392.

while in reasoned activity this source is remembered and a high degree of consciousness of the relation between stimulus and image exists. This does not mean that the overt activity in the case of pure or unconscious suggestion is a totally unconscious activity, but only that the relation between stimulus and response is unperceived immediately by the actor. Very intense consciousness may arise in connection with carrying out the activity that is, wherever anything problematical arises in the adjustment that is being made of means to ends. But consciousness is present only when there is some conflict of stimuli, and in the type of suggestion under discussion there is no such conflict of stimuli, only one stimulus being present as stimulus. This is what the "narrowing of consciousness [or attention] upon the suggested idea," referred to by Baldwin, means.

It is clear from the above account and from Woodworth's description of the act that the newspaper can function in suggestion in various ways, in all the ways, in fact, in which it can influence the nervous set. In any one act it may have entered into the constitution of the nervous set as "a factor of long standing," in the composition of a "habit"; it may constitute one or more of the "sensations of the moment," or complex of these sensations; it may be present as a "recent perception," or as a "thought lately present in consciousness." The newspaper as stimulus may be, therefore: (1) either the source of initial images or ideas that have now come to constitute either part of the fringe of a present act or the focus of a present act; or (2) it may be a present stimulus calling up images, ideas, already in the nervous set, as where a present newspaper account of a crime sets the person to committing that crime, or, when he has determined upon a crime, gives him his method. In the former of the two phases of newspaper influence the idea or motor tendency may lie dormant and not come into consciousness at all, or it may take the form of a fixed idea, in which case the person frequently even seeks stimuli which bear upon it. [20]

But acts of pure suggestion not only form a large number of the cases of suggestion, but, as was stated in the beginning of this chapter, enter into less purely suggested acts and into reasoned acts. The difference between a suggested act and a reasoned act, neurologically speaking, is the absence or presence of conflicting stimuli-processes. Every act, however, is a complex of many previous acts, and, as has been pointed out, involves, at any one moment, the total set of the nervous system of that moment. The neural set,

---

[20] Well-known examples of this unconscious suggestion are to be found in epidemics of crime of various sorts, suicide epidemics, murders, highway and bank robberies, etc. See latter part of chap. vi.

as described by Woodworth, includes a complex of past and present neural experiences into which suggestion has entered more or less frequently.[21]

Suggestion, consequently, is a process that is continually going on in the form of responses to surrounding stimuli. "The fact is," to quote Cooley, "that the main current of our thought is made up of impulses absorbed without deliberate choice from the life about us or else arising from hereditary instinct or from habit."[22] And this again is built up "without deliberate choice from the life about us."

The questions of social importance here are: Under what conditions is suggestion likely to occur? That is, (1) In what sorts of people is this process frequent and habitual; (2) What sorts of stimuli are apt to be suggestive and in what form or through what medium? That is to say, a psychological analysis of objective social conditions as stimuli and of the subjective individual to whom these are stimuli must be made.

Psychology has some evidence as to the kind of stimuli that are likely to set up associations. In general, the more concrete the stimulus the more likely it is to be remembered and to be responded to. More definitely still, frequency, vividness, recency, coexistence, are the objective conditions which have been found experimentally to be most conducive to suggestion.[23] In a later chapter it will be pointed out in greater detail how these conditions operate in the daily newspaper, through its featuring, in the use of varieties of type, wording, position, coloring, illustration, etc.

We have now to consider what types of people, external factors, suggestions, can incite to anti-social acts. Given the objective conditions already mentioned, whether a person exposed to them gets a suggestion or not depends, in general, upon the type of person he is—whether his previously ingrained experience is of such a character as to leave him open to such stimuli.[24] It will leave him open to anti-social stimuli if the rest of the stimulation in his experience has been of a similar character, or if he has had no strong

---

[21] "There are numbers of people in the community who feel the temptation to approach the brink of crime who need only a slight incentive to convert the impulse into action. The man who killed the Duke of Buckingham happened to be passing a hardware store and saw displayed in the window a huge knife with a keen edge. It was enough. He bought the knife and flayed the duke." S. W. Pennypacker, *op. cit.*, 590. The phrase "feel the temptation to approach the brink of crime" does not mean that people are conscious of such a feeling, but merely that in the presence of a stimulus to certain criminal acts they have an impulse to perform them.

[22] *Op. cit.*, 30.

[23] Boris Sidis, op. cit., 28; also E. B. Titchener, *Experimental Psychology* (Students' Qualitative Manual; Macmillan, 1896), 201.

[24] A. Moll, *op. cit.*, 68.

counter-stimulation or training in evaluating stimuli. In other words, the objective and subjective conditions of suggestion revolve themselves, first into a question of how the attention can be attracted, how the eye or ear can be caught. And here, psychology tells us that novel stimuli, stimuli that appeal to organic appetites or native instincts, stimuli that appeal to special acquired interests, are the ones that catch the attention and thus enable the first step toward suggested activity to be taken. [25]

The objective and subjective conditions of suggestion revolve themselves, secondly, into a question of how these stimuli are evaluated, that is, related to social standards. Whether, the attention once caught, these stimuli *are* evaluated by the individual depends, as has been shown, upon his training for such evaluation. Young people whose habits and ideas are in process of formation, the weak and unstable of all ages, are not in a position to estimate these stimuli critically. McDougall says,

> The suggestibility of any subject is not of the same degree at all times; it varies not only according to the topic and according to the source from which the proposition is communicated [he is speaking here of verbal suggestion only], but also with the condition of the subject's brain from hour to hour. The least degree of suggestibility is that of a wide-awake, self reliant man of settled convictions, possessing a large store of systematically organized knowledge which he habitually brings to bear in criticism of all statements made to him. Greater degrees of suggestibility are due in the main to conditions of four kinds: (1) abnormal states of the brain, of which the relative dissociation obtaining in hysteria, hypnosis, normal sleep, and fatigue, is the most important; (2) deficiency of knowledge or convictions relating to the topic in regard to which the suggestion is made, and

---

[25] Illustrations of how the attention is got in these various ways are to be found, for example, in the yellow journal which represents an appeal both to organic appetites and to a desire for the novel (W. I. Thomas, *op. cit.*); in various forms of advertising, such as pictures of women on cigar boxes, suggestive pictures of women in the windows and on the walls of saloons, bill board signs, notably the illustration for *The Girl from Rector's*, played in Chicago in 1909, which some members of the Chicago Women's Club and of the Juvenile Protective Association took measures to have removed, a very suggestive picture advertising *The Girl in the Taxi*, and others. In addition, a number of advertisements in newspapers are based upon this same appeal. A Colorado paper displayed a picture of Ruth St. Denys dancing followed by the statement that "Some people have called this dancing immoral," and other remarks to that effect, ending with "But whatever you think about the dancing, groceries at—are the ones you want." Book reviews of the type of those generally written by Jeannette Gilder are apparently based on the same principle. Books, such as *Elizabeth's Visits to America* and *Lady Cardigan's Recollections*, are reviewed in the daily papers at some length by her, in advance of their publication. The suggestive and immoral portions are liberally quoted and dwelt upon, with the result that there is usually a wide demand for the books when they appear.

imperfect organization of knowledge; (3) the impressive character of the source from which the suggested proposition is communicated ("prestige suggestion"]; (4) peculiarities of the character and native disposition of the subject.[26] [...]

It is also true that people are differently suggestible, according to their types of imagery.[27] But the newspaper includes more than one type of suggestion. And this again increases its influence i.e., where more than one sensation area is stimulated, there is more likelihood of response. There are verbal suggestion, which contains indirect suggestions of other types, and visual suggestion in the form of illustrations, colors, differences in the form and size of type, etc.[28] In short, the modern newspaper, especially the so-called yellow and sensational elements in the modern newspaper, represent a mechanics of expression, a world of sensuous appeal, to eye, and ear, which has grown up slowly in other times and in other situations and which is a distinct excitant in ways which frequently are no longer socially useful. Anything which dramatizes, makes for a break in monotony, such as the patrol-wagon, policeman, etc., is a stimulus, is exciting, and is apt to be suggestive to the small boy or to older people of the mental pattern of the small boy. The motor or activity stimuli in the modern newspaper are of just this sort, and, on account of the important part they have played in the development of the race, make a strong appeal.[29]

On the basis of the psychology of suggestion as above developed, a direct causal connection may be established between the newspaper and crime and other anti-social activities.

---

[26] *Introduction to Social Psychology*, 98.

[27] W. D. Scott, "Difference in Suggestibility," *Psych. Rev.* (March, 1910), 147–54.

[28] There is no experimental evidence in psychology to show through which of the senses people are more commonly or easily suggestible, but it is an admitted fact that in modern life the eye has come to be the most important organ for picking up and mediating impressions. A common illustration of this fact is to be found in the effect of certain pictures, such as those representing abnormal activities, which often produce kinesthetic or activity effects in the person viewing them.

[29] "For the great majority of the public the emotion felt in connection with the brutal and exact details with which the press describes the most atrocious crimes vanishes after the first moment of astonishment and horror and we return tranquilly to our own thoughts and affairs; but for the lowest minority, the thing does not end so soon. A few—the predisposed, the degenerates—feel this emotion for a long time; the crime described so minutely has strongly impressed them; they think about it incessantly, it becomes a nightmare; and some day they give way to the obsession as the assassin Lemaire did, who after having stabbed a child to death, said calmly to a police agent who arrested him: 'I read in a newspaper the description of an act similar to that which I have performed, and I wished to imitate it.'"—Scipio Sighele, *Literature et criminalite* (Giard & Briere, Paris, 1908), 210.

It is not possible to measure this influence quantitatively, but it is none the less real because it cannot be so measured, as can, for example, the numerical results of advertising suggestion, [30] which is an analogous case of the influence of suggestion.

It is necessary, therefore, to make, on the one hand, a careful estimate of the matter dealing with crime and other anti-social activities in the newspapers, and on the other hand an analysis of actual and typical cases in which the newspaper is known to have suggested criminal and other anti-social acts. In the following chapter the method of analysis used in tabulating the matter in the newspapers will be discussed.

CHAPTER IV: METHODS USED IN THE PRESENT STUDY

Two kinds of fact regarding the influence of newspapers upon the growth of crime and other anti-social activity have been collected in this investigation: direct evidence of newspaper suggestion, consisting of cases in which the cause and effect relation between the newspaper and anti-social activity is known to have existed; and analyses of the relative amounts of space devoted by newspapers to anti-social and other matter. The latter constitutes a study of the possible objective sources of the stimuli in the newspaper to anti-social activity; the former some of the responses to these stimuli. Both studies are necessary preliminaries to any adequate control of the anti-social activity under consideration here.

The direct evidence was collected from all the available sources, from newspapers themselves, from persons who came in contact with criminals or other anti-social persons, or with juvenile offenders, and from court records. In addition 201 question-lists were sent out, 74 to prison and reformatory

---

[30] "The actual effort of modern advertising is not so much to convince as to suggest . . . . the idea is suggested by the advertisement and the impulsiveness of human nature enforces the suggested idea, hence the desired result follows in a way unknown to the purchaser [unconscious suggestion]."—W. D. Scott, *Psychology of Advertising* (Small, Maynard & Co., 1908), 83. "Advertisers are, in general, wise businessmen and are usually able to tell whether their advertising pays or not. If it pays, they continue it; if it does not, they cease advertising," says Professor Scott (*ibid*, 180). The brewers spend enormous sums in advertising to show, on physicians' and even on preachers' authority, that beer is nutritious and non-poisonous. They make a close calculation as to approximately how much money this suggestion will cost them and profit them. They advertise especially during local option and anti-saloon agitations, as a means of contra-suggestion. Advertising here has a direct causal connection with the sale of beer. Mail-order houses and department stores advertise only in papers of large general circulation and in those which circulate among certain classes of people, different in the two cases. Also certain forms of "fake" and other miscellaneous advertisements are known to be carried principally, or wholly, by the cheap literary papers which circulate in the rural districts. Cf. *Success Magazine* (June, 1909), 412.

officials, 75 to juvenile court judges and other judges, 45 to chief probation officers, and 7 to other persons. [...]

CHAPTER VII: CONCLUSION

I. *Summary and conclusions.*—The object of the present study has been to show a causal connection between the news paper and crime and other anti-social activity. In how far and in what manner this has been done a summary of the previous chapters will show. [31] [...]

It appears from chap. vi that the newspaper leads to antisocial activity in a number of ways. These may be summed up by saying that it influences people directly, both unconsciously and consciously, to commit anti-social acts. It also has a more indirect anti-social influence on public opinion during criminal trials through its accounts of these trials and through its partisan selection of evidence; and, finally, it aids in building up anti-social standards, and thus in preparing the way for anti-social acts.

Finally, the results from the analyses of the papers are based upon a comparatively extensive number of issues of papers (203), comprising 57 different American newspapers. The per centages, therefore, constitute representative figures, both as to number and kind of papers and total number of issues studied.

The evidence collected for chap. vi unquestionably establishes the *existence* of suggestion to anti-social activity, and indirectly suggests its *extent*. Cases of direct newspaper suggestion to crime and other anti-social activity, cases of exactly analogous suggestion through the similar medium of literature, also similar cases of suggestion through moving-picture shows, theater representations, etc., along with a large body of facts testifying to a wide experience and conviction on the part of experts and others that the suggestion exists, were presented in support of the argument. [...]

III. *Recommendations for Changes in the Newspaper*

(I) The newspaper is a tremendous influence in the community. Its stimuli reach an enormous number of persons and reach them frequently and insistently. It should, therefore, be an educative and dependable medium. Its possible educative value has scarcely been realized. Suggestive anti-social matter should be excluded from it. This does not mean that all mention of

---

[31] The concluding chapter was written to accompany chap. vi in its original form with the entire mass of evidence and detailed discussion of evidence included.

anti-social matters should be excluded. It is desirable that the public should be informed on all matters which they can assist in improving. But the news which gives them the information should not be couched in terms or presented in forms and details which make it criminally suggestive or factually misleading. It is possible to deal with anti-social matters in such a manner as to minimize the possibility of suggestion to anti-social activity by confining the treatment to bare statements of fact, by selecting such facts only as are necessary to constructive action in the matter. It is likewise possible to use all of the media which contribute so largely to anti-social results in gaining increased social results. Many of these methods constitute a technique ready made for educative purposes. Large type, vivid and picturesque writing, illustrations, colored type, diagrams, etc., are just as easily the media of social as of anti-social suggestion and when the content conveyed by them is of a social character they are indispensable for readers who are fatigued, or who read in poor light. [...]

(4) Therefore it is important to consider methods possible at present.

(*a*) We need new and adequately enforced laws defining strictly the power of newspapers to deal with news, laws analogous to those already in operation in regard to the use of the mails, billboards, etc. Such laws would, as a matter of fact, in many cases be mere formulations of practices already in vogue. Courts both in the United States and England have already shown their power to restrain newspapers from, or to punish them for, detailing certain types of anti-social facts.

(*b*) Judges should recognize in their decisions the facts already known regarding anti-social suggestion.

(*c*) Public opinion needs to be educated to secure support for constructive legislation along this line and to support such laws as we have or as may be made.

(*d*) Further investigation of the relation of newspaper suggestion and other suggestion to crime and other anti-social activity should be made, and public officials, such as probation officers, juvenile court judges and other judges, superintendents of institutions, etc., should be encouraged and required to keep records of cases of such connection. In this way a better basis for activity regarding the newspapers could be established.

PART THREE

Applications

CHAPTER TWENTY-THREE

The Psychology of Persuasion (1920)

William Macpherson

London: Methuen, pp. 70–74, 135–55 [with elisions].

EDITOR'S INTRODUCTION

Unlike the scholarly Fenton, William Macpherson (see note) was writing for a popular audience. He was "an assistant master of method" at London Day Training College, University of London, in the 1920s and 1930s, teaching classes in literature and the arts, but applying a psychological filter to his subjects. He is interesting here for his early examination of cinema and advertising as vehicles for persuasion.

In fact, and in contrast to most of the literature of the time, his term of preference for the process of attitude formation and modification was "persuasion," foreshadowing the change in nomenclature brought about in the 1940s. At the same time, he also used "suggestion," and in the following excerpt, reviews the literature on both, sometimes combining the terms, and arguably even conflating them. For Macpherson, both are non-rational and emotional phenomena, but "suggestibility," "the capacity that we all possess of accepting beliefs without any rational demonstration of their truth," is the core mechanism in the process of persuasion.

Along with others noted previously, he also foreshadows the cognitive selectivity process and confirmation bias of contemporary social psychology.

"The starting-point," he states, "of all persuasion, of ourselves or others, is a belief or wish. Holding a certain belief; or desiring that a certain course of action shall be pursued, we set out to justify our belief and the conduct that it implies."

In the second half of the excerpt, Macpherson moves to a detailed discussion of "the persuasion of the cinematograph." Movies were a relatively new form of the popular arts at the time; talking pictures weren't introduced until the late 1920s. Macpherson examines the use of cinema as a propaganda tool in World War I and then considers the unique characteristics of the medium, such as its ability to collapse time and space through editing, which enhance its manipulative capabilities.

He puts a similar lens on advertising and "publicity campaigns," again using wartime experiences as examples and "demonstrating conclusively" the efficacy of advertisement as a means of persuasion.—*P.P.*

Note

No additional biographical information is available.

The Psychology of Persuasion (1920)

CHAPTER I: THE PROCESS AND ELEMENTS OF PERSUASION

MAN has been described as a *reasoning* animal; and every one likes to think that the description is applicable to himself. The instinctive and impulsive side of our nature, as contrasted with the rational, has been apt to be ignored both by the man in the street and by the writer on psychology: it has been considered, perhaps, to be not quite respectable. In recent years, however, writers on psychology have come to recognise fully the important part that impulse and emotion play in human life. As a matter of fact, men do not, usually, act rationally in the sense that they first carefully calculate the means that will enable them to realise their end, and only then act; and, whether they calculate thus or not, the fundamental source of their actions is always some instinct or emotion that they seek to satisfy. To say this is to say nothing derogatory to human nature; indeed, as we all know, to act on impulse is often much more respectable than to act from calculation. If much of the wrong-doing of the world may be attributed to the uncontrolled working of selfish impulses, it should also be remembered that impulse is the source of art and science, and of many of the best things in life.

Impulse is one of the non-rational elements in our nature, but this does not imply that it is necessarily irrational, or that it works against reason. In this chapter an attempt will be made to show that the process of persuasion is, fundamentally, a non-rational process, dominated much more by the emotional and impulsive part of our nature than by the rational. But this circumstance, while it accounts, partially, for the extreme ease with which we are able to delude ourselves and others, must not be regarded as in itself a condemnation of the process, or as implying that it is, of necessity, irrational.

The starting-point of all persuasion, of ourselves or others, is a belief or wish. Holding a certain belief; or desiring that a certain course of action shall be pursued, we set out to justify our belief and the conduct that it implies. Thus, before he begins to speak, the orator whose aim is persuasion has already present in his mind a belief or wish, fully formed, from which all his arguments and appeals flow; and the effectiveness of his persuasion will be proportionate to the clearness and fulness with which the belief has been defined, and the degree of conviction with which it is held. When we persuade ourselves, also, it is no less true that the belief or wish we seek to confirm is given before hand. In this respect persuasion differs from the process of rational logic.

When we employ the process of rational logic our object is either to discover or to demonstrate. We may desire, for instance, to discover the conditions under which a candle will burn, and this we may do by a process of induction from a series of experiments. The mere fact that here we are seeking to *discover* a true conclusion indicates that it is not given beforehand! Again, when logical demonstration is our aim, a proposition is advanced hypothetically, no pre-supposition being made as to its truth or falsity, and the whole course of the reasoning is directed to furnish proofs of its inherent validity. The methods of logical discovery and demonstration are most successful when they are applied to natural phenomena on which we can experiment, but they are also applicable to human affairs: men do reason logically and disinterestedly about human conduct (especially other people's conduct), discriminate between alternatives, and refuse to assent to beliefs the implications of which they have not investigated. The method of persuasion, however, is much more common. In it we start from a belief or wish that is given beforehand: instead of following, the belief precedes the process. Superficially, indeed, the logic of persuasion may resemble, or simulate, a logical demonstration, but in reality, starting not from a hypothesis but from a belief already fully formed and accepted, and destined to dominate it through out, it is quite different.

Our effective beliefs regarding human life and conduct are determined not by reasoning but by many unconscious and frequently irrational factors. We believe because we wish to believe, so that we may satisfy our instincts and emotions and sentiments, because our environment and education have made certain beliefs seem necessary, because our fathers have believed before us, or because it is convenient and expedient to think as our neighbours do. In self-persuasion the belief from which the process starts is often held by us quite unconsciously, having its origin in many remote factors, and the process itself may be to a large extent unconscious. In the persuasion of others we begin with a conscious belief, and the subsequent process is a conscious, deliberate, and more or less systematic attempt to impress our belief on others. But always, alike in the persuasion of ourselves and others, our purpose is to gain approval, our own or that of other people, for beliefs or wishes already formed and accepted by us.

We have used the terms 'belief' and 'wish' as if they were synonymous. Our beliefs and our wishes, indeed, are inextricably interwoven; or rather, they are not really to be distinguished. The state of mind from which persuasion starts implies an intellectual element, which we may express by the term 'belief,' and at the same time a practical element, a reference to conduct and action, which we may express by the term 'wish'; but in an ultimate analysis those elements are seen to coalesce, the essence of both being that they are latent courses of action by which our environment may be modified. When a politician makes a speech in which he advocates the nationalisation of land, we may indicate the state of mind from which his persuasion starts by the term 'belief,' or by the term 'wish,' indifferently; he believes, and also wishes, that land should be nationalised; the fundamental character of his belief or wish is that it is a latent course of action. The object of persuasion is to make explicit and definite the course of action implied in the initial belief or wish, and to furnish adequate motives and justification for it. [...]

Our beliefs and wishes, from which the process of persuasion starts, our latent and premeditated courses of action, depend mainly on the emotional elements in our nature. The motive force that impels men to action is always some instinct, tendency, emotion, sentiment, or passion. We accept a belief or wish, and act so that it may be realised, primarily with a view to satisfying some aspect of our emotional nature. [...]

The fundamental character of persuasion, as a process that aims at modifying conduct and inducing action, is that it is an emotional process. In this respect, again, it differs from the process of rational logic, which should have no tincture of emotion, or so little, and of such a character, as, having exercised no diverting influence on the course, of the reasoning and on the conclusion ultimately reached, may be considered negligible.

CHAPTER III: GROUP PRESSURE AND THE SENSE OF POWER-METHODS OF IMPRESSION AND EXPLOITATION

AT no previous period of the world's history has the human tendency to associate in groups been so marked as it is at present, and for this reason the influence exercised by group-pressure on men's persuasions has never before been so widely and deeply operant. In every aspect of life evidences of the increasing tendency towards group-effort may be observed. [...]

That the loyal co-operation of individuals within a group is calculated to gain the immediate ends in view cannot be doubted. It makes for practical efficiency. Whether its results will be good or evil depends entirely on the nature of the ends sought and the means employed to realise them. Of co-operation as a mighty influence for good more will be said later; in this chapter we shall deal mainly with the evil influence that it frequently exercises in the form of organised group-pressure.

The tendency of man to associate in groups is closely connected with the quality of suggestibility: the capacity that we all possess of accepting beliefs without any rational demonstration of their truth, because they are held, or have been held, by other people. It is man's innate tendency to suggestibility that makes social life possible. And this quality operates fundamentally, also, in the process of persuasion: in the first place, it dictates to a large extent the beliefs from which the process starts, while those beliefs, with their underlying emotions, may dominate absolutely the course that the process follows; and, in the second place, it is mainly on this quality that the speaker or the writer who aims at persuading others relies to enable him to attain his end. The potency of suggestion varies according to the individual, and women are supposed to be, in general, more suggestible than men; but it holds sway over us all, in every individual, and at all places and times. Its power is, however, most strikingly exhibited when people are gathered in crowds. Then the art of suggestion may be employed with immediate or startling effect, and the orator and the demagogue find their profit therein: men's natural kinship declares itself, and they are moved, often impulsively and irrationally, to common action. Similarly, the power of suggestion over an individual may be especially strong if he belongs to a particular group having for its aim the promotion of certain interests or supposed interests. In such cases, supported by the opinions of their fellows and by the power behind an organised combination of forces, buoyed by the atmosphere of suggestion that sustains all collective effort, men may easily persuade themselves wrongly: specious arguments, and irrelevant appeals to imagination and emotion, may readily be enlisted in the service of the desired end, any argument, and any appeal, being considered valuable if only it seems likely to promote the realisation of the end. The members of a group are united by the bond of a common object to which great importance is attached, and their loyalty as members is proportionate to the thoroughness with which they identify themselves with it. Under those circumstances, it is obvious that there will be a natural human tendency, greatly augmented by the force of suggestion, to reject as of no value any considerations unfavourable to the interests of the group, and to emphasise unduly, as of great value, all favourable considerations.

It is difficult, or impossible, for the members of a group, who are pledged to afford one another mutual support, to exercise complete independence of judgment, or to resist the opinions of the majority. An individual member who persists in acting contrary to the opinions or mode of action dictated by his group is liable to be ejected therefrom, and so to lose the comfort and support, and the material advantages, conferred by his membership. Thus the professions of medicine and law, which are practically close corporations, have each its own "etiquette," its system of rules, forming a kind of written or unwritten law which all the members are pledged to obey; and those who choose not to conform to the prescribed code, ceasing to be recognised as members of the profession, may lose their means of livelihood—a serious consequence, tending to induce members, even if they should disagree absolutely with certain of the prescribed usages, to waive their disagreement, and conform.

Suggestibility may play its part here also, and encourage the members of a group to abandon, or refrain from stating, their private beliefs. Suppose for instance, that the activities of a group involve the employment of secret methods of impression, and that the opinions and feelings of some member are wholly opposed to such action: so compelling is the force of suggestion that, meeting his fellow members frequently and coming under their influence, he will be apt presently to fall into line with them, and end by approving the plans that originally he had condemned. And in this change of front, even if there might still survive in his mind some feeling of repugnance to the methods employed, he would readily be assisted by the specious reflection that, at any rate, he was acting for the support and protection of his fellow members. As we have noted in the preceding chapter, the belief that "the end justifies the means" often serves to justify unscrupulous conduct, not only in groups, but in individuals: on that ground, for instance, Napoleon's arbitrary acts have often been defended. We have already examined this principle, and found it to be radically fallacious. It often serves merely as an excuse to enable people to satisfy their desire for power, or their instincts of cruelty and revenge, under a specious appearance of altruism.

Suggestion may work in a group through any of the emotions, and sometimes it works through fear: it may happen that the members of a group are positively afraid to commit any action that might seem antagonistic to the general group-principles. This is especially likely to be the case if secret methods of impression or punishment are employed by the group. Mr. J.M. de Beaufort, in *Behind the German Veil*, remarks that there is no cause for wonder in the fact that the Germans were afraid of one another, for even before the war they spent £4,000,000 a year on their spy system; and he adds that the employment of secret methods had bred in them a kind of subtle reliance on co-operation, quite opposed to freedom of action and personal courage—the single-handed German would adventure little, but joined (and watched) by his fellows he would dare almost anything.

The persuasions of those who have been caught fast in the machinery of a system are almost of necessity stereotyped, and, in some instances, to attempt to escape from the controlling machinery would be even danger-ous. There is evidence that at the beginning of the War many of the German soldiers shrank from committing the cruelties and barbarities enjoined on them by the policy of "frightfulness," but were constrained to obey, as men inextricably involved in the machinery of a powerful system.

One of the main characteristics of groups is that they are powerful: from that circumstance, partly, they originate. Most individuals, as individuals, possess but small, power to impose their ideas and will on others; but as members of a group they share a common strength. The desire for power is almost universal; and, when once power has been acquired, it is not relin-quished willingly. As members of a group, many people who, of themselves, in virtue of their own qualities or capabilities, could never hope to exercise any considerable influence on the opinions and lives of others, are enabled to experience the sense of power, and find it precious—perhaps the more precious in precise proportion.

CHAPTER IV: THE RIGHT DIRECTION OF PERSUASION

ANY one who studies the process and elements of persuasion, and the manifold aberrations of which it is capable, cannot but be liable to a kind of cynicism; and, indeed, for that matter, who that looks into his own heart could be other than cynical at times? The process of persuasion, as we have analysed it, is seen to be fundamentally a non-rational process. Its very starting-point derives from the non-rational, the beliefs or wishes from which our persuasions start being accepted by us, not because they have been proved by rational demonstration to be true, but, ultimately, to satisfy some aspect of our instinctive nature. For most of us, the strongest motive to belief is furnished by the herd instinct in one form or another. We tend to accept as true the opinions and beliefs of the herd, or that portion of it with which we are in most intimate contact, and to reject antagonistic beliefs as untrue. The most potent factors in the determination of our beliefs are our primal instincts, race and rationality, education, books, newspapers, and the immediate circle of our neighbours and friends. Further, we are, as a rule, entirely unconscious of those, the real, sources of our beliefs, and flatter ourselves that we believe on exclusively rational grounds. The mental process, also, that follows the initial belief in persuasion may be described as being non-rational, since it is essentially an emotional process. Consisting in a series of judgments the value of which is proportionate to their capacity to reinforce and justify our belief, it follows throughout an emotional bias in the direction of the end proposed: underlying all the judgments that constitute it are instincts, tendencies, emotions, sentiments, or passions that we seek to satisfy. In the course of our persuasions we are apt to accept unquestioningly all ideas that harmonise with and reinforce those emotions, while such as appear to be inconsistent with them we reject.

Described in those terms, the process of persuasion, on first consideration, might easily be regarded with suspicion, as one not likely to lead us to true conclusions or just actions. In any case, the very birthright of an Englishman entitles him to feel afraid of a process that can be described as emotional. In this connection, however, it may be comforting, and it is important, to bear in mind that the non-rational is not necessarily irrational, and that, more often than not, fortunately for us, the non-rational processes of mind work on the side of, and not against, reason. The wisdom of past ages may be none the less wise because it has descended to us from the past; and the beliefs that we accept through suggestion, not from logical demonstration may be just and true. Were this not so, humanity would be in a sad plight indeed. Further, because a process is emotional, it is not therefore irrational: the instincts and tendencies that are most deeply rooted in our being may work on the side of reason, and preserve and develop the life both of individuals and communities. The really irrational method of dealing with a human problem is to neglect any of its essential conditions, among which always, are emotions and sentiments. In the consideration of any question bearing on human life and action, it is the merely logical person, not he who includes within his view the emotions and sentiments inherently involved, whose persuasions are futile. More and more it is coming to be recognised that (in Mr. G. K. Chesterton's phrase) from reason in itself nothing rational has ever proceeded. Following out this line of thought, Mr. Benjamin Kidd asserts that the cause of all human progress is "psychic emotion." "The great secret of the coming age of the world," he says, "is that civilisation rests not on Reason but on Emotion. . . . It is clearly in evidence that the science of creating and transmitting public opinion under the influence of collective motion is about to become the principal science of civilisation, to the mastery of which all governments and all powerful interests will in the future address themselves with every resource at their command. . . . The immature imaginings of the past about the place of reason in the world will all be put aside. . . . Civilisation has its origin, has its existence, and has the cause of its progress, in the emotion of the ideal."[1] [...]

A form of pictorial persuasion which is of special interest at the present time is the persuasion of the cinematograph. During the War several Government Departments employed the moving picture extensively as a means of conveying information and making propaganda: thus both in our own and in allied countries steps were taken to impress on people, by means of the cinema, the true causes of the War, and the nature of German atrocities in the conduct of the War. Again, such films as "Where are my Children?" illustrate the value of the cinematograph as a means for presenting social questions in a striking and dramatic form.

The principal element of persuasion in the representations of the cinema is narration. The film is well adapted to unfold to us vividly a series of actions, events, or incidents: it excites our emotions through the senses

---

[1] *The Science of Power.* By Benjamin Kidd. Methuen & Co., Ltd.: London, 1918.

and the imagination, depicting imaginary situations or situations that have actually occurred.

The plastic arts generally, it has been already remarked, contain some of the elements, and may be employed as instruments, of persuasion; but the cinema has enlarged the boundaries of pictorial art, and created a fresh form of expression, more fully adapted to realise the purposes of persuasion. Painting and sculpture, employing as signs colours and figures in space, can only express properly objects which are coexistent, or the parts of which coexist—that it to say, bodies. They may represent actions, since all bodies exist not only in space, but also in time, and at each moment of their existence may assume a different appearance; but they can do this only suggestively, through the medium of bodies, and can represent only one particular moment of an action. They cannot represent movement absolutely; they fix a momentary aspect or arrangement of bodies, and give to it a character of permanence—so that Keats can say appropriately of the lover and the maid carved on the Grecian urn "forever wilt thou love and she be fair." The proper domain of the plastic arts, then, is space; they are strictly limited in regard to the category of time.

The cinematograph, on the other hand, is not so limited: it may depict a series of events the duration of which is supposed to extend through months or years, and, in a single picture, it may represent the successive appearance of a situation, as seen in the varying groupings and attitudes of the actors. It resembles painting in so far as, the signs it employs being figures in space, it is well adapted to represent bodies, and, through them, simultaneous actions; but it transcends painting, and approximates to the art of verbal narration, in that it can represent effectively successive action in time.

In some respects, indeed, the moving picture is even better fitted than narration to exhibit the time-relations of events. For instance, two events significantly related to one another and happening simultaneously may be brought before us with telling effect in almost an instant of time, while in narration lengthy successive explanations would be required to make clear their proper relation. In a propagandist film that has been widely exhibited, "My Four Years in Germany," one of the pictures having represented a banquet given in honour of the United States ambassador by high political personages in Berlin, who profess the utmost good-will towards America, the next picture shows, in effective contrast, a simultaneous meeting of the German military authorities, at which the real hostility and the secret plans of Germany are made clear. This is a typical instance of the methods of persuasion to which cinematographic representation is well adapted: the sequence of the pictures is intended to produce in the spectator a particular emotion favourable to a particular belief.

The comparative freedom that the cinema possesses in the representation of time-relations is illustrated in another characteristic device, which expresses also the freedom from time-limitations that is characteristic of thought. We all know how, in a given situation at a particular moment, our thoughts may revert to the past or project themselves into the future, and how this retrospection and prevision may affect our persuasions: this faculty of mind the film is naturally fitted to illustrate. When the United States ambassador is informed that he will not be handed his passports until he has given an undertaking that all German ships interned in American ports shall be restored, there passes before his mind's eye a vision of the dinner-table, adorned with American flags, at which he had recently sat, and he recalls the cordial professions of friendship made by his hosts and fellow-guests-his memories are represented concretely on the film, on which the picture of the banquet again takes visible form, and vanishes, as quickly and silently as it had-passed before the ambassador's mental vision. Or, again, in a similar propagandist film, when the hero, a young American, is invited to undertake a dangerous twelve 'honest men and true' the man who seems to you to be the most intelligent, and who appears to take the most interest in the case. Your whole object should now be to *capture him*. . . . But you must not leave the other eleven gentlemen out in the cold, because if they think you are taking no notice of them, they, decent men as they are, will be hurt and feel slighted at you, a learned limb of the law, giving them no notice." [2] The main object of the salesman, too, is to "capture" his client; and to achieve his purpose he must apply discretion and good judgment, adapting his words and manner to the customers personality. Above all, remembering that the public are only too ready to impute to him exclusively interested motives, he should not be obtrusive: in some customers, such an attitude would at once arouse 'contrariant' ideas, hostile forces with which persuasion of every kind frequently has to reckon.

Advertisement is similar to salesmanship in many respects as a form of persuasion. The ordinary trade advertisement seeks, as a rule, to stimulate and reinforce in individuals some generally felt want or need, and it is prompted, primarily, by the desire for gain. As being written, however, and

---

[2] *Forensic Eloquence; or, The Eloquence of the Bar.* By P. J. Cooke (of the Middle Temple). London: 1897.

not spoken, advertisements afford less scope for the exercise of the more personal qualities that may appear in salesmanship. On the other hand, they are more completely, if more formally, organised, and may employ as signs pictures as well as words. They embody, in miniature, all the elements, and exemplify many of the principles and methods, of written persuasion generally.

The aim of most advertising is to induce the reader to buy some particular commodity; but in recent years its scope has been greatly enlarged. The "advertising agent" is now dubbed a "publicity expert," and he is held to be qualified not only to help traders to sell their wares, but to propagate ideas on questions of public and national interest, to assist, for example, a local authority to carry on a campaign against a public abuse or danger, or a political party to persuade the electors, or the State itself to appeal to its individual members. In this country, some of the "publicity campaigns " that were initiated during the War by Government Departments led to remarkable practical results, demonstrating conclusively the efficacy of advertisement as a means of persuasion.

With a view to illustrating certain characteristics of advertisement generally, the following typical sentences may be quoted from a lengthy advertisement issued by the Ministry of National Service in 1917:—

> NATIONAL SERVICE: INDUSTRIAL ARMY: 1917.—Defeat the enemy's attempt to starve you. . . . Place yourselves—free men and uncompelled—at the disposal of National Service. . . . Britain MUST become as nearly self-supporting as possible. . . . Help to bring a speedy peace by releasing fit men to fight. Enrol to-day. Go NOW apply at the nearest Post-Office or National Service Office for Voluntary Service Form—and; sign it NOW.

It has been stated in Chapter I that the process of persuasion always starts from a belief or wish in the speaker's or writer's mind. In this instance the writer's persuasions set out from the belief or wish that as many men as possible should volunteer for national service.

Underlying this belief were certain sentiments and tendencies which the writer sought to arouse also in his readers: the individualistic instinct of self-preservation, threatened by the possible curtailment of food-supplies; the sentiment of patriotism; anger at Germany's declaration of war on the sea-traffic of the world; moral indignation at her disregard of law and humanity; and fear of the consequences. Those emotional tendencies formed the motive-power and directing force of all the writer's persuasions, and he sought to induce them in his readers, as being fitted to lead to the desired action.

A more intellectual element also appears: the writer supports his case by simple arguments. Men who volunteer, he says, will be fulfilling a patriotic duty, since they will be helping to avert starvation and defeat the enemy; and their action will also assist in bringing peace more quickly.

In the formal expression of the advertisement the most conspicuous features are the simple, direct, and striking style of presentation, the use of bold type to emphasise the need for immediate action, the repetition of such suggestive words as "the Enemy," and the frequent employment of urgent and imperative phrases—"defeat the Enemy's attempt to starve you," "Britain *must* become self-supporting," "Place yourselves at the disposal of National Service," "Help to bring a speedy peace," "Enroll to-day." "Sign now." This use of the direct and imperative form of address is in accordance with the principle noted above, that in all effective persuasion a definitely personal note must be struck: the appeal must be driven home to each of the individuals addressed. In any form of national propaganda this principle is specially important, for, while we all acknowledge certain social or national duties that are incumbent on us, our acknowledgment of them is often merely passive and implicit: the publicist's function, then, in making national propaganda, is to transmute the vague and general recognition of duty to the State into a particular purpose tending to definite and individual action—he must lead each of his readers to perceive a direct relationship between himself and the obligation predicated.

Ordinary trade advertisements illustrate the same principles and methods. They appeal, however, mainly to individualistic instincts and tendencies, and their essential aim is the gain of the advertiser. Here again the imperative is frequently the mood; and as the appeal made is often to primitive tendencies, such as the need of food and drink, or the desire for health and enjoyment, little is required in the way of argument to enforce it. But particular instances of the beneficial results produced by the wares advertised, or testimonies of approval, are often cited. The most common form of "argument" in advertisement is merely strong assertion, which by frequent repetition exercises in itself a suggestive and persuasive power. [...]

CHAPTER TWENTY-FOUR

The Control of the Social Mind (1923)

Arland Deyett Weeks

New York: D. Appleton, pp. 205–19 [with elisions].

EDITOR'S INTRODUCTION

W here Fenton concerned herself with suggestion and antisocial behavior, Macpherson used World War I examples of political propaganda in his analysis, which was more typical of the period. Concern with the potential force of propaganda became, according to Sproule (1997), nearly a public obsession following the war, generating waves of writing from social commentators and academics alike and even giving rise to a dedicated organization of scholars and researchers, the Institute for Propaganda Analysis (IPA). Arland Weeks (1871–1936) offers an example of an academic whose work on the subject was crafted for both a scholarly and a popular audience.

Weeks was dean of the School of Education at the North Dakota Agricultural College in the 1920s and early 1930s. He authored a number of books, both academic and popular, including *The Psychology of Citizenship* (1917), *Social Antagonisms* (1918), and *The Control of the Social Mind*, from which the following excerpt is taken.

As with Macpherson's book, Weeks's text was aimed in part at public consumption. In his critical, albeit charitable review of the text, Floyd Allport (1924) allowed that Weeks's "psychology" was "inspirational rather than of a scientific or research character." And in that "inspirational" character, Weeks's writing expresses deep concern about the potential impact of media to bend and shape public perception, at the same time finding in social psychology grounds for hope.

In the following passage, Weeks reviews, in lay terms, "the law of suggestion" and its ability to exert "virtual control of behavior." He adds a new note to the analysis in locating the roots of suggestive power in "a tendency of people to economize their efforts and follow the line of least resistance." In this, he arguably anticipates the cognitive heuristics of the contemporary Elaboration Likelihood Model.

While observing that "one can no more resist the bombardment of suggestions from the press, from history, and from social contact than he can resist the influence of the weather upon his skin," he nonetheless argues, echoing Tarde, that newspapers provide time and space for public deliberation and thereby ameliorate the potentially ruinous consequences of mob suggestion.

Despite, then, a concern about the susceptibility of the public to various forms of control, the overall tenor of the book is optimistically prescriptive, advancing various recommendations designed to prevent or offset the effects of propaganda. Noted one reviewer: "The author is typically American in his belief in progress and the omnipotence of Education" (Jastrow 1925, 751).—*P.P.*

References

Allport, Floyd. 1924. "Review of *The Control of the Social Mind* by Arland Weeks." *Journal of Abnormal and Social Psychology* 19: 309–11.

Jastrow, Joseph. 1925. "Review of *The Control of the Social Mind*." *American Journal of Sociology* 30, no. 6: 751.

Sproule, J. Michael. 1997. *Propaganda and Democracy: The American Experience of Media and Mass Persuasion*. Cambridge: Cambridge University Press.

Weeks, Arlan. 1917. *The Psychology of Citizenship*. Chicago: A.C. McClurg.

Weeks, Arlan. 1918. *Social Antagonisms*. Chicago: A.C. McClurg.

The Control of the Social Mind (1923)

XIV: THE POWER OF SUGGESTION

To one brought up in cannibal society, with no opposing ideas in circulation, cannibalism would seem just and right. The kind of civilization is determined by the prevailing kinds of ideas. The most abhorrent practices, as for example, the drinking of warm blood from the cut necks of horses strung up by the heels, a Patagonian custom, would look proper to us if this were approved by our elders and we were instructed to this end from infancy. There is little that is inevitable in social evolution; a great deal is due to the ideas that chance to be presented. Man does not inherit any set idea against eating his relatives and neighbors; but a Christian civilization, which is a large body of ideas, forbids. We may not even eat small children, the tidbits of orthodox cannibalism. We may, however, employ them in factories. It is all a matter of ideas. The history of ideas is the history of mankind; modern social conditions are largely a product of suggestion. What ideas rule within the mind, and whether one idea or another pulls the trigger of behavior, is determined very largely by the agencies of suggestion.

Any presentation of ideas to consciousness constitutes suggestion. As conscious or voluntary action is in response to ideas, the determinative influence of suggestion is evident. By control of range and character of ideas presented, virtual control of behavior is ordinarily effected. The control of ideas results in the domination of decisions and actions—as may be readily observed in the conduct of children or in responses of individuals in public meetings. The idea of an act may be regarded as the onset of a force that naturally eventuates in corresponding performance.

The power of suggestion has its root in a tendency of people to economize their efforts and follow the line of least resistance. It is often easier to act than to think; hence an idea that once gains the focus of attention tends to result in corresponding movements and to govern conduct. If a person were restricted to one idea his action could be predicted, for he would have no alternative except to carry out a single thought. Where there is a variety of ideas or suggestions in a given period of time a selection has to be made, as not all can be carried out. The hypnotist controls the behavior of his subject by limiting the latter's field of ideas. Restricted to a single idea, such as that of crowing like a rooster, the subject proceeds to crow; he cannot do otherwise if his mind has only the idea of crowing.

The essential fact to note is that all behavior that is consciously directed is in response to images and ideas. If the idea of murder never entered any person's mind, homicide would cease. If no one thought war, the occupation of the warrior would be gone. The actual selection of ideas determines civilization and governs the individual.

Differences appear in the susceptibility of persons to suggestion, some responding quickly and readily, while others show greater resistance and seem relatively immune. This difference in resistance is correlated with the number and strength of inhibitory ideas, many of which have originated in painful experience. The child is highly suggestible because he has fewer ideas derived from experience to hold against the fresh suggestions. A person whose memory is meager or enfeebled as in sickness is rendered more suggestible, as his remembered stock of opposing ideas is less than normal. But all people no matter how virile and mature are suggestible. One can no more resist the bombardment of suggestions from the press, from history, and from social contact than he can resist the influence of the weather upon his skin. The greatest men of the past have been strangely like the men of their time in most of their ideas and in general outlook; if more advanced in some particulars they have been of the mass in others. The pressure of suggestion is like the pressure of atmosphere, resistless even if not recognized. Li Hung Chang, Chinese viceroy, acclaimed one of the greatest men of his generation, showed in his outlook on life but slight divergence from the prevailing set of ideas of his day and land.

A distinction may be made between positive and negative suggestion. If a person is told not to do a thing, he is given a suggestion of doing it coupled with the suggestion not to do it. In practice the constructive suggestion is better than the negative caution. It is better to say, "Sit up straight," than to say, "Do not sit bent over." The latter form presents the idea of sitting bent over; one has an image of this position, and the negative may not neutralize the improper image. So with the "movie" that shows a burglary of a railroad station, with the burglar ultimately captured and brought to justice; that the burglar is caught may not wholly neutralize the impression left by showing the commission of the crime. Depraved suggestions may be imparted under the guise of moral lessons. Safety lies in the avoidance of the expression of ideas associated with things society does not want done. It is doubtful if preaching against war on the ground of its idiocy and horror would be nearly so effective as saying nothing about war and putting emphasis upon constructive and antithetical measures of civilization.

The early Romans used biography as a source of suggestion. The Roman culture was brought down for centuries by instruction based upon the careers of former statesmen and leaders. Biography is a prolific source of ideals—and its use is capable of forming one generation very much like preceding ones. Literature and history are effective vehicles of suggestion. If literature and history are presented with scientific impartiality and fullness, bad examples as well as the good are brought to attention. Perhaps the scientific historian would oppose obliviscence for masses of historical material, informing, say, regarding the Roman arena, the exposure of infants, and human slavery; but one cannot be enthusiastic over parading suggestions which, carried into action, would plunge us back into barbarism and savagery. At any rate it is a fair inference that there is need of cultivating resistance to suggestion, and, in the case of the young, of noting closely what their reactions actually are to questionable types of culture materials.

It is not possible to know in advance what suggestions will prevail; an example may be imitated or it may provoke defiance. A suggestion that falls in with tendencies is of course much more likely to be acted out than one that goes against desires. In his essay on Liberty, John Stuart Mill maintained that the appearance of drunken men on the streets had a good moral effect as an object lesson for sobriety. There is such a thing as getting wholesome lessons from unworthy examples, but the risk is great. The reaction against the bad example may be violent at first but change later. Given examples of inebriety, the young man might come to regard getting drunk as quite the proper thing, no matter how repulsive the original example appeared. The strange practices of foreign peoples at first strike one as being beyond the possibility of imitation; but no one can be sure that in a given social environment he would not at last quite fully assimilate what at first seemed repulsive and immoral. [...]

The application of the law of suggestion in health and sickness is noteworthy. One can be made to feel ill by suggestion, and he can be made to feel well by suggestion. It would be attempting too much to expect that suggestion would make a man with a broken leg feel comfortable and whole, but within limits ideas have wonderful power over physical conditions. Patients accustomed to injections of morphine to allay pain are sometimes given without detection a "shot of water" instead. Physicians who have little faith in drugs have found it impossible to practice medicine successfully without some show of medicine bottles, powders, and pills; they lose practice if not sufficiently recognizing the appeal to the imagination of a display of curative agents. Cripples have been known to throw away their crutches under the powerful suggestive influence of sacred shrines and relics. The cheering presence of a well-fed and optimistic physician is often worth more than any medicines he prescribes. But tell a sick person how ill he looks, or advocate the advantages of a sandy soil for burial and the tables are turned.

Of course it will not do to blink facts and deny that evils exist. The emotional response, however, may be directed toward cheerfulness and courage. It is sometimes difficult to decide how far to go in recognizing and denouncing evils, as for example, graft exposures. Take the case of an official who, making purchases for the government, pays a top price for materials and secures an unlawful rebate by dealing with a certain company. Does the description of such a practice tend to honesty or dishonesty? In dealing with matters of this type care needs to be given to the emotional response. The offense would need to be dissected and its bearings shown.

The idea that dishonesty is smart would need to be checked by fuller considerations. It is a matter of practical judgment as to how far to go in publicity in dealing with matters of this sort. A good deal of the discretion required for getting along in society without undue friction consists of a practical recognition of suggestion, lest a casual comment arouse undesired associations. Some imagination is required to say the thing that does not give, even indirectly, an undesired suggestion.

Attitude, dress and manner give suggestions. A cringing attitude invites censure; a confident manner carries with it the idea of success and efficiency. It is often difficult to know when to apologize and how much to apologize. Abject apology may suggest to the injured party that his injury was greater than it was. More than one person has got himself into a tangle by attempting explanations of small matters that might better have been disregarded. The advantage of saying nothing, when that is the best thing to do, appeals to one whenever he notes an example of an unexpectedly perverse association of ideas.

The individual is one person when alone and another when in the presence of others. Let anyone turn his mind inward upon itself, and he will discover how changed he becomes by joining with others. Here is a man who in solitude reaches certain conclusions which he confidently expects to urge at a public meeting. He strides zealously to the forum with his convictions bristling. The murmur of the crowd reaches his ear, whereupon he hastily reviews his program of utterance and smooths out a few wrinkles. He joins his fellows and experiences a psychological influence from the antagonistic unanimity of the crowd. His individuality of conviction suffers a strange and sudden shrinkage in the face of massed difference. His ideas, which stood distinct, authentic, and reputable, in solitude, now encounter all the countervailing ideas that an assembly may represent. The invader may now hold to his convictions and declare his faith in the single tax, but he is under strain. His feelings are not what they were in his study, and his utterance will show dips and evasions and placating phrase. The influence of the many is to strip the individual of individuality and assimilate him into the group. The spell of the crowd may be resisted, but there is no man living who does not become a different person in quality of consciousness when in a group.

There is the compulsion to win the favor of the group. Deep in instinctive inheritance is the need to stand in favor with one's fellows, lest they turn and rend. Man is gregarious and always has been one of the herd—he dreads to be homed out of it and left to batten on the moor. True, he may flout one group, having his eye on some other group for its approval. But every man is playing to a gallery and cannot live without applause.

Spurred by group admiration, the individual will dare what would terrify him when alone. Men in crowds will face dangers and undergo discomforts that as individuals they would flee. Under the stimulus of others' eyes men choose physical hazard as the lesser of two evils, for most men would prefer to risk being killed than to live under scorn. Bathers who would not dream of going into cold water unsupported by mob psychology will affect a fine abandon when of a party of campers. The crowd acts as an anesthetic. The highest type of courage is that of flouting crowd force and opinion. So-called physical courage is as nothing compared with the courage of holding to individual conviction and conduct, with the crowd antagonistic. The crowd is the coward's refuge; the man who is brave only with the pack is the fundamental coward.

Representing a relatively primitive level of mentality and emotion, the crowd supplies ideal conditions for conflagrations of suggestion. Ideas run through compact groups with facility. Such quickness of response and unity of reaction were no doubt conditions for survival in prehistoric ages. A strangely instantaneous unity of movement may be witnessed in the flight of flocks of birds, a flock turning, rising and alighting as if the different members were held together by invisible wires. Something like this instinctive harmony and dominating oneness attaches to man in the mass, with slaughtering effect upon individuality.

Add to the primitive abasement of mob psychology the possible accompaniments of bad air, physical contact, inclosure, fatigue, hunger, and hypnotizing oneness of stimulus, as the silver tongued, the band, the spectacle—and it becomes a miracle that the tribe has been saved from itself. Happily radio promises to make the building of large auditoriums less likely, and the extension of the ballot to nominations should reduce the number of occasions for crowd orgy in political assemblages.

Something approaching conditions of crowd psychology is implied in the extension of modern means of communicating ideas; but there is the saving factor of interval. Nothing abates crowd psychology so much as a day for deliberation. With time the bowed branches and withered leaves of personal intelligence revive. Anything that makes for delay between suggestion and reaction is therefore a means of grace; time means time to think. Inhibitory ideas come with the dawn; herrings swim across the waters in the meantime. We can be civilized by acting from suggestion, but only from such as the best intelligence certifies.

Conditions that discourage the unanimity of mob mind are auspicious; the opposition of leaders and a diversity of group ideals contribute to the ultimate welfare through affording range for variations of opinion. Free thought came into the world in the gap between the two great branches of the church, a gap which widened into scientific development. Opportunity for social development appears in conflicts of prestige and denials of jurisdiction. It is a happy augury when complaints are heard touching the uncertainties of fashion. That one city rivals another in ultimate authority over what is correct to wear is an advantage. Happy day, when standards are "up in the air"—when no one knows what real poetry is, nor any one knows the ultimate ideals in education, or the true position of women. Inability to know one's place is not without a certain kind of promise; it has the merit at least of preserving us from blasting finality. When there is no one to tell us exactly what to think, we are perforce compelled to think for ourselves. Convinced of the electrical equality of suggestion, its potency to make behavior and to form institutions, one is impelled toward censorship. But no censorship can prevent partial disclosure, and the surreptitious has strange power to charm. Not in censorship by legal methods can suggestion best be governed for social welfare. The free sifting of ideas, free speech and yet more freedom of speech, free discussion and yet more—these are the means of social safety, just as freedom without stint or limit has been the indispensable condition for the development of science. The scientist is only too ready to disavow a false hypothesis. Yet in the search for economic and social knowledge there is less confidence that the stream will run clear. An error in social theory is as sure of detection and disavowal as a scientific error. The major technic of science can wisely be imitated for social progress. Society can profitably use a larger supply of constructive and rational suggestions and socially salutary ideas. The best way to dispose of a perverse suggestion is to oppose to it a better one, and keep up the process until the people are competent judges of ideas.

CHAPTER TWENTY-FIVE

"Control of Propaganda as a Psychological Problem" (1922)

Edward Kellog Strong, Jr.

Scientific Monthly *14, no. 3: pp. 234–52..*

EDITOR'S INTRODUCTION

A similar piece, again authored by an academic but aimed at a popular audience, was published in *Scientific Monthly* in 1922 by Edward Strong, Jr. (1884–1963), a well-regarded professor of applied psychology at Stanford University. Strong had an undergraduate and master's degree from the University of California and took his PhD in psychology at Columbia University (1911). He worked initially in an advertising firm and during World War I in the Army's office of personnel, before settling in at Stanford in 1923.

He was, therefore, well placed to review the "problem" of propaganda, especially as it reached its crescendo of public distress in the interwar years. In the following piece, Strong addresses the myriad ways in which propaganda was used in the war, for good purposes and bad, and looks at the continuing efforts to sway opinion in politics and commerce, where he also makes some effort to distinguish advertising from political messaging.

He explains to his readers that the psychological process whereby attitudes and sentiments can be molded is "suggestion," the "non-rational influencing of others," and he describes various categories, emphasizing the importance of emotion and motivation in the process.

Like Weeks, his aim is to submit proposals to offset or control propaganda, and he suggests that government regulation, counter-propaganda via pro-social publicity campaigns, and education could be useful in this regard. Unlike Weeks, however, he finds that each has its limits, and in the end, he concedes defeat, or at least discouragement. "Society today," he concludes, "has no way to handle it."—*P.P.*

"Control of Propaganda as a Psychological Problem" (1922)

An interesting phenomenon of the last few years has been the unanimity with which millions of men and women have conformed in their thinking and in their actions to what certain leaders wanted. Vast sums of money have been raised for liberty and victory loans, for the Red Cross and for many other agencies. Citizens of the United States consented to universal conscription, cut down their daily use of sugar, closed down their factories on certain days, and went without gasoline for their autos voluntarily and enthusiastically. To an extraordinary degree men and women in nearly all the countries of the world have cooperated in carrying out programs necessitating radical changes in their everyday life; and they have done so not because they were ordered to do so, and so were forced to it, but because they freely responded to suggestions presented in skillfully conducted propaganda.

Because of the surprising success of all this propaganda, the innumerable times it has been employed and the ease with which it has been carried out, people generally have become conscious of propaganda as a great tool or method for influencing others. Propaganda has, of course, existed for ages. But it has not been comprehended so clearly by the mass of people as it is to-day. And certainly it has never before been employed on such great numbers of men and women. To-day it is a clearly recognized method of social control.

If propaganda were a means of influencing others along lines only of benefit to society, it could be hailed with great acclaim. But unfortunately it can also be employed for dishonest and socially vicious programs, just as well as for honest and worthwhile movements. At the present time the advertising of patent medicines that cannot possibly cure, and of stock in companies formed for no other purpose than to defraud the public, appears in altogether too many of our publications. Federal authorities estimated that in five years, 1910–15, the 2,861 swindlers that were arrested had defrauded the public of $351,000,000, averaging a dishonest gain of $123,000. All authorities are agreed that such swindling increased very greatly during the war, and possibly reached its climax sometime after the armistice. If so, it is now on the decline. Let us hope so! [...]

The question naturally arises, is there no way of controlling propaganda? Certainly there are ways and they are enforced more or less in the case of certain types of propaganda. But there are other types which are not so easily evaluated and consequently not so easily handled.

A perusal of literature on this subject gives one the impression that very few to-day are sincerely interested in the matter, except those apparently who desire to control or eliminate propaganda directed at their own. It is still viewed as highly ethical for us to sort and reject and trim in the name of our own view of truth, justice, democracy and loyalty to our group. But it is anti-social for the other fellow to do so. If we are Republicans we want the editor of our newspaper to give us good Republican views and to damn the Democrats. If we are Democrats, we want the reverse. We really want "facts" that support our views. It is too uncomfortable to be confronted with many counter "facts."

Naturally as a psychologist, I view this matter as an interesting psychological problem. It is my purpose in this place to discuss certain psychological aspects of the subject and to point out some of the ways in which propaganda may be controlled. It is also my purpose to call attention to certain types of propaganda which at present I see no way of controlling, in the hope that others may become interested in the subject and labor to work out some adequate methods.

First of all let us clarify the use of certain terms which are employed in discussing the subject and at the same time come to an understanding of the psychological elements which are involved.

The word "propaganda" means essentially the spread of a particular doctrine or a system of principles, especially when there is an organization or general plan back of the movement. Propaganda differs from "education" with which it is purposely confused, in that in the case of the former the aim is to spread one doctrine, whereas in the case of the latter the aim is to extend a knowledge of the facts as far as known. Advertising men have never been able to agree on a definition of "advertising" and I should not want to attempt here what they have failed to do. But I think we can distinguish between advertising and propaganda by saying that advertising is usually concerned with making known and desirable a definite commodity or service with the definite aim of leading many individuals, as such, to acquire the commodity or service. Propaganda includes many types of advertising, but it is mainly concerned with the subtle presentation to the public of information so chosen and so focused that among many individuals there develops a general "point of view" which is favorable to the aim of the propagandist and leads to action in that general direction. A further distinction between these two methods of influencing people pertains to the *methods* employed rather than the *object*. The advertiser buys space upon which appears his message, and the reader knows it a paid advertisement. The propagandist may advertise, but he especially aims to employ space he did not buy, at least directly, and not to permit the reader to know that the material is propaganda. He believes his material will have greater effect when its source is unknown.

It is clear that both advertising and propaganda make use of argument and suggestion. And much has been written and said as to these two methods of influencing others. We have no quarrel in this paper with argumentative or "reason-why" appeals to the public. But we are very much concerned with appeals involving suggestion.

The term "suggestion" has been employed in a great variety of ways, sometimes in a narrow sense, but usually in a rather broad and indefinite way. Frequently it is used to cover all the means of imparting information and exerting influence other than through reasoning. Without going into the subject here, let us recognize three phases of non-rational influencing of others. In the simplest form one or more ideas are presented which are known to be associated in the minds of the audience with another idea not mentioned. The audience thinks the non-mentioned idea because of their established habits of thought. In this way a speaker may denounce most viciously and unfairly a prominent man without giving his name, by skillfully referring to one or more of his known characteristics. The desired effect is accomplished and without making it possible for the prominent man to reply. Then there is the more complicated phase of suggestion where an *action* is brought into the mind of the audience—the action being a familiar one and also one that will be desired as soon as mentioned. Thus a school boy at recess says, "Let's get a drink." The other boys might not have gotten a drink if they had not been reminded of the action. But as soon as it is called to mind, they feel the desire and so go. So also a nation like Germany, all primed for war, as in 1914—I don't refer here to her military preparations, but to the state of mind of her citizens—was ready to act immediately when her leaders said "Let's fight." It was the absence of just such a mental state in the United States that kept us out of war. Later on the attitude was developed—almost over-developed before it had a chance to function—and we were eager to act when the word was given.

In both these phases of suggestion the effect is produced because there exists within the mind of the person being influenced certain habits of thinking and action and when the proper stimulus or cue is given the associated thinking and acting immediately follow. There is still a third phase of suggestion, which I prefer to call motivation, in which a person is led to do something which is unfamiliar or which he would not do if it were merely mentioned. It is because of this third method of influencing others that the control of propaganda is so difficult. [...]

Motivation involves two elements—first, the arousal of a strong desire, and, second, the presentation of a certain action which appears to be a satisfactory way of expressing the aroused desire. Moreover the action in such cases is not one that the individual would perform if it were merely suggested.

The question has often been discussed: Could the United States have declared war in 1914? I think there is no doubt that there was insufficient war sentiment at that time to have permitted mere suggestions from the President to be effective. But I think there is also equally no doubt that proper propaganda would have motivated the country into war. The years 1914 to 1917 may be looked upon as a period in which such sentiment developed and was finally put into action in a calmer and far less emotional manner than usually prevails at such a time.

Recent work in psychology has emphasized the distinction between an "idea" and a "sentiment." The sentiment, according to Rivers, is an idea emotionally toned. "House" is thus an idea, whereas "home" is a sentiment, for home always includes an emotional consciousness of mother and father, brothers and sisters, old familiar associations and the like. When the sentiment becomes suppressed and lost to consciousness it is called a "complex." Sentiments and complexes, we are coming to see more and more are extremely important in explaining behavior; much of abnormal conduct being traceable to the existence of complexes.

Motivation is thus the process of deliberately developing a sentiment, of deliberately associating an idea with an emotion, of tying together in the mind of another the love for wife and the idea of buying a vacuum cleaner, or of sympathy for the Belgians and hatred of the Germans, and the idea of war.

The aim of propaganda is to develop sentiment and then precipitate action through mere suggestion. Let us consider some implications which are involved in all this.

First of all let us note that theoretically any emotional element can be associated with any specific line of action. Practically, certain combinations are difficult to accomplish, but theoretically they are possible. Thus, the correspondence school arouses the boy's love for his mother and challenges him to make her proud of him and "funnels" the aroused emotional desire into taking a correspondence course. The same appeal could be utilized to get young men to go to church, to quit gambling, to work harder for their employer, to enlist when war is declared, to do anything the boy could be made to believe his mother would approve of. [...]

Propaganda depends upon this psychological process of motivation for its success. And motivation, as we have seen, is the deliberate process of arousing one's emotions and desires and then suggesting a line of action by which these desires may be expressed. And we have seen further that any emotional element can be associated with any specific action; and that when one is well motivated he ignores intellectual considerations touching upon the honesty of the statements or the efficacy of the program.

So much for our analysis of motivation—the principal psychological process in propaganda. Now let us consider how propaganda may be controlled by society so that dishonest and pernicious campaigns may be prevented without interference to worthwhile propaganda.

The most convenient method of considering the many angles of the subject will be through discussing propaganda in terms of the following three aspects: First, propaganda considered with regard to the truth or falsity of the statements in which it is presented; second, with regard to the action suggested as the means of satisfying the aroused desire; and third, with regard to the emotional element, the desire that is aroused. The matter of control can accordingly be discussed in terms of these three questions: First, how far can propaganda be controlled in terms of the validity of the statements which are made? Second, to what extent can propaganda be controlled in terms of the action which is proposed? And third, to what extent can propaganda be controlled in terms of the emotional elements that are involved?

First of all, then, how far can propaganda be controlled in terms of the validity of the statements which are made?

Society has long dealt with false statements and already has postal regulations, laws against slander, libel and the like. To protect politicians the English law provides a fine not to exceed £100 if the name and address of the printer and publisher is omitted from a poster relating to the candidature of any person for Parliament and other offices. The Association of Advertising Clubs of the World carries on a steady campaign against dishonest advertising and has accomplished a great deal of good against this type of propaganda. At this time, thirty-six states have passed the Printers' Ink Statute or a modification of it, thereby facilitating convictions in such cases. And the Association of Advertising Clubs of the World is spending money and effort in enforcing it. Control of propaganda publicly making dishonest statements can clearly be taken care of.

But unfortunately many undesirable propaganda will not fall under the class of propaganda publicly making dishonest statements. One very undesirable sort is spread by word of mouth. No one knows from when it comes, and exactly what is back of it. We had many stories thus circulated against the Germans during the war, and we have the same sort of thing carried on against prominent men almost all the time. Stories of Roosevelt's excessive drinking were thus circulated. And it was not until they were publicly expressed that he had an opportunity of disposing of them through law suit. Such word of mouth propaganda is fostered in times of emotional stress and particularly wherever people believe they are not being told all the facts. The best possible cure for it is publicity of the sort that makes people *believe* they are getting all sides to the question.

But in addition to this sneaking underhand propaganda there are all sorts of campaigns which are very undesirable, but which adhere technically to the truth. They cannot accordingly be prosecuted for dishonesty. Some of them, however, give false impressions just the same. This is so because the human brain does not necessarily think in a logical manner. [...]

To require that propaganda contain truths and not falsehoods is a desirable regulation, but it will not stop undesirable campaigns.

Let us consider second to what extent propaganda can be controlled in terms of the action which is proposed.

If the proposed action is that of buying, it is not difficult to evaluate the propaganda, or advertising as it would usually be in this case, upon the grounds that the individual did or did not get value received. But if the proposed action is that of giving money for some cause or charity, justification upon such grounds is far more difficult. If a woman, very fond of cats, wants to endow a hospital for them, run by thoroughly incompetent people whom she likes, isn't that sufficient to justify her action and the propaganda, as far as she is concerned? It is hard to attack such action in terms of the rights of individuals, but it is being more and more attacked upon the grounds of social welfare. Businessmen through their Chambers of Commerce in sheer defense are increasingly investigating such propositions and, in many places, list the charities that they will countenance. Out of the war has come the Community Chest movement whereby all social agencies in a district make up their budgets in advance and after they have been gone over by both disinterested and interested parties, a single united effort is made to raise the total amount in one campaign for the year. Such plans help the worthy cause and interfere with the unworthy one. But they do not eliminate the unworthy campaigns.

The establishment of bureaus, whose business it is to investigate all organizations asking for funds—organizations like the National Information Bureau—renders it easier to determine whether any organization is desirable or not. Can society go farther here? Can society not only positively help the worthy cause, but put the unworthy, inefficient or unnecessarily duplicating agency out of business? There is no question but that many individuals are being fooled every year and much money squandered through such non-worthwhile causes. But at the same time, we must remember that most new uplift movements have encountered great opposition at the start, and to increase this opposition still more through the establishment of legal regulations may do society in the long run more harm than good.

In addition to campaigns to sell a commodity or service or to obtain gifts, there are other campaigns devoted to accomplishing specific actions of a sort much more difficult to estimate fairly. Political campaigns aim to secure votes for certain men; propaganda appears from time to time to influence citizens to vote for or against certain measures; propaganda appeared in many forms a short time ago, appealing to citizens of the United States to intervene in Mexico; lobbies are familiar accompaniments to our legislatures, each one aiming to accomplish a specific program; unions appeal to public opinion to aid them in winning a strike and companies appeal to the same public to help them prevent or break the strike, etc. We are so accustomed to our political machinery that we do not often stop and ask ourselves whether it is geared up so as to serve society in the best way. Only when some enthusiastic social uplifter boasts that she and four others alone put a measure through a state legislature by the use of skillful lobbying, or a secretary of a business man's organization calmly announces months in advance that Congress will do away with a bureau because his organization is demanding such action, and his prophecy comes true, does one wonder whether some sort of control of propaganda would not be worthwhile even here. And one waxes quite indignant, as did a former Secretary of War, when he comes to realize that much of the propaganda for bringing back the bodies of our dead soldiers was instigated by the journal of the undertakers and casket makers.

To control such propaganda we must have facts and we must have a body to review the facts. This we do not have in many cases. A political campaign on a clean-cut issue is supposed to be a trial as to the merits of the two sides before all the citizens who through their votes decide the issue. This is the theory of democracy. It works pretty well in many cases, surprisingly well in some. But in most campaigns the issue is not clean-cut and in nearly all campaigns the political strategist endeavors to confuse the issue, so that many a time a citizen votes against what he really wants. And then there are many measures coming up in our fearfully complex life of to-day upon which the average man is not at all competent to pass judgment. Except in a few instances, society has not yet organized itself so as properly to handle such matters. In the case of struggles between capital and labor, we are steadily advancing toward the insistence upon both sides that they shall present the facts as they see them and also toward the establishment of tribunals which shall weigh all the facts and decide the issue. The impartial chairmanship program maintained by the clothing industry in Chicago and other cities has worked very satisfactorily and seems to be the ideal machinery for controlling propaganda in that field. Its greatest merit lies, it seems to me, in the fact that complaints are studied and evaluated very shortly after they arise, thus eliminating the getting under headway of extensive propaganda with all the arousal of emotions that propaganda assures. [...]

So far we have considered the possibilities of controlling propaganda from the two aspects: first, as to whether the statements in it were true or false; and second, as to whether the proposed action was socially worth while or not. This discussion has seemingly emphasized the necessity of taking motives into account. Now let us consider the third aspect of the subject—the element of aroused desire, the emotional background and psychologically true cause of the action.

We have seen that theoretically any emotion may be aroused as the basis for stirring one to act and that there needs be little or no rational connection between the two. The detailed suffering of a little girl and her kitten can motivate our hatred against the Germans, arouse our sympathy for the Armenians, make us enthusiastic for the Red Cross, or lead us to give money for support of a home for cats. The story may be true or concocted for the purpose; the inferences against the Germans or for the home for cats may be also true or false; the organization carrying on the propaganda may be efficiently administered or not—all these considerations little concern us. We feel the emotion, we want to do something because by acting we will feel better, and away we go regardless of mere intellectual considerations.

Here is the real psychological problem concerning propaganda. Take away the emotional element and society need have no fear of propaganda. For man is always very slow to act in terms of ideas alone. Witness his indifference when he really knows the political organization in control of his municipality is flagrantly dishonest. He does nothing until his emotions are aroused by a whirlwind speaker, or by personal injury. So long as a radical writes or speaks in a philosophical manner society can rightly be indifferent. But when he discards the intellectual aspects of his views, seizes upon some slogan and fills his writings or speeches with concrete tales of human suffering and the arrogance of the rich, society rightly becomes alarmed. For now the radical is setting fire to dynamite and neither he nor any one else can tell what may result.

At the present time the prospects do not appear over bright of controlling propaganda through regulation. There is, however, a method of weakening its influence, and that is by fighting one propaganda by another, or by general publicity. The trouble, however, with fighting bad propaganda by good propaganda, aside from the very practical consideration that the former is usually better equipped financially, is that seldom is the public supplied with facts upon which a real conclusion can be thought out. Instead it is inflamed to take sides and a deadlock results, or the matter is settled by some sort of resort to force. Just in this way arose the turmoil about the League of Nations program. Instead of thinking it through and arriving rationally at a real conclusion, Wilsonites and anti-Wilsonites became emotionally aroused and it was voted down because the latter group had the greater force measured in votes. Both sides know the real issue is not dead, and the Republicans who defeated Wilson's program are now attempting at Washington to find the conclusions we should have reached months ago. Fighting propaganda with propaganda is not likely, then, to give us satisfactory results.

Can propaganda be controlled through publicity? Yes, if we had perfect publicity. But that, apparently, we cannot have. Hence, we can only hope to have partial control by this means. It has been suggested that propaganda could be controlled by national control of all publicity. Would such regulated and censored publicity help here? [...]

Possibly publicity is the one best cure we have today for handling those forms of propaganda which are not readily controlled by other means. But if this is the case it means that more of our newspapers and magazines will have to convince the public that what they print is not controlled by certain interests. At the present time I should judge that great numbers of citizens believe most newspapers, if not their own, distort the facts to fit their purposes. And again, if publicity is to cure the evils of propaganda, it means that society must work out some more satisfactory method than now exists of providing the groups of poor people with adequate publicity to offset the enormous advantage that groups composed of wealthy people have in commanding the printed page. Too few newspapers print to-day, and too few can ever afford to print, the detailed testimony in a labor controversy, yet unless the laboring man feels his side is presented, he will have supplied to him and will read wild denunciations of capital instead of the sworn testimony of his leaders as given before a board of arbitration.

Another means of controlling propaganda lies in educating the public to an understanding of the methods employed in propaganda. It is thought that man likes to feel he is being appealed to on logical grounds: that he resents being "soft-soaped." And that he does not want to be "worked" or to have something "put over on him." Possibly, it is contended, articles such as have appeared recently in our magazines recounting the methods by which propagandists have fooled men and women may educate the public to see through a publicity campaign. Personally, I do not believe that very much can be accomplished in this way, for, as Barnum claimed, the public likes to be fooled; and secondly, clever appeals to the emotions will nearly always win when pitted against intellectually held convictions.

In closing, I want to emphasize one point. It is possible today for a group to carry on a very subtle propaganda with the immediate aim of developing some sentiment. There is no machinery to stop them, whether the sentiment is socially good or bad. For sentiment is an emotional state of mind and as long as no action results, society today has no way to handle it.

CHAPTER TWENTY-SIX

"The Theory of Political Propaganda" (1927)

Harold D. Lasswell

American Political Science Review *21, no. 3: pp. 627–31 [with elisions].*

EDITOR'S INTRODUCTION

While research and commentary on propaganda was voluminous in this period, one of the few works still remembered by contemporary media scholars (for some, perhaps, the *only* work) was by Harold Lasswell (1902–1978). Lasswell's undergraduate (1922) and doctoral (1926) degrees were from the University of Chicago; he spent most of his academic career on the faculties of the University of Chicago and, after World War II, Yale University.

Lasswell was an historic figure in media studies and in political science. According to one biographer, he "ranked among the half dozen creative innovators in the social sciences in the twentieth century" (Almond 1987). Schramm, as noted earlier, rather famously anointed him one of the four "founding fathers" of mass communications research, along with Hovland, Lazarsfeld, and Lewin. His contributions to the field included the "Who (says) What (to) Whom (in) What Channel (with) What Effect" functional model of analysis, the advancement of the content analytical method, and his early work on propaganda.

While some described his 1927 *Propaganda Technique in the World War* as the origin of the "magic bullet" model (Lubken 2008), Lasswell, in fact, characterized propaganda in that classic text as the "direct use of suggestion," noting that "propaganda is concerned with the management of opinions and attitudes by the direct manipulation of social suggestion" (9).

Propaganda, like the above entries, was a work designed both for academics and for the general public. In a companion article in the *American Political Science Review*, reprinted below, Lasswell goes into greater theoretical detail, for the academic community, on the psychological mechanisms of opinion change. He describes the process from various perspectives, including behavioristic stimulus-response, cultural, and suggestion theory. Here he stipulates a pronounced difference in his definition of suggestion compared with that typically used by social psychologists. "Suggestion," he states, "is not used as it is in individual psychology to mean the acceptance of an idea without reflection; it refers to cultural material with a recognizable meaning."

His preferred approach throughout is cultural and psychoanalytic (influenced by Freud). "Propaganda is the management of collective attitudes by the manipulation of significant symbols," he explains. He adopts the concept of "collective attitudes" from anthropology to distinguish social beliefs and opinions from the metaphysical forms of French crowd theory, and he describes in detail the myriad ways in which propagandists representing all types of public and private organizations harness the mass media for the practical manipulation of attitudes.

His piece is more analytical than prescriptive, although later in his career Lasswell advocated the application of social science to the improvement of democratic processes.—*P.P.*

References

Almond, Gabriel. 1987. "Harold Dwight Lasswell." In *Biographical Memoirs*: Volume 57, edited by the National Academy of Sciences, 249–76. Washington, DC: National Academies Press.

Lubken, Deborah. 2008. "Remembering the Straw Man: The Travels and Adventures of Hypodermic." In *The History of Media and Communication Research*, edited by David W. Park and Jefferson Pooley, 19–42. New York: Peter Lang.

"The Theory of Political Propaganda" (1927)

Propaganda is the management of collective attitudes by the manipulation of significant symbols. The word attitude is taken to mean a tendency to act according to certain patterns of valuation. The existence of an attitude is not a direct datum of experience, but an inference from signs which have a conventionalized significance. We say that the voters of a certain ward resent a negro candidate, and in so doing we have compactly summarized the tendency of a particular group to act toward a particular object in a specific context. The valuational patterns upon which this inference is founded may be primitive gestures of the face and body, or more sophisticated gestures of the pen and voice. Taken together, these objects which have a standard meaning in a group are called significant symbols. The elevated eyebrow, the clenched fist, the sharp voice, the pungent phrase, have their references established within the web of a particular culture. Such significant symbols are paraphernalia employed in expressing the attitudes, and they are also capable of being employed to reaffirm or redefine attitudes. Thus, significant symbols have both an expressive and a propagandist function in public life.

The idea of a "collective attitude" is not that of a super-organic, extra-natural entity. Collective phenomena have too often been treated as if they were on a plane apart from individual action. Confusion has arisen principally because students have been slow to invent a word able to bear the connotation of uniformity without also implying a biological or metaphysical unity. The anthropologists have introduced the notion of a pattern to designate the standard uniformities of conduct at a given time and place, and this is the sense of the word here intended. Thus the collective attitude, as a pattern, is a distribution of individual acts and not an indwelling spirit which has achieved transitory realization in the rough, coarse facts of the world of sense.

Collective attitudes are amenable to many modes of alteration. They may be shattered before an onslaught of violent intimidation or disintegrated by economic coercion. They may be reaffirmed in the muscular regimentation of drill. But their arrangement and rearrangement occurs principally under the impetus of significant symbols; and the technique of using significant symbols for this purpose is propaganda.

Propaganda as a word is closely allied in popular and technical usage with certain others. It must be distinguished from education. We need a name for the processes by which techniques are inculcated—techniques of spelling, letter-forming, adding, piano-playing, and lathe-handling. If this be education, we are free to apply the term propaganda to the creation of valuational dispositions or attitudes.

The deliberative attitude is capable of being separated from the propagandist attitude. Deliberation implies the search for the solution of a besetting problem with no desire to prejudice a particular solution in advance. The propagandist is very much concerned about how a specific solution is to be evoked and "put over." And though the most subtle propaganda closely resembles disinterested deliberation, there is no difficulty in distinguishing the extremes.

What is the relation between propaganda and the changing of opinions through psychiatric interviews? Such an interview is an intensive approach to the individual by means of which the interviewer gains access to the individual's private stock of meanings and becomes capable of exploiting them rather than the standard meanings of the groups of which the individual is a member. The intimate, continuing relationship which is set up under quasi-clinical conditions is quite beyond the reach of the propagandist, who must restrict himself to dealing with the individual as a standard member of some groups or sub-groups which he differentiates upon the basis of extrinsic evidence. [1]

Propagandas may be classified upon the basis of many possible criteria. Some are carried on by organizations like the Anti-Cigarette League which have a definite and restricted objective; others are conducted by organizations, like most civic associations, which have a rather general and diffused purpose. This objective may be revolutionary or counter-revolutionary, reformist or counter-reformist, depending upon whether or not a sweeping institutional change is involved. Propaganda may be carried on by organizations which rely almost exclusively upon it or which use it as an auxiliary implement among several means of social control. Some propagandas are essentially temporary, like the boosters' club for a favorite son, or comparatively permanent. Some propagandas are intra-group, in the sense that they exist to consolidate an existing attitude and not, like the extra-group propagandas, to assume the additional burden of proselyting. There are propagandas which are manned by those who hope to reap direct, tangible, and substantial gains from them; others are staffed by those who are content with a remote, intangible, and rather imprecise advantage to themselves. Some are run by men who make it their life work, and others are handled by amateurs. Some depend upon a central or skeleton staff and others rely

---

[1] Advertising is paid publicity and may or may not be employed in propaganda.

upon widespread and catholic associations. One propaganda group may flourish in secret and another may invite publicity.

Besides all these conceivable and often valuable distinctions, propagandas may be conveniently divided according to the object toward which it is proposed to modify or crystallize an attitude. Some propagandas exist to organize an attitude toward a person, like Mr. Coolidge or Mr. Smith; others to organize an attitude toward a group, like the Japanese or the workers; others to organize an attitude toward a policy or institution, like free trade or parliamentary government; and still others to organize an attitude toward a mode of personal participation, like buying war bonds or joining the marines. No propaganda fits tightly into its category of major emphasis, and it must be remembered that pigeon-holes are invented to serve convenience and not to satisfy yearnings for the immortal and the immutable.

If we state the strategy of propaganda in cultural terms, we may say that it involves the presentation of an object in a culture in such a manner that certain cultural attitudes will be organized toward it. The problem of the propagandist is to intensify the attitudes favorable to his purpose, to reverse the attitudes hostile to it, and to attract the indifferent, or, at the worst, to prevent them from assuming a hostile bent.

Every cultural group has its vested values. These may include the ownership of property or the possession of claims to ceremonial deference. An object toward which it is hoped to arouse hostility must be presented as a menace to as many of these values as possible. There are always ambitious hopes of increasing values, and the object must be made to appear as the stumbling block to their realization. There are patterns of right and wrong, and the object must be made to flout the good. There are standards of propriety, and the object must appear ridiculous and gauche. If the plan is to draw out positive attitudes toward an object, it must be presented, not as a menace and an obstruction, nor as despicable or absurd, but as a protector of our values, a champion of our dreams, and a model of virtue and propriety.

Propaganda objects must be chosen with extreme care. The primary objects are usually quite distinct. Thus war propaganda involves the enemy, the ally, and the neutral. It involves leaders on both sides and the support of certain policies and institutions. It implies the control of attitudes toward various forms of participation—enlistment, bond buying, and strenuous exertion. These, and similar objects, are conspicuously entangled in the context of the total situation, and the propagandist can easily see that he must deal with them. But some are contingently and not primarily implicated. They are important in the sense that unless precautions are taken attention may be inconveniently diverted to them. The accumulating unrest of a nation may be turned by social revolutionaries into an outburst against the government which distracts the hostility of the community from the enemy, and breakdown ensues. War propaganda must therefore include the social revolutionist as an object of hostility, and all propaganda must be conceived with sufficient scope to embrace these contingent objects.

The strategy of propaganda, which has been phrased in cultural terms, can readily be described in the language of stimulus-response. Translated into this vocabulary, which is especially intelligible to some, the propagandist may be said to be concerned with the multiplication of those stimuli which are best calculated to evoke the desired responses, and with the nullification of those stimuli which are likely to instigate the undesired responses. Putting the same thing into terms of social suggestion, the problem of the propagandist is to multiply all the suggestions favorable to the attitudes which he wishes to produce and strengthen, and to restrict all suggestions which are unfavorable to them. In this sense of the word, suggestion is not used as it is in individual psychology to mean the acceptance of an idea without reflection; it refers to cultural material with a recognizable meaning.

Whatever form of words helps to ignite the imagination of the practical manipulator of attitudes is the most valuable one. Terminological difficulties disappear when we turn from the problem of choosing propaganda matter to discuss the specific carriers of propaganda material. The form in which the significant symbols are embodied to reach the public may be spoken, written, pictorial, or musical, and the number of stimulus carriers is infinite. If the propagandist identifies himself imaginatively with the life of his subjects in a particular situation, he is able to explore several channels of approach. Consider, for a moment, the people who ride the street cars. They may be reached by placards posted inside the car, by posters on the billboards along the track, by newspapers which they read, by conversations which they overhear, by leaflets which are openly or surreptitiously slipped into their hands, by street demonstrations at halting places, and no doubt by other means. Of these possible occasions there are no end. People walk along the streets or ride in automobiles, trams, and subways, elevated trains, boats, electrical or steam railways; they congregate in theatres, churches, lecture halls, eating places, athletic parks, concert rooms, barber shops and beauty parlors, coffee-houses and drug stores; people work in offices, warehouses, mills, factories, and conveyances. An inspection of the life patterns of any community reveals the web of mobility routes and congregating centres through which interested fact and opinion may be disseminated.

Propaganda rose to transitory importance in the past whenever a social system based upon the sanctions of antiquity was broken up by a tyrant. The ever-present function of propaganda in modern life is in large measure attributable to the social disorganization which has been precipitated by the rapid advent of technological changes. Impersonality has supplanted personal loyalty to leaders. Literacy and the physical channels of communication have quickened the connection between those who rule and the ruled. Conventions have arisen which favor the ventilation of opinions and the taking of votes. Most of that which formerly could be done by violence and intimidation must now be done by argument and persuasion. Democracy has proclaimed the dictatorship of palaver, and the technique of dictating to the dictator is named propaganda.

CHAPTER TWENTY-SEVEN

The Psychology of Advertising (1913)

Walter Dill Scott

5th ed. Boston: Small, Maynard, pp. 1–6, 80–88 [with elisions].

EDITOR'S INTRODUCTION

A long with political propaganda, commercial propaganda, or advertising, was of great interest to early social scientists and developed its own stream of literature. Of those scholars addressing the issue in the early 1900s, the preeminent figure was Walter Scott (1869–1955). Scott was a man of considerable energy and professional achievement. He earned his BA at Northwestern University in 1891, then traveled to Germany to study under the noted psychologist and philosopher Wilhelm Wundt, receiving his PhD from the University of Leipzig in 1900. He returned to Northwestern and in 1909 was appointed head of its new Department of Psychology. He was elected president of the American Psychological Association in 1919 and the following year named president of Northwestern.

In 1902, Scott published *The Psychology of Advertising in Theory and Practice*, following it in 1908 with his first edition of *The Psychology of Advertising*. He would issue five more editions of the latter text over the following years and, according to one biographer, "dominated the field of advertising psychology until 1910–1911" (Kuna 1976, 348). At the heart of Scott's psychology was the doctrine of suggestion. He recognized and appreciated appeals to reason in advertising but saw greater effectiveness in suggestion. "The actual effect of modern advertising," he declared, "is not so much to convince as to suggest." Scott took his research to the industry, not as a critic, but as an adviser. He founded a consulting firm in 1919, which operated for about four years, and much of his published work was in the form of instruction and guidance for advertising professionals.

"Scott's theory of advertising," said Kuna, "with the law of suggestion as its central tenet was *the* psychology of advertising during the formative era in that subject's history" (353, italics in the original). A flavor of this psychological approach to advertising is captured in the following excerpt from Scott's (1913) fifth edition of *The Psychology of Advertising*. The applied, pro-business character of the writing is apparent from the start: "Advertising has as its one function the influencing of human minds. Unless it does this it is useless and destructive to the firms attempting it." The science of psychology, he then argues, can be most useful in helping achieve positive commercial goals.

He treats the theory of suggestion in detail, although the book comes early in suggestion research and lacks some of the nuance of conditionality common in later writing. Again, practical advice dominates Scott's discussion, and he closes with a note of optimism for his professional audience: "It seems that no form of action can be suggested by an advertisement that does not successfully challenge the reader to do what is proposed."—*P.P.*

References

Kuna, David. 1976. "The Concept of Suggestion in the Early History of Advertising Psychology." *Journal of the History of the Behavioral Sciences* 12, no. 4: 347–53.

The Psychology of Advertising (1913)

I. INTRODUCTION

The typical business man is an optimist. For him the future is full of possibilities that never have been realized in the past. He is not, however, a daydreamer, but one who uses his imagination in formulating purposes which lead to immediate action. His power of execution often surpasses that of his imagination, and he is frequently surprised to see his vision realized in less time than he had even dared to hope.

The advertiser may well be regarded as typical of the class of American business men. At a time when advertisements were poorly constructed and given limited circulation, certain enterprising men saw the possibilities of advertising and began systematically to improve the whole profession of advertising. Artists were employed to construct appropriate illustrations, and skilled typographers vied with each other in setting up the text in the most artistic and legible manner possible. Business system was used in ascertaining the amount of circulation of various publications as well as the kind of circulation. Advertisements were keyed, and other means were employed to discover the exact value of each style of advertisements and of each medium in which advertisements were inserted.

These improvements have been as beneficial as the most sanguine could have hoped for, but in and of themselves they were not sufficient to place advertising upon a scientific basis. Advertising has as its one function the influencing of human minds. Unless it does this it is useless and destructive to the firms attempting it. As it is the human mind that advertising is dealing with, its only scientific basis is psychology, which is simply a systematic study of those same minds which the advertiser is seeking to influence. This fact was seen by wise advertisers and such conceptions began to appear in print and to be heard in conventions of advertising men some ten years ago. Occasionally one who was especially optimistic prophesied that at some time—perhaps in the distant future—advertisers would turn to psychology for guidance. [...]

Although the attitude of the advertising world has changed and even though much has been done to present psychology in a helpful form to the advertisers, the work of the psychologist is not yet available to the business world because the material has not been presented in any one accessible place. Contributions are scattered through the files of a score of American and European publications. Some articles appearing under this head are of minor significance, while others are so important that they should be collected in a place and form such that they would be available to the largest possible number of readers. The psychology of advertising has reached a stage in its development where all that has thus far been accomplished should be reconsidered. The worthless should be discarded and the valuable brought out into due prominence in systematic arrangement. In view of this condition of affairs the author has assumed the pleasing task of systematizing *the* subject of the psychology of advertising and of presenting it in such a form that it will be of distinct practical value to all who are interested in business promotion. [...]

VI. SUGGESTION

The mental process known as "Suggestion" is in bad repute because, in the popular mind, it has too often been associated on the one hand with hypnotism and on the other with indecency and vulgarity. Hypnotism in the hands of the scientist or of the fakir is well known to be a form of suggestion. A story which does not specifically depart from that which conforms to the standards of propriety but which is so constructed that it leads the hearers to conceptions that are "off color" is said to be suggestive. In this way it has come to pass that the whole subject of suggestion has been passed by with less consideration than is due it.

There is no uniformity in the meanings that are attached to the term *suggestion* even among the most careful writers. If I were sitting in my office and considering the advisability of beginning a certain enterprise, I might say that one idea "suggested" a second and this second a third, etc. A scientific definition would not allow this use of the term but would substitute the expression "called up" for "suggested." Thus I should say that one idea "called up" the second, etc. *Suggestion must be brought about by a second person or an object.* In my musings and deliberations I should not say that one idea suggested another, but if the same idea were called forth at the instigation of a second person or upon the presentation of an object, I should then call it suggestion—if it met the second essential condition of suggestion. This second condition is that *the resulting conception, conclusion or action must follow with less than the normal amount of deliberation.* Suggestion is thus a relative term, and in many instances it might be difficult to say whether or not a particular act was suggestion. If the act followed a normal amount of consideration after a normal time for deliberation, it would not be suggestion, while if the same act followed too abruptly or with too little consideration it might be a true case of suggestion.

Every normal individual is subject to the influence of suggestion. Every idea of which we think is all too liable to be held for truth, and every thought of an action which enters our minds is likely to result in such action. [...]

Thought is dynamic in its very nature and every idea of an action tends to produce that action.

The most perfect working of suggestion is to be seen under hypnosis and in crowds. In hypnosis the subject holds every idea presented as true, and every idea suggested is acted out with no hesitation what ever. Here the mind is so narrowed by the artificial sleep that no contradictory or inhibiting idea arises, and hence no idea can seem absurd and no action seems out of place. There is no possible criticism or deliberation and so we have the extreme case of susceptibility to suggestion.

The effect of a crowd upon an individual approaches that of the hypnotizer. The individual is affected by every member of the crowd and the influence becomes so overpowering that it can hardly be resisted. If the crowd is a "lynching party" the whole atmosphere is one of revenge, and everywhere is suggested the idea of "lynch the culprit." This idea is presented on all sides. It can be read from the faces and actions of the individuals and is heard in their cries. No other idea has a chance to arise in consciousness and hence this one idea, being dynamic, leads to its natural consequences.

It was once supposed that suggestion was something abnormal and that reason was the common attribute of men. Today we are finding that suggestion is of universal application to all persons, while reason is a process which is exceptional, even among the wisest. We reason rarely, but act under suggestion constantly.

There has been a great agitation of late among advertisers for "reason why" copy. This agitation has had some value, but it is easily over-emphasized. Occasionally customers are persuaded and convinced, but more frequently they make their purchases because the act is suggested at the psychological moment. Suggestion and persuasion are not antagonistic; both should be kept in mind. However, in advertising, suggestion should not be subordinated to persuasion but should be supplemented by it. The actual effect of modern advertising is not so much to convince as to suggest. The individual swallowed up by a crowd is not aware of the fact that he is not exercising a normal amount of deliberation. His actions appear to him to be the result of reason, although the idea, as presented, is not criticised at all and no contradictory or inhibiting idea has any possibility of arising, in his mind. In the same way we think that we are performing a deliberate act when we purchase an advertised commodity, while in fact we may never have deliberated upon the subject at all. The idea is suggested by the advertisement, and the impulsiveness of human nature enforces the suggested idea, hence the desired result follows in a way unknown to the purchaser. [...]

The second most effective class is probably the ideas suggested by the words of our companions. Advertisements that are seen frequently are difficult to distinguish in their force from ideas which are secured from the words of our friends. Advertising thus becomes a great social illusion. We attribute to our social environment that which in reality has been secured from the advertisements which we have seen so often that we forget the source of the information.

Street railway advertising is especially effective at this point because the suggestion is presented so frequently that we soon forget the source of the suggestions and end by attributing it to the advice of friends.

In advertising some commodities argumentation is of more importance than suggestion, and for such things booklets and other similar forms of advertising are the most effective. Such commodities are, however, the exception and not the rule. In the most successful advertising argumentation and forms of reasoning are not disregarded, but the emphasis is put upon suggestion. Inasmuch as more of our actions are induced by suggestion than by argumentation, advertising conforms, in this particular, to the psychological situation. It puts the emphasis where the most can be accomplished and subordinates those mental processes which hold a second place in determining our actions.

As stated above, those suggestions are the most powerful which we receive from the actions and words of other persons. The successful advertiser seems to have worked upon this hypothesis in constructing many advertisements. He has also taken advantage of the fact that we soon forget the person who originally suggested the idea and become subject to illusions upon the matter. [...]

It seems that no form of action can be suggested by an advertisement that does not successfully challenge the reader to do what is proposed. The suggested idea haunts one and even though the action may be absurd, it is difficult to resist.

CHAPTER TWENTY-EIGHT

"The Conditions of the Belief in Advertising" (1923)

Albert T. Poffenberger

Journal of Applied Psychology *7, no. 1: pp. 1–9.*

EDITOR'S INTRODUCTION

A somewhat different approach to the psychology of advertising was taken by Albert Poffenberger (1885–1977). Poffenberger was a Bucknell University undergraduate, receiving his PhD from Columbia University in 1912. He then joined the psychology faculty at Columbia, where he stayed until his retirement in 1950. During his career he helped pioneer applied psychology and served as president of the American Psychological Association (1935) and the Social Science Research Council.

While Scott drew support for his analyses from industry practice and extant literature, Poffenberger experimented. Both conducted their studies in support of the profession, but Poffenberger was a bit more dispassionate. In the following passage, he starts with a puzzlement: "The fact that the American people are each year induced to squander many millions of dollars in worthless securities through the medium of advertising in some form, and that warnings seem quite ineffective in protecting them, makes one curious about the basis of belief in advertising."

In answer to his implied question, he proposes three conditions that advance a belief in an advertising message: (1) that the "ideas aroused by an advertisement must not conflict too sharply with the reader's experience," (2) according to the "well-known law of suggestion," the message should come from an authoritative source, and (3) the message should arouse desires, fears or "emotions generally." Poffenberger organizes substantial experiments and surveys around his first two conditions, employing real-world advertisements. One, interestingly, involved a cosmetic product containing radium (a naturally occurring radioactive material). The advertising campaign failed and Poffenberger found support for the hypothesis "that the suggestion to apply radium on the skin for toilet purposes conflicted too sharply with people's (pre-existing) opinions about radium."—*P.P.*

"The Conditions of the Belief in Advertising" (1923)

A reader of the literature dealing with the Psychology of Advertising finds numerous articles written upon the effectiveness of various mechanical devices, the attention and memory value of size of space and the position on the page, the influence of color, style of type and its arrangement, the effectiveness of repeating the advertisement, etc. The problem of arousing the confidence of the consumer in the article advertised, the conditions on which it depends, how belief in advertisements may be created and how it may be measured have been very lightly touched in experimental studies. The importance of these matters is emphasized in every textbook on advertising. The fact that the American people are each year induced to squander many millions of dollars in worthless securities through the medium of advertising in some form, and that warnings seem quite ineffective in protecting them, makes one curious about the basis of belief in advertising. It is not enough to say that the American people like to be fooled and that there is no scheme too wild to arouse the confidence of a large proportion of them. The advertiser should know that action is dependent upon belief and that belief in advertising depends upon conditions, some of which at least are under his control.

Belief is indeed a complex mental state and it may depend at any time upon a great variety of factors, the most common of which are listed in textbooks of psychology and advertising. It is not the purpose of this report to repeat such lists but to cite some experimental evidence from the field of advertising to show the importance of a few of the conditions of belief for success in advertising.

1. Belief is rarely the result of reasoning. One does not go through the processes of logic to establish his beliefs. If logic is used at all it is to justify a belief already established. A striking illustration of the separation of reasoning and belief is found in the case of the insane patient who firmly believed himself to be the son of a king, and yet whose reason was intact enough to enable him to solve complicated mathematical problems.

The advertising of the New Gillette razor offered a good opportunity for studying the relation between belief and reasoning. On May 16, 1921, the Gillette Razor Company announced "a new triumph of American inventive genius of startling interest to every man with a beard to shave." The advertisements state that the "fulcrum shoulder, overhanging cap and channeled guard" were the three innovations which made possible "for the first time in any razor, micrometric control of blade position." A diagram showed "how the blade is biflexed between overhanging cap and fulcrum shoulder. It is flexed once into the inside curve of the cap. This is the minor flexure—the curve for easy gliding, action and play of the wrist in shaving. It is flexed a second time—more sharply and in a shorter radius—by the grip of the overhanging cap the whole length of the fulcrum shoulder. This is the major flexure." This arrangement provided an exactness of adjustment to 1-1000 of an inch. Advertisements containing the above information and well illustrated were given to fifty seven men, college students and university graduates, together with a series of seven questions intended to test both their belief in the new razor and their understanding of it. The answers to these questions showed that all the students agreed that the new razor was better than the old one, and that they would rather pay $5.00 for the new one than $1.00 or $2.00 for the old one. In supporting their belief they were allowed to consult the advertisement as much as they wished. They quoted the "fulcrum shoulder, overhanging cap and channeled guard," which made possible "micrometric control of blade position," but not one of them could explain how the micrometric control was obtained or what advantage there would be in having such micrometric control. They believed that the "channel guard" was an improvement although they could not tell why it was an improvement. As to the importance of major and minor flexures they were entirely ignorant. Five minutes examination of an enlarged diagram of the new razor improved their understanding of the razor little—or not at all.

Here is a belief effective for the purpose of the advertiser in spite of the inability of the reader to support his belief with reason. This experiment is quoted not to show that the advertisement is poor, but merely to show that in advertising reasoning is not needed to create belief. Whether the space in the advertisement devoted to argument might have been more profitably filled, is however an interesting question.

2. It is not necessarily that which is true that is believed. The fact that a statement in an advertisement is true will not guarantee belief on the part of the readers of it. The truth may be too startling and surprising to be believed, and in some cases it might be more effective to tell half the truth than the whole truth. [...]

Thus far the negative side of the question has been presented. If belief in an advertisement does not depend upon the truth of the statements made and does not depend upon the reasoning of the reader, on what does it depend? To state the matter simply, we may say that ideas which are present in the mind and are not interfered with by any opposing ideas will be believed. This is merely a bare statement of the law of suggestion and to comply with it in advertising, conflicting ideas should be prevented from entering the mind. There are many conditions on which such undisturbed acceptance of ideas depends. Only three will be mentioned here.

1. The ideas aroused by an advertisement must not conflict too sharply with the reader's experience. Introspections volunteered by many of the 100 subjects who served in the experiments just described indicated that their past experiences with trunks, vacuum bottles and phonographs furnished conflicting ideas which the advertisements were not sufficiently powerful to overcome. This was especially true in the case of the phonograph advertisement where doubt was expressed in a large percentage of the cases.

An experimental study of an advertising campaign that failed showed clearly the need for complying with the conditions of belief. "Radior Products," a series of toilet preparations were introduced into this country by an English firm. The appeal contained in the advertising may be illustrated by the following quotation taken from one of the advertisements: "Radior is the magic new word in the book of beauty. It means the triumphant union of the finest complexion preparations with actual radium. Its content of radium works the miracle of nature. It purifies the skin, gives it the health to regain 1ts youthfulness and loveliness." The container of these preparations was represented as emanating rays which were very suggestive of bolts of lightning. These toilet preparations could not be sold—the campaign had failed.

Why? One possible reason for the failure was that the suggestion to apply radium on the skin for toilet purposes conflicted too sharply with people's opinions about radium. In order to discover what people believed about radium, a questionaire was carefully prepared in the form of a True-False test and submitted to 400 people, comprising a well-to-do, well-educated group, a group of average intelligence and financial standing and a special group of persons working in "Beauty Parlors." [...]

Nothing need be said here concerning the difference in the reactions of the different groups to the questionaire, except that the most intelligent group had the strongest reaction against radium-containing products, and that the "Beauty Parlor" workers had the least antagonism. Inquiry among these people indicated that some of them had confused radium with the violet ray which was at the time a very popular form of treatment with them. The results of the study of the questionaire may be summarized as follows:

Forty-eight per cent of the persons tested believed that radium is a deadly poison; 80 per cent believed that it causes burns when it comes in contact with the skin; 89 per cent believed that radium preparations should be used only upon the advice of a physician; 71 per cent said that they would not buy any kind of toilet preparation that they knew contained even a minute quantity of radium; 90 per cent thought of radium as a substance used for the treatment of cancer. The whole experiment may be summed up in the statement that about 70 per cent of all the replies indicated opinions unfavorable to radium-containing products as toilet preparations. The basis of this unfavorable reaction could easily be traced to the people's accumulated experiences of radium. Clippings of all articles dealing with radium and appearing in newspapers and magazines were collected for a short period. Practically all of them emphasized the harmful effects of radium and the dangers incurred in handling it, instead of any beneficial properties it might possess.

This is a clear case of the inability of an advertising campaign to overcome the resistance established by experience. To create a favorable attitude toward radium-containing products as toilet preparations by an educational campaign conducted in newspapers and magazines might conceivably have been possible. But it certainly would have been impracticable.

2. Ideas that are to create belief must come from an authoritative source. This is a well-known law of suggestion. The hypnotist can do nothing without his air of authority and the subject's recognition of it. We are accustomed to believe the statements made by a person in whom we have confidence,

and to believe what is printed in a medium which we consider authoritative. Even if there is conflict with one's own experience, he will sometimes accept the contrary experience of another person as a basis for belief if he have sufficient confidence in the other person. But even then the new experience may not be too conflicting. Advertisers have for years striven to develop an atmosphere of confidence and authority by all the devices at their command. The present experiment was intended to measure in a tentative fashion the degree of confidence which an advertisement can create in comparison with other forms of publication. I have compared the degree of belief or doubt aroused by the three advertisements previously described (namely Taylor Trunks, Stanley Vacuum Bottles and Edison Phonographs) with the belief aroused by essentially the same statements coming from a reputable journal. In order to make such a comparison, the facts stated in each advertisement were prepared in the form of a news item abstracted from an engineering magazine. One such abstract will illustrate the character of all. These abstracts were presented to a group of 100 persons of the same general character as those tested in the earlier experiments, but who knew nothing of those experiments or nothing of the purpose of the present experiment. Along with the abstract of each advertisement was a series of questions as nearly as possible like those used in the test with the advertisements. As far as we were able to ascertain, no one doubted the authenticity of the news abstracts. Instead of reporting the results of the three questionnaires in detail, it will be sufficient to compare for each of the three cases the number of replies indicating doubt in the advertisement, and doubt in the news item. [...]

In two of the cases it will be noted that there was greater confidence in the advertisement than in the news clipping, while in the third there was greater confidence in the news clipping. An examination of the three advertisements did not afford an entirely satisfactory explanation for the shift of belief in the case of the third advertisement. It seems safe to conclude from these records that although belief in certain advertisements may be low, they may carry at least as much authority in presenting a set of facts as can be conveyed by a news article. The doubt in the cases we have studied is the effect rather of conflict of ideas with experience, than the effect of the use of an unauthoritative medium of expression. Introspections volunteered by the subjects suggest that illustrations and especially photographs used in the advertisements tend to strengthen belief. Unless one suspects trickery, as some of our subjects did, looking at a picture ought to carry with it greater weight in establishing belief than merely reading printed matter. Even if

Mark Twain was right in advising that one believe only half that he sees and nothing that he hears, the advantage in favor of the picture is obvious.

3. There is a third important condition of belief, namely, that we tend to believe what arouses our desires, our fears and our emotions generally. I have no experimental evidence to offer in this connection, and know of none in the field of advertising. But evidence for the importance of this factor may be drawn from psychology. Wm. James has said, "A man who has no belief in ghosts by daylight will temporarily believe in them when alone at midnight, he feels his blood curdle at a mysterious sound or vision, his heart thumping and his legs impelled to flee." In strong emotion we might find the condition responsible for the belief in the bargain counter. The politician finds no difficulty in honestly believing what best fits in with his aspirations, while his opponent may as honestly believe the opposite and for a like reason. If one really wants a certain suit of clothes or an automobile which costs more than he should pay, he may honestly believe that he is making an economical purchase. Once a belief has been established m this way, logic and reasoning may be used to support it.

These three conditions of belief which I have described represent three important variables in the formula for advertising success. For most advertising situations they are unknown variables which may interact in a very complex manner. But they may be discovered by careful examination. That they are not always sought or discovered, is clear from the cases I have cited which were taken from advertising already used. Three questions might well be asked about every advertisement: (1) What adverse beliefs and experiences does it have to meet in the minds of consumers? (2) Will the authority which it wears by its mode of presentation or by the medium in which it appears enable it to create belief? (3) Does the appeal used arouse desires which will in turn create belief in the advertised article? These are human behavior questions that psychological methods will enable the advertiser to answer before the advertising is used as well as after the money has been spent upon broadcasting it.

CHAPTER TWENTY-NINE

The Psychology of the Audience (1935)

Harry L. Hollingworth

New York: American Book, pp. 141–58 [with elisions].

EDITOR'S INTRODUCTION

In 1935, suggestion theory was at its zenith. It was the preferred psychological explanation for political propaganda and commercial advertising. As noted earlier, Leonard Doob's manifesto on propaganda and the first major work on the effects of radio by Hadley Cantril and Gordon Allport, both published that year, rested on the psychology of suggestion.

Harry Hollingworth's book *The Psychology of the Audience* was also released in 1935 and provides a fitting close to this collection. Like Scott and Poffenberger, Hollingworth (1880–1956) was a pioneer in applied psychology, putting his research skills to work in business and industrial settings throughout his career. He received his doctorate in psychology from Columbia University in 1909 and joined the faculty at Columbia's Barnard College, where he eventually rose to head of the Psychology Department. In 1927 he was elected president of the American Psychological Association. He was said to have written nearly a book a year during his career, on topics ranging from functional neuroses, to psychology and ethics, to vocational psychology. He developed a particular interest in the psychology of advertising and wrote *Advertising and Selling* in 1913, produced as an instructional text for those in business and promotion.

Similarly, *The Psychology of the Audience* is a handbook for those in public speaking and promotion, but one informed by decades of research in social psychology. In the following passages, Hollingworth offers advice for the public speaker and salesperson, starting with an exposition on "The Laws of Suggestion." He lists seven operational principles, including the use frequency, indirect versus indirect suggestion, and the establishment of authority, noting, again, that high speaker prestige can result in the adoption of suggestions "even when they are unsupported by sufficient reason."

He separates from Le Bon in describing the typical attributes of a congregation, especially with respect to the thoughtfulness and intelligence of the gathered individuals, and, adopting an individual-based analytical lens, rejects the idea of a group mind. He cites experimental work, including his own, to examine the efficacy of the "prestige of the group" versus that of the expert, summarizing then-established findings that results will vary by topic and circumstance. He concludes with a dozen recommendations designed to aid the public speaker in "directing the acts and verdicts of the audience."—*P.P.*

References

Cantril, Hadley, and Gordon G. Allport. 1935. *The Psychology of Radio*. New York: Harper.

Doob, Leonard. 1935. *Propaganda: Its Psychology and Technique*. New York: Henry Holt.

Hollingworth, Harry. 1913. *Advertising and Selling*. New York: D. Appleton.

The Psychology of the Audience (1935)

CHAPTER IX: Directing Action

DEFINING THE ACT

The principles involved in directing the action of the audience will vary considerably, no doubt, with the type of audience, the occasion for action, and the actual authority of the speaker. There is little that can be enumerated here beyond the simple rules of suggestion which apply to all human relations. Whether the action is to take place at once, as in the case of a deliberative assembly called on to vote on an issue, or whether the action is deferred until a time subsequent to the dispersal of the audience, as in the case of a political campaign, one principle should never be forgotten. This is the principle of suggesting in specific and definite terms the nature, place, and method of the desired response.

The treasurer of a society was frequently observed to rise at periodic intervals during the year and, pointing out the urgent need for funds, in the form of regular membership dues, to request that members kindly pay their assessments. No specifications were given beyond this gentle and vague suggestion, and as a consequence few assessments were paid, in spite of the frequent requests. The treasurer should have closed the first request by indicating at which door she would stand at the close of the meeting, or by writing her name and address on the board, or by some other such specific device should have suggested definite action at definite time or place. Such an illustration is to be sure a far cry from the field of oratory, but it represents one of the real cases in which an audience must be effectively handled if it is to be won.

It is in just this spirit that the salesman always has his order book ready and requests the converted prospect immediately to "sign on the dotted line." The advertiser places a coupon in the corner of the page, or is sure to give his firm name, address, or place of business. Revival meetings which succeed provide specific altar directions—"Married men gather at the right of the platform," "All the dentists in the congregation now sing the third verse," "March up the aisle while the choir sings Onward Christian Soldiers." The climax of this specification of response is seen in the most completely polarized audience that we have described, that of the organized team or regiment or orchestra.

THE LAWS OF SUGGESTION

In much the same way, the remaining general laws of suggestion, which have been frequently formulated and illustrated, apply as fully to the winning of an audience to action as they do to the handling of individuals. We need here do no more than suggest these by a brief statement indicating the nature of each of the principles.

1. The strength of a suggestion depends in part on the degree to which it seems to be of spontaneous origin, an act of the individual's own initiative. Arrogance and domination are at once and instinctively resented and

resisted. The more indirect the suggestion, the more it can be made to be an original determination or plan or conclusion on the part of the listener, the greater its dynamic power.

2. Within the limits of the law just indicated, the dynamic power of a suggestion will be the greater, the more forcefully and vividly it is presented. This is especially true when the suggested act is in harmony with the pre-established habits and tendencies. When the suggestion violates life-long habits and instincts, attempts to be forceful and vigorous usually lapse into arrogance and thereby defeat their own purpose.

3. It is more effective to suggest the desired response directly than it is to argue against a response that is not desired. Suggestion is most active at its positive pole, and the negative suggestion tends to defeat its own purpose. The Old Covenant with its "Thou Shalt Not" was readily displaced by the New Covenant with its simple, positive "Thou Shalt."

4. The action power of a suggestion varies directly with the prestige of its source. The more we revere a speaker, for any reason whatsoever, the greater confidence we tend to place in anything he may say, and the more prone we are to imitate him and to adopt his suggestions, even when they are unsupported by sufficient reason.

5. The strength of a suggestion will be determined in part by the degree of internal resistance it encounters. That suggestion will be most effective which can call to its aid or appropriate the dynamic force of some other impulse that is already active or latent. Suggestions to violate life-long habits, firmly fixed moral feelings, and sacred relationships are impotent, even during the pronounced suggestibility of the hypnotic trance.

6. The strength of a suggestion varies with the frequency with which it is met. But mere mechanical repetition avails little unless the repeated suggestion is attended to with interest. Experiment shows that repetition of advertising appeals is twice as effective when the form, style, and expression is varied, with constant theme, as when exact duplication of previous appeals is used. Repetition accompanied by sufficient variety to lend interest but with sufficient uniformity to acquire a constant meaning, produces a genuine cumulative effect.

7. In appealing over the short circuit for a specific line of action, no interference, substitute, rival idea, or opposing action should be suggested. Such an idea merely impedes the action power of the first suggestion, by inviting comparison and thus involves deliberate choice and hesitation. There is an apparent contradiction between what we have just said concern-

ing the advantages of repetition with variety and LeBon's[1] assertion that "Affirmation has no real influence unless it be constantly repeated, and so far as possible in the same terms." Both principles, however, are valid. The apparent contradiction arises from the fact that a suggestion or affirmation may have two very distinct functions.

PSYCHOLOGY OF THE SLOGAN

For the purposes of maintaining attention and interest, of linking up the impression with the individual's background of experience, and of persuading him toward a general course of action, repetition with variation seems to be the most effective measure. But another function of the suggestion, and an important one, as we have seen, is that of specifying and giving precise definition to the act. Here the principle of repetition in the same terms, of duplication instead of variation, has its advantages. This is what is involved in the psychology of the slogan. "Swat the fly," an exhortation constantly reiterated, defines the act, and serves effectually to perpetuate the decision beyond the immediate occasion of its formation. It crystallizes the propaganda of a whole evening's program, remains with the auditor as a succinct formula of action. Becoming a slogan, it unites in a common decision audiences geographically remote from each other and readily spreads to individuals not present at the local program.

Along with the demand for a concrete symbol,—a seal, a flag, a color, a badge, trademark, battle cry, or other single device for representing and suggesting the essence of an abstract principle or a group enterprise,—goes the popular craving for a terse slogan which will take the place of careful description, conceal the lack of real understanding, identify, and rally the devotees of a leader or party, and serve as a convenient challenge to the enemy. Political leaders, as well as juvenile organizers and advertisers, have learned the practical utility of the slogan, and the individualism and partnership of enterprise and control give the practice respectable standing in spite of its dubious psychological implications.

HATE AND FEAR

Along with the power of the slogan should be mentioned the unifying effect of participation in a common punishment or deprivation. The levy of a tax at once establishes bonds of community between individuals who are

---

[1] LeBon, G. *The Crowd*, Macmillan. By permission.

liable to it, however dispersed they may be. Limitations and regulations imposed on the individual's personal ration of sugar, flour, or milk go far toward arousing to active belligerency a population apathetic or resistant to the progress of military operations and the plans of the chief of staff. In the fusion of heterogeneous elements of a population into an effective social group nothing is more potent than a common hatred or a common fear. Any common emotion tends to have this consolidating effect on an audience, but on the whole it is said that mobs are more easily organized for malicious than for ennobling enterprises. [...]

AUDIENCES AND MOBS

It has been popular, in the literature of group psychology, to belittle the function of intelligence in the mental processes of an audience. Thus Le-Bon [2] insists that:

> As soon as a few individuals are gathered together they constitute a crowd, and although they should be distinguished men of learning, they assume all the characteristics of crowds with respect to the matter outside their specialty. ... From the moment that they form part of a crowd the learned man and the ignoramus are equally incapable of observation.

Again he refers to:

> the slight importance of the mental level of the different elements composing a crowd, so far as the decisions it comes to are concerned. ... When a deliberative assembly is called upon to give its opinion on a question not entirely technical, intelligence stands for nothing. For instance a gathering of scientific men or artists, owing to the mere fact that they form an assemblage, will not deliver judgments on general subjects sensibly different from those rendered by a gathering of masons or grocers. ... The decisions affecting matters of general interest come to by an assembly of men of distinction, but specialists in different walks of life, are not sensibly superior to the decisions that would be adopted by a gathering of imbeciles.

This assumed "mental inferiority of all collectivities," whatever their composition, leads LeBon to emphatic advice on the way to influence assemblies to action:

---

[2] LeBon, G. *The Crowd*, Macmillan. By permission.

> Crowds are not to be influenced by reasoning and can only comprehend rough-and-ready associations of ideas. The orators who know how to make an impression on them always appeal in consequence to their sentiments and never to their reason. . . . An orator wishing to move a crowd must make an abusive use of violent affirmation. To exaggerate, to affirm, to resort to repetition, and never to attempt to prove anything by reasoning, are methods of argument well known to speakers at public meetings.

LeBon attributes special potency to the seduction of the audience by images,—to "the magic force of words and formulae, independent of their real sense." "The chief concern of a good counsel," he says, "should be to work upon the feelings of the jury, and, as with all crowds, to argue but little or only to employ rudimentary modes of reasoning."

We need not concern ourselves with the naïve explanations which this writer gives for the tendencies he attributes to all assemblages. It is clear that the composition of the "average audience" usually suffices to explain such phenomena when they actually occur. There is no necessity to invoke a "mental leveling," a "collective consciousness," a "brain paralysis," or "the unconsciousness of the mob."

The truth is that men are less different from each other in their physical make-up and anatomy, and in their original instinctive and emotional reactions, than they are in intelligence and wisdom, or in their acquired skills and standards. Men who agree in their repugnance to a given odor or their fear in danger may yet differ remarkably both in intelligence and knowledge. In so far as verdicts and acts relating to what LeBon calls "matters of general interest" are based on the fundamental interests, and such common inclinations as those toward mercy, justice, revenge, jealousy, pride, there is nothing either surprising or mysterious in the agreement of "the artist and the grocer." Their difference will lie rather in the type of object or situation most likely to arouse such reactions.

But the conception of the assembly as a mob which the speaker invariably seeks to stampede to some tumultuous act or verdict, to be recalled perhaps with chagrin on the morrow or in history, is far from representing the audience or the enterprise which most speakers will confront. To present the frenzied and vociferous delivery of magical formulae, striking images, and seductive metaphors as the goal of public speaking is, to say the least, woefully to underestimate the varieties and occasions of public congregation.

MAJORITY VERSUS EXPERT OPINION

It is well known of course that individual opinion is influenced not only by strictly relevant data and personal evaluation, but also to a considerable extent by the suggestive influence of the opinions of others. The knowledge that the majority hold a given opinion inclines many individuals favorably toward the majority's decision. Similarly the verdict of an expert in the field in question gives a bias to the individual's judgment. Is the majority or the expert more potent in thus deflecting the individual opinion? Is the audience more susceptible, in general, to the statement of public opinion or to the quotation of authority?

In an experiment conducted in 1910, the writer attempted to measure the effectiveness of various types of appeal in the case of the description of marketable products. Among the thirty main interests or instincts represented were two which bear on the point just raised. Thus three appeals based their claim on the prestige of the group, thereby suggesting the desirability of the article. Two appeals, on the other hand, were based on the recommendations of prominent persons, who, in the public eye, might well represent expert opinion. If a perfect appeal, that is, one which for every member of the experimental group was the most effective of the series, be considered to have a value of 100 per cent, then, on this basis, the recommendation scores only 14 per cent whereas the Group Suggestion scores 50 per cent. The suggestion of the group is in this field apparently much more effective than is the opinion of the expert.

An experiment of H. T. Moore's[3] is directed toward a similar point. This investigator studied three types of situations; viz., speech, morals, and music.

> Ninety-five subjects were given eighteen paired comparisons for each of three types of situation. The instructions for the linguistic judgments were that the subjects check the more offensive one of each pair of expressions. . . . The ethical judgments involved the checking of the more offensive of two traits of character in each of eighteen pairs. ... The musical judgments involved an expression of preference for one of two resolutions of the dominant seventh chord, played on a reed organ. Eighteen paired resolutions were played, and the preferences recorded after each.

---

[3] Moore, H.T. "Comparative Influence of Majority and Expert Opinion," *American Journal of Psychology*, July 1917.

After these opinions had been recorded and a time interval of several days had elapsed, a repetition of the experiment showed the chance of reversal for such judgments, when no suggestive influence was used. On later occasions this second half of the experiment was accompanied in each case by a statement of what the majority opinion had been on the original occasion. In a third case the statement was used instead of the opinion of some expert in the field of question. The investigator now inquired whether the suggestion of group opinion and of expert opinion produced a greater number of reversals of judgment than came by chance alone, and how these two influences compared in this respect, in the three fields of speech, morals, and music. [...]

The author concludes:

> If we now take as our unit of measurement the per cent recorded as the chance
> of reversal, we find, as indicated . . . that the probability of reversing favorably
> to the majority in matters of speech and morals in approximately five times
> chance; whereas in matters of musical feeling the probability is only about twice
> chance. By majority is meant here of course only the special type of majority
> provided in the experiment, but if generalization is permissible on the basis
> of the evidence available, we may venture the statement that a man is two and
> a half times as individualistic in his musical likes and dislikes as in his moral
> and linguistic preferences. Similarly we may conclude that expert and majority
> opinion hold about equal sway over the individual in morals and music, but
> that the chances are about ten to seven in favor of majority prestige in matters
> pertaining to speech. [...]

THE DETERMINANTS OF BELIEF

In the long run the final test of belief is the readiness or the willingness to act. Indeed some psychologists have been convinced that the experience of belief is nothing more than the feeling of this readiness for action. However this may be, inducement to act must proceed either through relying on a belief explicitly or implicitly held, or else through the establishment of a new belief. Even the emotional appeal operates through the utilization of a native or long-acquired value, interest, preference, or conviction.

The psychology of arousing action thus involves in part the psychology of belief, and it would be useful in this connection to know what are the most effective determinants of our convictions. Such information would be of specially practical value in the endeavor to establish a new belief in the minds of one's audience, inasmuch as it would enable the speaker to take advantage of thought habits and lines of least resistance. Very little is known quantitatively or experimentally as to the relative potency of the different determinants of conviction, and this constitutes a field in which exploration will surely be profitable. [...]

PRACTICAL CONCLUSIONS

1. The first principle for directing the acts and verdicts of the audience is that of indicating specifically and definitely rather than vaguely and generally the precise nature, place, time, and method of the proposed act.

2. The strength of a suggestion varies directly with its spontaneity, vividness, positive form, prestige, and frequency.

3. The strength of a suggestion varies inversely with the internal resistance it encounters and with the number of rival suggestions operating.

4. Repetition with variation promotes conviction; repetition with duplication better specifies and defines the response to be made.

5. A slogan or catch-word crystallizes a whole program and remains with the audience as a succinct formula of action.

6. If audiences are more easily aroused to malicious than to ennobling acts or verdicts, this is in part because anger, hate, and fear are emotions most easily recognized in others and propagated through their demeanor.

7. The mobilization of an audience depends no more upon the actions of the leader than upon the contributory signs afforded one another by the auditors, through their attitudes and visible expressions.

8. The traditional "mental inferiority of all congregations"eis only a result of the fact that people are more alike in the simple, primitive, concrete structural, and fundamental traits than they are in complex, more recently acquired, symbolic, functional, and derived traits.

9. The prevalent "mob conception" of the nature of an audience woefully underestimates the varieties and occasions of public congregation.

10. There is no "mind of the audience"; there are only the individual people with their individual minds; but in a congregation special stimuli and hence special behavior occur which are absent when the individuals are alone.

11. Whether the opinion of the public or the judgment of experts has higher prestige with an audience, varies with the subject matter of the discourse.

12. People prefer their acts to appear rationally determined; they suppose their own acts to be more rationally determined than the acts of others; they suppose their own acts to be more rationally determined than they actually are.